ENCOUNTERING TORAH

ENCOUNTERING TORAH
Reflections on the Weekly Portion

RABBI VERNON H. KURTZ

Encountering Torah: Reflections on the Weekly Portion
By Rabbi Vernon H. Kurtz
Published by North Suburban Synagogue Beth El
1175 Sheridan Road, Highland Park, Illinois 60035
© 2013 Vernon H. Kurtz

All rights reserved. No part of this work may be reproduced, in any form or by any means, without permission in writing from the copyright owner.

ISBN 978-0-9886786-0-6

Some of the material in this book has been published in a different form in the *Chicago Jewish News*.

The author is grateful to the following publishers for permission to reprint selections from their books:

Quotes from *Tanakh: The Holy Scriptures*. Reprinted from *Tanakh: The Holy Scriptures* by permission of the University of Nebraska Press © 1985, 1999 The Jewish Publication Society, Philadelphia.

Quotes from *Etz Hayim*. Reprinted with permission from *Etz Hayim: Torah and Commentary*, ed. Rabbi David L. Lieber © Rabbinical Assembly, 2001.

Quotes from *Siddur Sim Shalom*. Reprinted with permission from *Siddur Sim Shalom*, ed. Rabbi Jules Harlow © Rabbinical Assembly, 1985.

Quotes from *Mahzor Lev Shalem*. Reprinted with permission from *Mahzor Lev Shalem*, ed. Rabbi Edward Feld © Rabbinical Assembly, 2010.

Quotes from *Likute Tefilah: A Rabbi's Manual*. Reprinted with permission from *Likute Tefilah: A Rabbi's Manual*, ed. Rabbi Jules Harlow © Rabbinical Assembly, 1965.

"Birth is a Beginning" by Rabbi Alvin Fine from *Gates of Repentance: The New Union Prayerbook for the Days of Awe* © 1978, 1996 by the Central Conference of American Rabbis. Used by permission of the Central Conference of American Rabbis. All rights reserved.

Quote from Maya Angelou. From WOULDN'T TAKE NOTHING FOR MY JOURNEY NOW by Maya Angelou © 1993 by Maya Angelou. Used by permission of Random House, Inc. Any third party use of this material, outside of this publication, is prohibited. Interested parties must apply directly to Random House, Inc. for permission.

Front, back, and interior images: "Jacob's Ladder" by Morris Dahan. Used by permission.
Cover design by Jennifer Klor.
Printed by G&H Soho.

With great respect for
Bernard C. (ז״ל) and Dorothy (ז״ל) Kurtz
Samuel (ז״ל) and Zena Wise

With deep abiding love for
Bryna Kurtz

With great pride in
Hadassa Michal (Haim Moshe) and Shira Miriam

And with immense hope in
Shmuel Binyamin, Meytal Dvora, and Anael Rina

We wish to thank the generous donors whose contributions supported the publication of this book. Their significant donations also help support North Suburban Synagogue Beth El's educational programs and youth scholarships.

PUBLISHER

Wendy and Steve Abrams

Annette and Jerry Blumberg

Dr. Gilbert Bogen in loving memory of Rosalyn Bogen

Joan and William Brodsky and Family

Andrew and Gail Brown

Mr. and Mrs. Benjamin B. Cohen

Larry and Barbara Field Family

The Field Family in memory of Eli and Dina Field and Max and Frieda Gaynes

Mr. and Mrs. Jeffrey Hecktman and Family

Hochberg Family Foundation

Michael and Karen Kesner and Family

Karen and Mitchell Kopin and Family

In memory of Mania and Jacob Levitan

Alissa, Jared, and Todd Neuhausen in loving memory of Benjamin and Madeline Neuhausen

North Suburban Synagogue Beth El Sisterhood

The Posen Family in honor of Faye, Sam, Helaine and Lawrence Posen

Andrea and Ken Saffir

Lynne and Howard Schechter in memory of their parents

Shirley Scheinman/Lansing Family in memory of "Izzy"

Lynn and Skip Schrayer

Mae and Mark Spitz in memory of Stanley Liebman and Michael Liebman

EDITOR

Harry and Harriet Bernbaum

Scott and Karen Bieber

Mr. and Mrs. Donald Chudacoff

Carey and Cheryl Cooper and Family

In memory of Janice Freedman

Elise and Ira Frost, Marc, Josh and Rachel Frost

Gary, David and Gabrielle Gordon and Marilyn Hirsch

Arnie and Nina Harris

St. Andrews Foundation established by Morris and Sara Hirsch

In memory of Elaine F. Krumbein from her family and friends

The Matthew Family in memory of Norman Matthew

Mally and Alan Rutkoff

Phyllis Shalowitz and Deborah and Bruce Cowans

Sara and Michael D. Sher and Family

Karyn and Bill Silverstein and Family

Yadelle Sklare in memory of Robert Sklare

Miriam and Morton Steinberg

In honor of Leonard Weitz

DESIGNER

Sally Aaron in loving memory of Willard Aaron

Susan and Joseph Ament

Harvey and Jackie Barnett

The Biller Family in memory of Rabbi Mordecai Simon

Melvin and Lenore Blum

Drs. Gordon and Carol Derman and Family

Charlene and Pierre Eilian

The Feinsteins-Steve, Linda, Sara, Matt, Carli and Melissa

Nancy and Maury Fertig and Family

Leonard and Rochelle Foxman

Lynn and Michael Froy and Family

Morris and June Back Frydman

Dr. Paul and Eileen (Rubenstein) Goldstein and Family

Mindy and Jeff Gordon and Family

In memory of Raymond S. Hara

Gwen, Scott, Jordan and Dana Heyman

The Hochwert Family

Edward J. and Ann Dee Holland and Family

Joan Holland and Eli Glassman

Carol and Joel Honigberg

Brenda and David Jackson and Family

Pearl and Joel Kagan and Family

Ruth and Malvin Kaufman, Leslie and Jonathan Kind, and Laura and Scott Kaufman

Edith and Bernard Kaye

In memory of Alexander S. Knopfler

Beth and Jeff Kopin

Mitch and Sari Kovitz and Family

Dr. Colman and Julie Kraff and Family

Jeffrey and Roberta Kwall and Family

Michael and Judy Lavin and Family

Jerry and Linda Lebovitz and Family

Jane and Scott Lederman and Family

The Levin Family honoring Betty Ann Levin and the memory of Dr. Jacob Louis Levin

Fran and Mark Levy and Family

Mr. and Mrs. Lorry Lichtenstein and Family

The Lidov Family in memory of Howard I. Lidov

Michael and Terri Lipsitz and Family

North Suburban Synagogue Beth El Men's Club

Janet and Gary Resnick and their children and grandchildren

Mr. and Mrs. Sidney Retsky and Family

Lisa, Jeff, Ben and Josh Rosenkranz

The Shapiro Family (Lori, David and Sara)

Fran and Jonathan Sherman and Family

Margaret and Alan Silberman

The Skidelsky and Winick Families

Rodney and Marilyn Slutzky

Robin and David Small in loving memory of Merle Mattenson

Sandy Starkman and Larry Pachter

Mr. and Mrs. James Stempel and Family

Bobbie and Len Tenner

Otto and Phyllis Hofman Waldmann

Diane and Loren Weil

Sheri and Sherwin Zuckerman

Table of Contents

Preface   ix
About the Sermons   xii

GENESIS / BERE'SHIT

Bere'shit: A Closer Look   3
Bere'shit: The World Gone Wrong   6
Noaḥ: Lurking Evil   9
Noaḥ: The Power of Words   12
Lekh Lekha: The Promised Land, Then and Now   15
Lekh Lekha: Abram, Melchizedek, and the Act of Giving   18
Va-yera: The Two Abrahams   21
Va-yera: Biblical Family/Modern Problems   24
Ḥayyei Sarah: The Passion of Abraham   27
Ḥayyei Sarah: The Last Days of Abraham and David   30
Toledot: Jacob or Esau?   34
Toledot: The Five Senses as a Source of Blessing   37
Va-yetse: Eyes to See   40
Va-yetse: The Dual Axis   43
Va-yishlaḥ: Jacob's Encounter   46
Va-yishlaḥ: Deborah's Legacy   49
Va-yeshev: Joseph's Core Values   52
Va-yeshev: The Challenge of Good Fortune   55
Mikkets: Joseph and Other Jewish Dreamers   58
Mikkets: Making a Difference   61
Va-yiggash: Responsible for One Another   64
Va-yiggash: Jewish Identity   67
Va-yeḥi: The Value of Tears   70
Va-yeḥi: The Secret of the Two *Yuds*   73

EXODUS / SHEMOT

Shemot: *Yihiye Tov*—"It Will Be Good"	79
Shemot: The Book of Names	82
Va-era: The Four Cups of Wine	85
Va-era: A People Who Dwell Apart	88
Bo: Beyond Remembering	91
Bo: The Challenge of Darkness	94
Be-shallaḥ—*Shabbat Shira*: The Ultimate Song	97
Be-shallaḥ—*Shabbat Shira*: Embodying Faith in Life	100
Yitro: To Listen and To Hear	103
Yitro: The Tenth Commandment	106
Mishpatim: Home, Sanctuary, Community	109
Mishpatim: *Derekh Eretz*	112
Terumah: It Depends on Us	115
Terumah: Bread on the Table	118
Tetsavveh: Who Is a Leader?	121
Tetsavveh: Using Knowledge for Good	124
Ki Tissa: Partners with God	127
Ki Tissa: Two Sets of Tablets	130
Va-yakhel: The Beauty of Shabbat	133
Pekudei: The Ideal and the Real	136

LEVITICUS / VA-YIKRA

Va-yikra: Good Manners	141
Va-yikra: Taking Responsibility	144
Tsav: The Path of Judaism	147
Tsav: Meaningful Effort	150
Shemini: Swimming Upstream	153
Shemini: Using Time Well	156

Tazria: Ultimate Wonder — 159
Metsora: Watching Our Words — 162
Aḥarei Mot: Adding Meaning to Life — 165
Kedoshim: The Holiness Code — 168
Emor: Looking Out for Others — 171
Emor: The Dignity of Work — 175
Be-har: The Gifts of Nature — 178
Be-ḥukkotai: Serious Torah Study — 181

NUMBERS / BE-MIDBAR

Be-midbar: Jewish Unity — 187
Be-midbar: The *Minyan* — 190
Naso: Trusting Relationships — 193
Naso: Lessons from the Priestly Blessings — 196
Be-ha'alotekha: Roses and Thorns — 199
Be-ha'alotekha: No Whining — 202
Shelaḥ-Lekha: Being Honest to Oneself and Others — 205
Shelaḥ-Lekha: The Sounds of Silence — 208
Koraḥ: Defining Wickedness — 211
Koraḥ: The Almond Tree — 214
Ḥukkat: To Whom Could Moses Turn? — 217
Balak: Simply *Tzniut* — 220
Pinḥas: Teaching by Example — 223
Pinḥas: The Wonder of Creation — 226
Mattot: Causeless Love — 229
Mase'ei: The Responsibility of Leadership — 232

DEUTERONOMY / DEVARIM

Devarim: The Meaning of Tisha B'Av — 237
Devarim: Constructive Criticism — 240
Va-ethannan: Re-experiencing Jewish History — 243
Va-ethannan: Loving Your Fellow, Loving God — 246
Ekev: Saying Yes — 249
Ekev: *Yirat Shamayim* — 252
Re'eh: The Prophetic View — 255
Re'eh: The Loving Parent — 258
Shofetim: The Sin of Indifference — 261
Shofetim: To Be Someone — 264
Ki Tetse: The Beauty of Small Deeds — 267
Ki Tetse: Remembering and Forgetting — 270
Ki Tavo: The Blessing of True Happiness — 273
Ki Tavo: *Tikkun Olam*—A True Story — 276
Nitsavim: Community and Faith — 279
Va-yelekh: No Regrets — 282
Ha'azinu: The Singular Soul — 285
Ha'azinu: *Mitzvot* of Heaven and of Earth — 288

Bibliographic Notes — 291
About the Author — 303

Preface

I feel very privileged to share my sermons and wisdom with my congregation and community. Since my graduation from the Jewish Theological Seminary in 1976, I have been extremely fortunate to have served two wonderful congregations in the Chicagoland area. For twelve years, I was a rabbi at Congregation Rodfei Zedek in Hyde Park, and for almost twenty-five years, I have had the great honor of serving as rabbi of North Suburban Synagogue Beth El in Highland Park. I have always taken my role as a preacher very seriously, and I pray that the lessons I have taught from the pulpit have enriched the lives of my congregants.

My favorite Biblical passage is Genesis 32:25. The text informs us that Jacob is ready to return to the land of Canaan after fleeing from his brother Esau. In preparation for their meeting, Jacob arises during the night and takes his wives and children and all of his possessions across the stream Jabbock. The Torah states: "Jacob was left alone. And a man wrestled with him until the break of dawn." This struggle, in the loneliness of night, forever changes Jacob. His name will no longer be Jacob, "but Israel, for he has striven with beings divine and human, and has prevailed" (Genesis 32:29). For me, this struggle never ends; every day we attempt to meet the challenges of life. Sometimes we prevail; other times we do not. Like Jacob, we walk away wounded, limping from the encounter, but blessed in the process.

Encountering Torah represents the challenge of creating a little bit of heaven on earth, utilizing the wisdom of our tradition to make this world a better place for all. This is not an easy task, and it is always a struggle. As a serious Jew, it is my responsibility, and indeed my privilege, to take on that struggle and transmit the wisdom of Torah to my community. In the over thirty-six years that I have been a rabbi, my congregants have challenged me to fulfill the roles indicated on my ordination certificate: "Rabbi and Preacher and Teacher in Israel."

PREFACE

The image on the cover of the book represents the beginning of Jacob's journey from Canaan. Jacob dreams that "a stairway was set on the ground and its top reached to the sky, and angels of God were going up and down on it" (Genesis 28:12). This particular image is personally meaningful, and this rendering by the Israeli artist Morris Dahan of Tzefat is especially significant, as an original painting with this same image graces a wall of our Jerusalem apartment. The symbolism of the dream, the journey, the ladder, and, eventually, Jacob's night-time struggle and his return to Canaan is not only part of the Biblical story but relates to the personal imagery of my life as well.

I have dedicated this book to members of my family, both past and present. My parents, Bernard (ז״ל) and Dorothy (ז״ל) Kurtz, as well as my in-laws, Samuel (ז״ל) and Zena Wise, have always been my greatest teachers. My wife Bryna is my best friend, my life partner, and my *ezer k'negdo*—my best supporter, and my chief critic. My daughters, Hadassa and Shira, as well as my son-in-law, Haim, have brought me great pride and *nachas*, and my grandchildren, Shmuel Binyamin, Meytal Dvora, and Anael Rina have given me immense joy. I dedicate this book to all of them.

I am grateful to many people who have assisted me in the publication of this book. I want to thank members of my community who have shown me great love and respect. I want to express my gratitude to my colleagues and staff members at Beth El with whom I work and who continue to challenge me to be a better rabbi. My assistants, Lennie Kay and Renee Hillman, have typed my work, made my life easier, and have supported me not only in preparing my sermons, but in conveying my teachings to our community.

I want to thank the *Chicago Jewish News*, its publisher, Joseph Aaron, and its managing editor, Pauline Dubkin Yearwood. Since the inception of the weekly newspaper eighteen years ago, I have contributed a monthly Torah column. This venue has allowed me to share my wisdom with the community. I have been able to refine many of these published sermons and include them in this book. I am grateful for their support.

I wish to thank the committee members who have worked with me to make this book a reality. Donna Becker has been of immense assistance in bringing this book to life. Her countless hours in the Beth El office and at home are much appreciated. Karen Bieber oversaw the printing, and I am extremely thankful to Karen who is one of my longest-standing congregants. I am thankful to Dr. Betsy Katz and Professor Roberta Kwall for their assistance in proofreading the text and offering very helpful comments. I wish to thank my editor Amy Gottlieb for her thoughtful work and careful editing, her wisdom, and her friendship. Jen Klor has been a wonderful designer of the book and its cover. I thank her for her expertise and her advice. I wish to thank our printer, James Harris, for his professional advice and for seeing the book to print. I also wish to thank the contributors whose names are found in the beginning of this book. They have not only supported this book's publication, they have also donated generously to support educational programs and youth scholarships at North Suburban Synagogue Beth El.

During the preparation of this book, my sister Janice Freedman (ז״ל) passed away. Her family, as well as my sister Renee's and mine, have been greatly diminished by her passing. I am extremely pleased that her name appears in the list of donors, and I am thankful to our many friends who made this possible.

Finally, I have been truly blessed by God, and for that I am eternally grateful. It is traditional to write at the conclusion of a Jewish book: *Tam v'nishlam shevaḥ le-El borei olam*—"The book is complete, praise be to God, Creator of the universe."

Rabbi Vernon H. Kurtz
February 2013 / *Shevat* 5773

About the Sermons

Many of my sermons include Biblical and Talmudic references, quotations from a variety of books and articles, and anecdotes. I have cited the primary sources in the text itself. In order to give interested readers suggestions for further reading, I have provided bibliographic notes at the end of the book. Sermonic material is often comprised of stories, sayings, and assorted teachings that a rabbi absorbs from all corners of life over the course of many years. As such, it is not possible to provide sources and citations as completely as one would in an academic work. The bibliographic notes do not in any way reflect the full complement of secondary material I've drawn upon in my sermons; they are intended to serve as mere guideposts for interested readers and should not be viewed as a definitive list of secondary sources.

For literary purposes, I have modified or paraphrased some quotations attributed to specific individuals. Those readers who wish to quote directly from these sources are encouraged to check against the original version. Substantial efforts also have been made to document the multitude of original sources mentioned in the text, and I take full responsibility for any inadvertent errors.

Please note that I have included two *divrei Torah*, two sermons, for each Torah portion, or *parashah*, except those that are commonly read together, where one sermon per portion is included. There is no sermon for *V'zot Ha-B'rakhah*, as it is read on Simḥat Torah, and I have never preached on it.

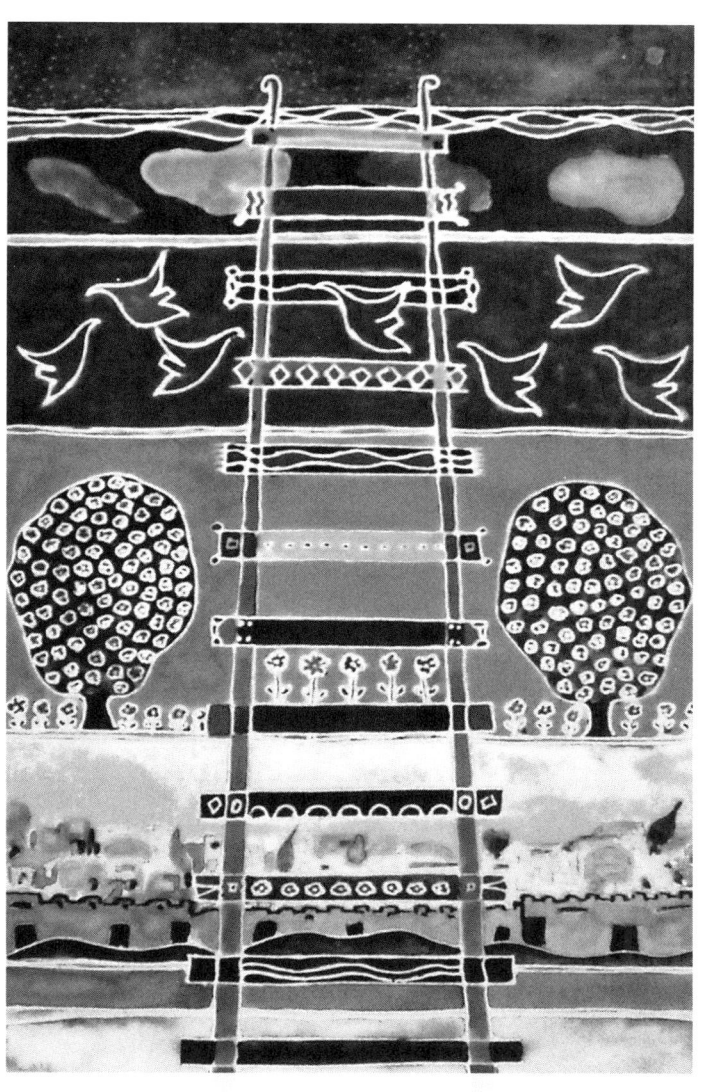

GENESIS
בראשית
BERE'SHIT

BERE'SHIT
A Closer Look

Two women visit an art museum. One is eager to go to lunch and cannot understand why her companion is spending her time examining one particular picture. "It looks just like a photograph; let's go," she says. But her friend persists. "Well, as long as we are here, let's look." She moves closer to the picture and studies it. "You know," she says, "there is really more here than meets the eye."

We are all alike. We think we are looking, but we don't really see; we believe we are hearing, but we don't actually listen. Life passes us by so quickly that we rarely stop to smell the flowers, observe the beauty of nature, relish the few moments we have with our loved ones. The video camera keeps shooting and tallies the minutes by tracking the feet of film we use. We have lost the ability to see the still photography of the moment, to appreciate its presence, and to observe the wonders that are always around us.

Shabbat *Bere'shit* marks the beginning of the Torah cycle. It always comes in the fall of the year as the season changes, and we, in the northern hemisphere, move toward the winter season. For those of us in the midwest, winter may be difficult, as it brings with it dark days and cold, but autumn is one of the most beautiful periods of the seasonal cycle.

When my family and I lived on the south side of Chicago and wanted to take visiting relatives and friends on a tour of the city and its metropolitan areas, we would drive north on Lake Shore Drive and continue our journey on Sheridan Road along Lake Michigan. This beautiful drive encompasses both urban and suburban areas. I recall, in particular, one drive in which we took our Israeli friends north on Sheridan Road during the fall season. They had never seen the beautiful colors of the fall artistry and the sparkling hues of the leaves. Seeing the foliage through their eyes gave us a renewed sense of wonder. Yet, now that I live on the north shore,

I neglect to enjoy that scenic drive and instead rush around, worrying about the current state of the roads and the traffic patterns.

Rabbi Milton Steinberg was one of the great rabbinic figures of the twentieth century. During World War II, while visiting the troops stationed in Texas, Steinberg suffered a heart attack. For months, he was confined to a hospital and was later permitted to stay in a hotel. The first Rosh Hashanah upon his return to his congregation, Park Avenue Synagogue in New York City, he delivered a sermon that became a classic of rabbinic homiletics. Remarking on his first venture into the outdoors after his hospitalization, he said, "How often I, too, had been indifferent to sunlight, how often, preoccupied with petty and sometimes mean concerns, I had disregarded it." Now he could describe the great joy the sunlight afforded him. Everywhere he looked he saw the golden glow of sunlight. That Rosh Hashanah, Rabbi Steinberg urged his congregation to hold on to life. There is so much for which we ought to be grateful if we only take the time.

On Shabbat *Bere'shit*, Steinberg's words ring true once more. We read the story of creation. Whether it happened as described in the Biblical account is immaterial. As Ronnie Schreiber commented on a Jewish listserv: "If He took 144 hours to do it, well, that's pretty impressive. And if He took ten billion years, well, the scope of that is also pretty impressive." What is much more significant is that we recognize that the miracles of creation are always around us: the world and its beauty; nature and its bounties; the universe and its vast mysteries. Creation was not a one-time event.

My favorite passage in our liturgy occurs in the first blessing preceding the *Sh'ma* in the morning service. Twice, both at the beginning of the blessing and at the end, the liturgist states that "God, in His goodness, renews Creation day after day." Each day, as we open our eyes, we should experience creation anew and observe its wonders. How magnificent it is to see the world through refreshed eyes and renewed vision. How important it is for all of us to look, listen, see, and observe.

Jack Borden was a TV journalist who formed a Boston-based organization called "For Spacious Skies." This organization grew out of Borden's street-corner survey in which he stopped twenty people in a row, put his hand over their eyes, visor-style, and asked, "How would you describe the present appearance of the sky?" None of the people surveyed could describe the beauty of the clear blue sky overhead. He immediately decided to launch his organization.

"The sky is something we just can't get away from," Borden explained. "It is evanescent, it's reborn every minute. Once we develop a perception of the sky as an everyday amenity in our lives, we're on a whole new visual diet, and we can see everything in a new way. Most people, though, never notice the sky. It's just background for them."

Sky awareness is an interesting concept. It instructs us to be more sensitive to the words of the prayer that we recite three times daily in which we thank God "for Your miracles which daily attend us and for Your wondrous kindnesses."

On September 9, 1858, the poet, essayist, and naturalist Henry David Thoreau wrote in his journal: "A man sees only what concerns him. A botanist absorbed in the pursuit of grasses does not distinguish the grandest pasture oaks. He as it were tramples down oaks unwittingly in his walk."

We are all guilty of the same transgression. Shabbat *Bere'shit* encourages us to open our eyes to the world around us, to its beauty and its mystery. Each morning, we are reminded once again to witness creation renewed and marvel at its freshness. Like the woman in the art gallery, all we need to do is take the time and examine what we see a little more closely. Then we, too, will be able to say, "There is really more here than meets the eye."

BERE'SHIT
The World Gone Wrong

Not even ten generations into the creation of the world, God is disillusioned with the crown of the creative process. On the sixth day of creation, when human life was created, the text states: "And God saw all that He had made, and found it very good" (Genesis 1:31). Yet by the time *parashat Bere'shit* ends and Noaḥ is born, the text tells us: "The Lord saw how great was man's wickedness on earth, and how every plan devised by his mind was nothing but evil all the time. And the Lord regretted that He had made man on earth, and His heart was saddened" (Genesis 6:5–6).

What a difference a few generations make. The story, which began in the Garden of Eden, is now so removed from Paradise that God is forced to regret what He created. While most people who read the text sense that the real downfall occurs with Adam and Eve eating of the forbidden fruit and being banished from the Garden, the real crisis of the first human family derives from Adam and Eve's children.

Cain and Abel were the first children born in a normal biological manner. As two brothers, they shared the entire world, a world that was at their fingertips. But they did not get along. In a verse pregnant with possibilities, the Torah tells us: "Cain said to his brother Abel … and when they were in the field, Cain set upon his brother Abel and killed him" (Genesis 4:8). Fratricide is already part of the human condition. Two human beings—before them the entire world—and one raises his hand to kill the other. What caused such hatred, enmity, and violence? The text only hints at possible responses. The Rabbis of the Midrash view this particular story as a prototype of man's inhumanity to man and delve into its meaning.

The Rabbis in *Genesis Rabbah* 22:7 read the text as an allegory for the origins of human aggression. Since both brothers had before them the entire world, Abel laid claim to the movable property and Cain to the land. But neither was satisfied. Cain said, "The land you stand on is mine," while Abel retorted, "What you are wearing is mine." One said, "Strip"; the other retorted, "Fly off the ground." And then, "Cain rose up against his brother Abel." A second interpretation suggests that they split the real estate of the world, and their struggle was over who would get the land upon which the Temple would be built. Their disagreement was intense: "Cain rose up against his brother Abel." A third interpretation suggests that the issue itself was sex. Since there were no women on the face of the earth besides their mother, "their quarrel was about the first Eve." Rabbi Huna explains: "An additional twin was born with Abel. One [Cain] said, 'I will have her because I am the firstborn.' The other [Abel] said, 'I must have her because she was born with me.'" The conclusion of the argument resulted in violence.

The Rabbis suggest that aggression and violence may occur because of envy, jealousy, and misunderstandings between human beings. Each of the Rabbinic comments highlights a possible cause for human aggression whose origins can stem from controversies over territory, religion, or sex.

Throughout the history of the world, nations have fought over territory. In the Middle East, for example, both Israelis and Palestinians claim the same land. From the earliest days of human existence, violence and aggression have occurred when there have been disagreements over control of territory. But it does not end there.

In our modern society, even neighborhoods are seen as territories. Very often, gang warfare ensues when a certain gang claims a neighborhood, a street, or an alley as part of its territory. Even young children, when they place their stakes on a piece of property—whether a tree house, a play area, or the corner of the sandbox—are prepared to fight in their own way to hold on to that which they think is rightfully theirs.

Unfortunately, religion has been used as a cause for hatred and enmity throughout history. Whether we look at the Crusades, the conquering wars of Islam, or the modern warfare fought in the name of religion, religion has been used as a crutch to hurt, maim, and wound. While it can serve as a salve, religion can also be used as a stick, and, too often, it has been. People have been killed in the name of religion throughout history, and, unfortunately, over the expanse of this globe, that type of violence still occurs.

And Freud was correct. We are an aggressive people, and sex often motivates aggression. Too often, violence in the home, or domestic abuse, is caused by petty jealousies and feelings of envy. Too many people have been killed in the name of love. Freud wrote that our first lust is for mother or father, though incest taboos usually keep that under control. But sexual desire is never totally dismissed, and too much pain, hurt, and injury have been caused because of it.

The ancient Rabbis recognized these dynamics of human personality. We can bring so much goodness to the world, but we can also bring destruction. Cain and Abel were the only two siblings on the face of this earth, and they could not live together. How sad that God is upset with His creation at this early moment of human history. As God looks down upon us on this day, are we any different? Have we improved our lot? Do we deserve once more to live in the Garden of Eden? Each time we read this selection in the Biblical story, we must ask ourselves these questions.

NOAḤ
Lurking Evil

We all know the story of Noaḥ, the flood, and the ark. According to the Bible, Noaḥ and everything that was inside the ark was saved. But according to a Rabbinic legend, there was also something saved outside of the ark. Og, an enemy of the Israelite people, was saved from the flood, and this individual's survival shaped the course of Israelite history in the times of the patriarchs and during the Israelite journey to the Land of Canaan.

A *midrash* in *Pirkei de-Rabbi Eliezer* 23 states that as Noaḥ gathered all of the animals into the ark, Og, one of the giants on the face of the earth, managed to save himself by hanging onto the ark. Og promised Noaḥ he would remain Noaḥ's servant for eternity if he could just hold on to the ark and last out the storm. According to the legend, Og saved himself because Noaḥ made a hole in the ark and gave him food during the flood.

According to Rabbinic interpretation, Og reappears during Abram's time when Lot, Abram's nephew, is captured in the war of the four kings against the five kings. An unnamed individual tells Abram of his nephew's misadventure: "A fugitive brought the news to Abram the Hebrew" (Genesis 14:13). This person, according to Rashi, was Og, and the *Targum Jonathan*, an Aramaic translation of the Bible, actually quotes this *midrash*, informing us that this was the very same Og who had survived Noaḥ's flood. In later Biblical history, Og, the King of Bashan, attempts to stop the Israelite advance to the Land of Canaan. The Torah tells us: "And King Og of Bashan, with all his people, came out to Edrei to engage them in battle" (Numbers 21:33). Og, the last of the giants, now 500 years of age, was defeated by the Israelites who made their way toward Canaan.

If God went so far as to destroy all humankind because of their corruption, why would Og, the embodiment of evil, have been spared? For what purpose was he the exception to the rule?

Og could have been left to die and evil would have been removed from the world, but that is not what life is all about. Life is a challenge to every human being who must inhabit the world, confront all of its temptations, and, yet, still manage to bring goodness, kindness, and gentleness to a universe that sorely needs it.

Perhaps the survival of Og reminds us that, even when God recreated the world, evil could not totally be subdued. Even as Noaḥ attempted to begin life anew, he represented the embodiment of both good and evil. He was a human being who constantly had to make decisions. Some of those decisions were appropriate. After all, Noaḥ was the only individual in his generation who was righteous. It was Noaḥ who built the ark to save humankind and animal life. On the other hand, Noaḥ was also the one who got drunk and led his family to dishonor and division.

It would be a boring world if we only had the capacity to do good. Instead, we must constantly challenge ourselves, channel our emotions, our drives, and our passions, recognizing that each time we make a decision, we must do it for good and not for ill. Our tradition understands that the evil inclination is part of the human soul. *Genesis Rabbah* 9:7 states: "If it were not for the evil impulse, no man would build a house or take a wife or beget children or engage in business."

We live in a world filled with a great deal of hatred and enmity. Unfortunately, there are individuals who refuse to appreciate that God created each and every one of us in God's image and who create havoc in our world with their bias, prejudice, and violent hatred toward others. How should we think of them, and how should we react toward them?

In *The Sunflower*, by famed Nazi hunter Simon Wiesenthal, Wiesenthal writes of his experiences as a young Jew in a concentration camp. One day, Wiesenthal is taken with his work detail from the camp to clean medical waste at a makeshift Army hospital. There he is taken to the bedside of a Nazi soldier whose head is swathed in bandages. The dying

Nazi blindly extends his hand toward Wiesenthal and begins to speak. Wiesenthal listens silently while the Nazi confesses to having participated in the burning alive of an entire village of Jews. The soldier, terrified of dying with this burden of guilt, begs absolution from Wiesenthal. Having listened to the Nazi's story for several hours, torn between horror and compassion for a dying man, Wiesenthal must decide how to react. Can he accept the apology of this dying Nazi, or should he refuse to exonerate him for his dastardly crimes? The encounter concludes as Wiesenthal finally walks out of the room without speaking.

How do we respond to evil in the world? Do we respond with more hatred or by modeling love, compassion, and care for others? There is no easy answer; the dilemma remains. I believe the Rabbinic *midrash* of Og surviving the flood is meant to tell us that evil will always be with us. We may attempt to subdue it or we may nurture it. Was Noah wrong by giving food to Og? Should he have thrown him off the ark altogether, letting him drown in the flowing waters, or should he have thrown him a lifeline and given him a chance to live?

What would you have done if you had been in Noah's shoes, or those of Weisenthal in the story of *The Sunflower*? This is the dilemma of the human condition. We don't have easy answers nor perhaps should we. The challenge of being human is not to negate the fact that evil is all around us. It is up to us to channel our drives, passions, and energy into goodness and to hope and pray that we can leave the world a little bit better than we found it. If we can do that, we will have accomplished our purpose here on earth.

NOAḤ
The Power of Words

Rabbi Shimon ben Gamliel said to his servant Tabbai, "Go and buy me good food in the market." Tabbai went out and brought back tongue. The rabbi told him, "Go out and buy me bad food in the market." Tabbai went out and brought back tongue. Whereupon the rabbi said, "When I told you to get good food, you brought me back tongue, and, when I told you to get bad food, you also brought me tongue." Tabbai replied, "Good comes from it and bad comes from it. When the tongue is good, there is nothing better, and when it is bad, there is nothing worse" (*Leviticus Rabbah* 33:1).

The power of the tongue is evident in *parashat Noaḥ*. The Torah tells us that the people of the earth wished to ensure that a flood would never again destroy the world, so they built a high tower that they hoped would reach heaven. God, enraged by their effrontery, decided to put an end to the project: "Thus the Lord scattered them from there over the face of the whole earth; and they stopped building the city" (Genesis 11:8).

Two questions have always puzzled me about this story. What horrible crime did the people commit to deserve such punishment, and, if their sin was so great, why were they not utterly destroyed like the generation of the flood? Some midrashic commentators, in searching for answers, focus upon the first verse of the story: "Everyone on earth had the same language and the same words" (Genesis 11:1). The last part of this phrase, *devarim aḥadim*, is very difficult to translate. One explanation in *Genesis Rabbah* 38:6 states: "They spoke against the Lord our God, the Lord is One (*eḥad*)" (Deuteronomy 6:4). Their sin was that they used words for evil purposes against God.

How can one sin against God with words? On the holiest day of the year, Yom Kippur, we stand before God and admit our transgressions as we recite the *Al Ḥet*, the long confessional. Over one-third of the transgressions on the list are sins of speech: "We have sinned against You in idle chatter … we have sinned against You by the way we talk … we have sinned against You through foolish talk … we have sinned against You by speaking ill of others." The *maḥzor* agrees with Tabbai that the tongue is a powerful and dangerous weapon. We must be careful how we use it and atone when we abuse it.

If we would only think before we speak, what a better world this could be. A proverb states: "A bird you set free, you may catch again, but a word that escapes your lips will not return." Remember the old limerick, "Sticks and stones may break my bones, but words will never hurt me"? We may have believed it as children; as adults, we know that it is not true. Words can and do hurt.

The tongue can offer words of kindness and compassion, it can offer support and aid to another human being, and it can offer encouragement to one who needs it. But it can also gossip, criticize, scold, and enunciate words that are destructive and devastating. This is why, I believe, the meditation at the conclusion of the silent *Amidah* states: "My God, keep my tongue from evil, my lips from lies."

The generation of the Tower of Babel, according to Rabbi Yoḥanan, used "sharp words" against man and, therefore, against God. They used the power of the tongue to injure, maim, and even destroy.

The *midrash* continues, "They were united in their possessions, what one possessed being at the other's disposal." They understood the concept of sharing with others; unfortunately, they used their resources for evil purposes.

In a caring society, we share our gifts with our fellow human beings, building upon the strength of community members to form model societies. Three men once came to the Angel of Fire and asked him to entrust them with his most precious possession, the white fire. He did so with the instruction, "Keep it well and use it wisely." The first man walked into a dark alley where people were groping in total darkness. He heard them cry, "If only someone would bring light to liberate us from this dark prison." The man kindled wood and made a huge fire so that all could see. The second man journeyed to a snow-capped mountain where people were freezing. Moved by their plight, he lit a fire to provide warmth for them. The third man wondered how he could keep the fire safe from the wind and rain. "I will hide it within my heart where no harm can come to it," he thought. When the three men returned to the Angel and reported to him how they used his gift, the Angel said to the first two men that their fires would never burn out, but to the third, he said, "Oh, poor man, my white fire can live only when it serves," and the Angel showed him that his fire had gone out.

It is not enough to keep our gifts inside our hearts. It is important to share them with others. The Tower of Babel generation was not destroyed because they knew what it meant to share their gifts with others, but they sinned when they were not inclined to use them for positive purposes that would benefit their society.

An anonymous quote reads: "The six most important words in the English language are: *I admit I made a mistake.* The five most important are: *You did a good job.* The four most important are: *What is your opinion?* The three most important are: *I appreciate you.* The two most important are: *Thank you.* The most important word in the English languages is the word *we,* and the least important word is *I.*"

The Tower of Babel generation understood the "we" but never used it for good purposes. May we share our resources to help others and use our words to uplift our fellow human beings.

LEKH LEKHA
The Promised Land, Then and Now

Parashat Lekh Lekha marks the beginning of the narrative of the Jewish people. Abram, as he is called at the beginning of this *parashah*, takes center stage along with his wife, Sarai, as they form the first family of our people. Their behavior continues to serve as a model of people of faith.

The first verse in the *parashah* begins the story: "The Lord said to Abram, 'Go forth from your native land and from your father's house to the land that I will show you'" (Genesis 12:1). Abram journeys from his familiar ancestral homeland and follows a God he does not know to the Land of Canaan. We may ask ourselves why Abram's journey is necessary. After all, if Abram was such a great individual and natural leader, could he not have brought monotheism to the world from his ancestral homeland? It should have been possible for him to accept the true God and follow God's dictates in any land.

If one assumes a Zionist mode of interpretation, the response is clear. Abram can only reach his full potential in the Promised Land: "Go forth … to the land that I will show you." It is only there that Abram can raise his physical, spiritual, intellectual, and emotional status. God tells Abram that his physical presence in the Holy Land will enhance his ability to be a person of faith and a leader of his nation.

Abram was the first *oleh*, the first immigrant to Israel. *Aliyah* should be considered one of the highest *mitzvot* of our generation. For 2,000 years, our people yearned to return to its ancestral homeland, to follow Abram's path. Today, we can live in a free democratic Jewish state that challenges us to build a society based upon Jewish values and democratic ideals. For those of us who live in the free world, this is an *aliyah* of choice whereby we take upon ourselves the special responsibilities and privileges of living in the land that God promised to Abram and Sarai. Within the Conservative movement, we have always been proponents of Zionism. We need to talk openly of the possibilities of *aliyah* within our congregations, institutions, and organizations and stress our ability to formulate a unique society that can serve as a model to Jews and non-Jews throughout the world. Abram and Sarai were the first to make *aliyah*, and we should at least contemplate following their example.

There are other interpretations to this verse. A Ḥasidic teaching suggests that this verse be read: "Go to yourself, go back to your roots," examine your past, and let it have an impact upon you in the present. As a people of history, it is essential that we know from whence we have come, for only in that manner can we begin to plan the future.

For those of us who decide to stay in North America, in the Diaspora, opportunities for a significant attachment to the State of Israel and its people should be a *sine qua non* of our ongoing activities. In order to understand our Judaism and the message of the Jewish people, we must have a constant attachment to the land, its history, and its destiny. Today we are accorded that possibility.

It is very easy today to be a participant in either short- or long-term programs in the State of Israel. Our own Conservative movement offers significant programs of which we can avail ourselves. Our Masorti movement in Israel is always ready to receive guests who can become part of Masorti congregations and communities on a short- or long-term basis. Our young people are afforded the opportunity to participate in programs during the summer, as well as semester and year-long programs.

To be actively engaged in Jewish life today means that we must have an ongoing attachment to the State of Israel and its people. If we truly want to understand what it means to be a Jew and to appreciate our ancestral roots, we should try to study in Israel or plan to spend significant time there as often as possible.

The Biblical commentator Rashi offers yet another interpretation of the verse. He suggests that Abram was asked to go to this new land for his "personal good and benefit." Abram's engagement with the Land of Canaan would be of great help to him in the establishment of his leadership and in the maturation of his character. The same can be said for us as well; attachment to the Land makes us better Jews and can make us better human beings.

If we don't make *aliyah*, or if for some reason we are not able to take advantage of long-term programs in Israel, we can still be actively involved with the State and its people. We should plan trips to Israel, either through our congregations or privately with our families, in order to feel connected to the Land. We can work on behalf of the institutions that serve our movement's needs in the State of Israel. We can be involved with the Zionist movement to promote Zionism as a vision to be actualized in a Jewish, pluralistic, democratic state. We can support Israel financially and politically from this side of the Atlantic and feel part of its ongoing enterprise. No task is too small in order to guarantee the safety and security of our people in the State of Israel and to assert our attachment to the Land.

Abram and Sarai were the first Jews to take a journey to the Promised Land. As the first family of the Jewish people, they serve as our models. May we take their lessons to heart and follow their example.

LEKH LEKHA
Abram, Melchizedek, and the Act of Giving

We think of Abram as a man of faith, but he was also a mighty warrior. In *parashat Lekh Lekha*, Abram is instrumental in rescuing his nephew Lot from captivity. In Genesis 14, a war takes place between four kings and five kings, with the former defeating the latter. In the process, Lot is taken captive. Abram is told of this occurrence and immediately goes into battle to rescue his nephew.

When he returns victorious, two individuals meet him: the King of Sodom and King Melchizedek of Salem. In those meetings, a great deal is told about Abram's character and values.

The Torah tells us that Melchizedek "brought out bread and wine; he was a priest of God Most High" (Genesis 14:18). Abram is blessed by Melchizedek, and, in turn, Abram gives a tenth of everything to the king.

The text then tells us that the King of Sodom said to Abram, "Give me the persons, and take the possessions for yourself." Abram immediately rejects that proposal and states, "I swear to the Lord, God Most High, Creator of heaven and earth: I will not take so much as a thread or a sandal strap of what is yours; you shall not say, 'It is I who made Abram rich'" (Genesis 14:21–23).

Why does Abram give a gift to Melchizedek and greet him with great honor, and, on the other hand, reject the King of Sodom's offer of including him in the spoils of war?

In the *JPS Torah Commentary*, Dr. Nahum Sarna suggests that there is a difference between the actions of the two kings and the text is very sensitive to that difference. The King of Sodom "came out" empty-handed to meet his benefactor, and the first word he uttered was "give." The

King of Salem "brought out" bread and wine and offered a blessing, even if he may have come to collect his tithe at the very same time.

Dr. Sarna suggests that there are "givers" and "takers" in this world. Melchizedek was a giver and was received with great honor by Abram who was more than pleased to give him tribute. On the other hand, the King of Sodom was a taker. He was pleased that Abram had helped win the war, and, though he would allow him to take some of the spoils, he was more concerned about obtaining his own portion first.

In truth, these concepts are with us to this very day. The world is comprised of givers and takers: those who use their talents, resources, and energy to help others, and those who see others simply as objects for their own purposes and personal gain.

Pirkei Avot 5:21 outlines the difference between Abraham (Abram), the giver and the King of Sodom, the taker. It states: "Whoever possesses these three qualities is numbered among the disciples of our father Abraham ... a generous spirit, a humble soul, a modest appetite."

In Rabbinic Hebrew, the term "a good eye," which is used in the Hebrew text, denotes a generous sense of benevolence, a wish to help others. This was part of Abraham's nature. He exhibited a humble soul when he spoke to the Lord and argued for the deliverance of the righteous people in Sodom and stated: "Here I venture to speak to my Lord, I who am but dust and ashes" (Genesis 18:27).

Finally, one who possesses a modest appetite or a lowly spirit will reject luxuries and excesses, preferring only life's bare necessities, seeing them as ample for his needs. He will be grateful for everything that is given to him, rather than attempting to take what may not necessarily be close at hand. *Pirkei Avot* 5:21 states that whoever follows those prescriptions deserves to be of the descendants of Abraham. One must be a giver. A generous spirit and a kind soul are a *sine qua non* of being a descendant of Abraham; modesty, humility, and generosity should be part of the DNA of each of his progeny.

On the other hand, *Pirkei Avot* 5:12 states that there are four kinds of people. "The first is the type of person who says: 'Mine is mine and yours is yours.' This is the average trait. However, some say this trait is characteristic of Sodom." Commentators have asked why someone who takes care of his own and allows another to take care of his own should be seen as a dweller in Sodom. After all, respecting the rights of others is commendable. However, there is a danger in this approach, fair and just though it be, as it may lead to closing a hand to those in need. One may say, "I am only concerned about myself; why should I be concerned about others? I don't need to be generous to other human beings; I need only to take care of my needs." If this is a general societal attitude, disaster is inevitable. The takers become unwilling to share their resources, energy, and efforts with other human beings. If that attitude prevails, then all of society suffers, and we are on our way to replicating the community of Sodom.

If the world can be divided into givers and takers, we must ask ourselves: "Where do we stand?" Are we so self-centered that we are concerned only for ourselves, or are we ready to share with others? Do we recognize our responsibility to those in need of friendship, kindness, and support? What is our attitude to those who are our neighbors, our friends, and the strangers in our midst?

Each of us is transformed when we give to others. We add goodness to the world and kindness to human society, and we gain humility and a sense of gratitude for the gifts that are ours. When we are merely takers, like the people of Sodom, we care little about other creations of God and instead start down the road to moral depravity. Where do we find ourselves between these two poles?

Abram felt an affinity to Melchizedek, the King of Salem, because he recognized him as a giver. As *Pirkei Avot* 5:21 states, if we truly want to be of the descendants of Abraham, we must carry on his attributes and characteristics. They must be part of our genetic code and our moral compass, motivating our lives and our spirits.

VA-YERA
The Two Abrahams

We all experience a singular epic and transformative event at some point in our lives. In *parashat Va-yera*, we read of that epic event in the life of *Avraham Avinu*, Abraham our patriarch.

In the story of *Akedat Yitzḥak*, the binding of Isaac, Abraham is asked to take his beloved son, "and go to the land of Moriah, and offer him there as a burnt offering on one of the heights that I [God] will point out to you" (Genesis 22:2). Abraham is ready and willing to sacrifice his son at the bidding of God. He brings the knife to Isaac's throat when an angel of God appears from the heavens and calls, "Abraham! Abraham!" (Genesis 22:11) and tells the patriarch that God does not want the sacrifice of his beloved son.

If we look closely at the text, the musical notations include a *pasek*, a momentary stop, between the repetitions of the name Abraham. Some commentators suggest that this separation is highly significant. The Zohar, the great mystical book of our tradition, states: "The latter Abraham was not like the former" (*Va-yera* 120 a–b). The text suggests that there are two Abrahams, the Abraham before the *Akedah* and the Abraham after the *Akedah*.

The first Abraham was the man who could argue with God. He was full of confidence, sure of himself, and was able to make treaties with Abimelech and pacts with Melchizedek. He had physical security; he had enormous wealth and power. Then an epic event occurred in his life. He was ready to sacrifice his most prized possession—his son—the key to his future and that of his nation. After the *Akedah*, Abraham was a different man. This second Abraham was a man who had lost his confidence: his wife died; he was alone, insecure, and worried about finding a mate for his beloved son.

These two Abrahams reflect two aspects of one personality. These forces within Abraham are found within each of us. With Abraham One, we can be confident and bold, satisfied with our achievements, striving for success. But with Abraham Two, we can be frightened, doubtful, and aware of our weakness and mortality. Many times, an epic event in the course of one's life changes one's perspective. This event can lead to personal fulfillment; it can also lead to a diminishment of self.

For some of us, the defining event may be a serious illness. We are never the same person again. With good fortune, we may return to physical health, but mentally and emotionally, we are never the same. Hopefully, we can learn positive lessons from the experience concerning the need to take care of our bodies and souls at the same time that we learn to experience the true gifts of life: appreciating a loved one, devoting ourselves to community service, or enhancing our personal growth.

For others, the defining event may be the death of a relative or a close friend. Life is never the same after the death of a loved one. We are forced to pick up the pieces of our shattered lives and attempt to repair them. It is never an easy task, but do it we must. Often we find a reserve of inner strength and courage we never knew we possessed.

The defining event can also be a crisis of faith. As we proceed through our lives, there will always be trials and tribulations that force us to re-examine our bonds with God. Sometimes we are led to doubt, but many times our belief system can mature and be strengthened in the process. Even Abraham must have experienced personal doubt on his journey from his birthplace in Ur of the Chaldees to the central event of this *parashah* on Mount Moriah. For example, in Genesis 15:2, Abraham doubts God's promise, as he is childless: "O Lord God, what can You give me, seeing that I shall die childless?" Like Abraham, each of us, if we take our belief in God seriously, will have those moments when we are confident that God is by our side and other times when we may feel abandoned. Hopefully, we can learn to put our faith in perspective and grow in the process.

Life is filled with events that are potentially transformative. Sometimes these events are caused by difficult circumstances: divorce, loss of employment, failure at a given task, rejection from the college of our choice, or simply finding ourselves totally unappreciated or severely criticized. Sometimes, however, life-changing events can be positive, such as a religious awakening, a successful achievement, or finding a new love. We are ever-changing people, hopefully always growing, learning, and expanding our horizons. The epic events of our lives are different for each of us. Initially they may be deemed positive or negative, but it is how they affect us that will determine their true influence.

The angel's call to Abraham is eternal. After the *Akedah*, Abraham was not the same person. The Zohar states: "The latter was perfected, the former was still incomplete" (*Va-yera* 120 a–b). After the *Akedah*, Abraham realized the full implication of his decision to follow God's path.

Abraham is the prototype for us all. Abraham responded to the call of the angel by saying, "Here I am" (Genesis 22:11). To the challenges in our lives, we too must respond, "Here I am," working to ensure that the epic events we experience can be sources of personal growth, deeper faith, and renewed commitment to the common good.

VA-YERA
Biblical Family/Modern Problems

Ask many non-Jews what impresses them about Jewish life, and they will very often respond, "the Jewish family." Traditionally, Jewish family life has been thought to be one of the jewels of our cultural heritage. The family was the conduit for teaching values, responsibility to others, and commitment to lofty ideals. Many of us were raised in circumstances that promoted positive extended family relationships. In my own childhood, along with my parents and sisters, my grandparents, uncles, aunts, and cousins were an integral part of my early family life, and there is no doubt that this large kinship group had a crucial impact on me during my formative years.

Unfortunately, that model is no longer the norm, and Jewish family life is under enormous strain. Divorce, intermarriage, tensions in relationships, mobility patterns, and modern technology have led to new family models that present new challenges to Jewish life today.

In reality, the perfect Jewish family was an ideal that may never have existed. The Biblical models reflect modern problems. Husbands and wives are in quarrelsome relationships: Abraham and Sarah; Isaac and Rebecca; Jacob and his two wives; Moses and Zipporah. Parents and children are often at loggerheads: Noah and his sons; Isaac and his two sons; Jacob and his twelve sons, to name a few. Sibling rivalry is constantly present: Cain and Abel; Isaac and Ishmael; Jacob and Esau; Joseph and his brothers; Moses, Aaron, and Miriam—all have their differences. And toward the end of *parashat Va-yera*, another modern scenario is described for us: "Some time later, Abraham was told, 'Milcah too has borne children to your brother Nahor'" (Genesis 22:20).

This statement is indicative of modern life. What does it mean that Abraham was told of the births in his brother's house? While it is true that there were no telephones, mail delivery, fax machines, e-mail, or social media at that time, it seems unfortunate that Abraham was never directly notified by his brother of the birth of nephews and nieces in his own family.

Two brothers, born of the same mother and father, had totally lost contact with one another. "It was told to Abraham." Who told him? The commentary *Or Ha-Afela* suggests: "by the Holy Spirit"; in other words, not even in a personal communication from his brother.

The Ramban, Nachmanides, was very sensitive to the nuances of this story: "Now from the text it would appear that Abraham had no knowledge of them except on that day. It would have been impossible for him not to have heard until this time, for the distance between Mesopotamia and Canaan is not great." The Ramban is bothered by the breakup of the family unit and its results. When does Abraham renew contact with his own family? Inevitably, he reaches out when he needs their help in searching for a wife for his son Isaac.

This is typical of the modern family. We live in an age of fragmented families: grandparents in Florida, parents in Chicago, children in California, and extended family around the world. Brothers and sisters live on different coasts and never see one another or their children; first cousins are perfect strangers. When there is a loss in the family, very often extended families meet each other for the first time. All too often, I have been present at tension-filled family gatherings with strained relationships apparent among siblings or different generations of the family circle.

In his book, *Nofet Zufim*, Judah Messer Leon writes, "One father can maintain ten children, but ten children cannot maintain one father." In our own time, we find that many of our communal organizations are charged with performing these tasks.

In recent decades, we have witnessed the decline of the American family as an institution, and Jewish life is the poorer for it. I once heard a story about a religious school teacher who looked up from a Bible story and asked her students, "Why do you believe in God?" The students offered a variety of answers until one young girl raised her hand and responded, "I guess it just runs in our family." For many of us, religious education comes from the family. When I consider my own upbringing, I realize that I was heavily influenced by my extended family, parents, and grandparents, who instilled in me my Jewish consciousness and values.

In his essay, "The Family Reunion," Dr. Leslie Farber states: "The family is, indeed, inescapable. You may revile it, renounce it, reject it—but you cannot resign from it; you are born into it, and *it* lives within and through you, to the end of your days. This may be inspiring, it may also be very annoying; in either case, it is humbling."

The story of Abraham and Nahor highlights the problems of family life. Two brothers have lost contact with one another and must rely upon a third party to inform them of the joys they have missed. We recognize that there are no perfect relationships in the Biblical story, as there are none in real life. As a didactic book, the Bible calls for us to learn from its description of past events. We need to strengthen our own familial bonds, even as the Jewish community needs to respond to the realities of modern life on a communal level. Family relationships are central to Jewish life, and they will have an impact on the Jewish future. Let us be among the builders and solidifiers of these relationships for our own good and for the good of future generations of Jews.

ḤAYYEI SARAH
The Passion of Abraham

The Torah reading cycle over the last few weeks, including *parashat Ḥayyei Sarah*, describes the story of Abraham, our patriarch. Throughout his life, Abraham exhibits passion and exuberance. He is told by God, "Go forth from your native land" (Genesis 12:1), and he does so with the full intention to complete his journey wherever it may take him. When he hears that his nephew Lot is taken captive, he immediately sets out to rescue him. His initiatives in the rite of circumcision, in the *mitzvah* of hospitality, and even in his supreme faith in the story of the *Akedah* reveal Abraham's total immersion in his mission of being "The Father of our Nation." Even in this *parashah*, the details of his purchase of a burial plot for his wife Sarah and his interest in finding a suitable wife for his son Isaac portray his single-minded purpose and devotion to the task at hand.

Abraham's death and burial are described at the conclusion of *Ḥayyei Sarah*. The Talmud in *Baba Batra* 91a states: "On the day when Abraham our father passed away, all the great ones of the nations of the world stood in a line and said: 'Woe to the world that has lost its leader and woe to the ship that has lost its pilot.'" Abraham was a true leader; people gravitated to him, and he made a difference in their lives. He was a leader, both in times of peace and in times of upheaval, much like the captain of a ship who leads it through tranquil and stormy waters.

Our lineage traces us all the way back to Abraham, and we are asked to emulate his characteristics and his actions. Like Abraham, we are bound by the covenant that was created between him and God. Like Abraham, we are asked to be hospitable and generous of nature and of spirit. Like Abraham, we are to be devoted to our faith and to the continuity of the Jewish people. Like Abraham, we are to stimulate others to follow in our path and recognize the true God, the God of Israel and of humanity.

Just like us, Abraham is not perfect. We cannot condone some of his actions with respect to his wife Hagar and his son Ishmael. We are uncomfortable with how he pretends his wife Sarah is his sister when his own immediate danger seems to frighten him into taking defensive action. And some of us are uncomfortable with his immediate reaction of subservience to God's demand to offer up his son on Mount Moriah.

Yet, as children of Abraham, we are bound to follow many of the wonderful attributes that truly made him "The Father of our Nation." Throughout the episodes in which he appears in Genesis, Abraham is a man of passion. And it is this passion that should inspire us to follow in his footsteps.

We need charismatic individuals like Abraham who display a passion for Jewish life and want to make a difference in the world. The Midrash tells us "God desires the heart" (*Yalkut Shimoni Shemini* 247). We are asked to place our bodies, our souls, and our hearts into our Jewish experiences; to make a total commitment to our faith and our people; and to improve the lot of humanity. In this way, we follow the path of Abraham and truly represent him as his descendants on this earth.

There is a cute story about a salmon and a chicken walking along the street looking for work. As they peer into a restaurant window, they notice an advertised special on lox and eggs. The chicken says to the salmon, "Let's go in and inquire." "Nothing doing," says the salmon. "Why not?" asks the chicken. The salmon replies, "I'm not going into that place. All they want from you is a contribution. From me, what they want is total commitment."

As descendants of Abraham our patriarch and Sarah our matriarch, we are asked for total commitment. We are asked to live our lives with dedication and passion as Jews and as human beings. Like Abraham, we are not perfect, but we can make a difference in the world. Jewish tradition teaches that each of us has the potential to make a powerful contribution to our world and to all humanity. We must embrace our Jewish heritage and feel it in our bones, sinews, and veins. We must work for the continuity of the Jewish people and our security around the world. We must accept our responsibilities to the State of Israel, the land to which Abraham was directed and that was promised as an everlasting gift to his descendants. And we must be hospitable to all, opening up our homes and our lives for the welfare of everyone. If we can express that commitment, dedication, and passion, we can truly emulate the lives of Abraham and Sarah, who, according to the Biblical record, touched souls and saved lives.

ḤAYYEI SARAH
The Last Days of Abraham and David

In Abraham's last days, he loses his wife and decides to bury her in Hebron at the Cave of Machpelah. The Torah then states: "Abraham was now old, advanced in years, and the Lord had blessed Abraham in all things" (Genesis 24:1). According to most commentators, Abraham was blessed not only with material well-being but also with his religious and moral integrity intact.

In the *haftarah*, we are told the story of King David's last few days: "King David was now old, advanced in years; and though they covered him with bedclothes, he never felt warm" (1 Kings 1:1). The text concentrates on David's loss of physical abilities and the schemes of his dependents for a stake in the future of the monarchy.

Abraham and David did not live easy lives. Abraham was asked by God to uproot himself and his wife and move to a new country. Even in the Land of Canaan, life was not easy for him. He was forced to travel to Egypt in order to provide for his family, and though he was blessed with two children, Ishmael and Isaac, their upbringing was filled with conflict.

David's life, too, was not simple. He was a young shepherd when he was chosen to serve in Saul's palace. While he became a good friend of Saul's son Jonathan, his prowess at war made Saul jealous. David had to flee from Saul, and later from the Philistines, and though he wished to build a temple in Jerusalem, his dream remained unfulfilled. Toward the end of his life, palace intrigue was part of his experience.

The Biblical text teaches that no life is without successes and failures. We can easily identify with the Biblical figures because they are so much like we are. No one has or will be granted a life symbolized by the proverbial rose garden. We know that all lives are filled with thorns, thistles, and weeds. Yet, it is up to us to determine how we confront the challenges with which we are presented. What is our attitude toward life, not only when things are going well, but also when they are not?

Viktor Frankl, a noted Viennese psychiatrist, was taken first to Theresienstadt in September 1942, and then to Auschwitz in October 1944. Assigned to a labor detail, he was able to observe his fellow prisoners. He wondered how certain inmates in the concentration camp were able to maintain a sense of hope and inner strength while others lost their will to live. In his book, *Man's Search for Meaning,* Frankl argues that we cannot avoid suffering, but we can choose how to cope with it, find meaning in it, and move forward with renewed purpose. Frankl's work teaches that there are people who melt at the slightest disappointment or setback. And there are those who suffer immeasurably and yet maintain an air of optimism and hope.

Frankl states: "Everything can be taken from a man but one thing: the last of the human freedoms—to choose one's attitude in any given set of circumstances, to choose one's own way." Frankl writes that human freedom "is not freedom from conditions, but it *is* freedom to take a stand toward the conditions." We may not be able to control our destiny, but we can most certainly control how we confront it.

Gates of Repentance, the Reform movement's *maḥzor,* contains Rabbi Alvin I. Fine's poem, "Birth is a Beginning." An adaptation of the poem also appears in the Conservative movement's *Maḥzor Lev Shalem.* This poem is often recited by rabbis at funeral services, as its words are extremely meaningful in describing the journey of life:

> Birth is a beginning
> And death a destination.
> And life is a journey:
> From childhood to maturity
> And youth to age;
> From innocence to awareness
> And ignorance to knowing;
> From foolishness to discretion
> And then, perhaps, to wisdom;

From weakness to strength
Or strength to weakness—
And, often, back again;
From health to sickness
And back, we pray, to health again;
From offense to forgiveness,
From loneliness to love,
From joy to gratitude,
From pain to compassion,
And grief to understanding—
From fear to faith;
From defeat to defeat to defeat—
Until, looking backward or ahead,
We see that victory lies
Not at some high place along the way,
But in having made the journey, stage by stage,
A sacred pilgrimage.
Birth is a beginning
And death a destination.
And life is a journey,
A sacred pilgrimage—
To life everlasting.

Life is indeed a journey. We hope that we will be blessed with good health, wonderful support systems, prosperity, love, friendship, and much success. Life can be challenging, as we cannot control everything that happens to us physically, mentally, emotionally, financially, or otherwise. However, the manner in which we accept it, live with it, confront it, and challenge it is in our control.

The juxtaposition of the last days of Abraham and David can teach us an important lesson. Although both of their lives were filled with many challenges, their last few days are recounted differently. Nachmanides suggests that Abraham felt blessed with health, wealth, honor, and children. He appreciated all the gifts that had come his way.

David, on the other hand, was embittered and despondent near the end of his life. In the first chapter of the Book of Kings, his situation gets worse. After Solomon has been chosen to succeed his father, David tells him what to do when he ascends the throne. On his death bed, David tells his son to take vengeance on those who crossed him in life.

Our lives are very much like those of Abraham and David. We pray that we have many successes, but we also know that there will be failures and difficult moments. How we respond to them will tell a great deal about our character. I pray that when we leave this world, we shall be blessed as Abraham was. As the Torah states: "And Abraham breathed his last, dying at a good ripe age, old and contented; and he was gathered to his kin" (Genesis 25:8). Abraham lived a full life, knowing he had accomplished his mission here on earth. May we be privileged to do the same.

TOLEDOT
Jacob or Esau?

From the opening verses of *parashat Toledot* through the end of the Book of Genesis, Jacob is a central figure in the patriarchal narrative. His father, brother, children, uncle, and wives each have their distinct personalities, yet their individual tales are intertwined with Jacob's life story.

In the opening verses of the *parashah*, Rebecca and Isaac are presented with twin boys. Even before their birth, Jacob and Esau commence their rivalry: "But the children struggled in her womb" (Genesis 25:22). The Midrash suggests that the characteristics of these two young children were already present in utero: "When Rebecca stood near synagogues and schools, Jacob struggled to come out; when she passed idolatrous temples, Esau eagerly struggled to come out" (*Genesis Rabbah* 63:6).

As they grew up, Jacob and Esau's lives took on different patterns. The Torah tells us: "When the boys grew up, Esau became a skillful hunter, a man of the outdoors; but Jacob was a mild man who stayed in camp" (Genesis 25:27). Though twins, Jacob and Esau were very different from one another. Esau was known as a hunter, a person of the field, and a violent individual who used his wiles and hunting expertise to bring game home to his father. Jacob was mild-mannered and, unlike his brother, not a man of the outdoors.

In works of Rabbinic exegesis, Jacob and Esau are portrayed as the ancestors of two different peoples. Esau represented Rome: conquerors and warriors who used the clash of arms to gain their victories. Jacob represented Israel. According to Rabbinic understanding, Jacob spent his time in study, living in the tent, and learning the ways of the Lord. Jacob, the ancestor of the Jewish people, set the stage for those who would follow him. He became a role model for those whose lives were filled with Torah study and pious behavior.

But the story does not end there. Jacob, on the advice of Rebecca, is told to take from Isaac the blessing that was rightfully Esau's. In a very dramatic scene, Jacob dresses up like his brother and approaches his blind, aged father. Isaac, sensing that something has gone awry, asks, perhaps in innocence, "Who are you my son?" (Genesis 27:18). Jacob replies, "It is I, Esau your firstborn" (Genesis 27:19). Rashi, not wanting to view Jacob as a cunning liar, interprets this text to mean that Jacob was saying to his father, "Father, it is I, your son Jacob; Esau is your eldest."

Avivah Gottlieb Zornberg points out that some commentators understand this statement as suggesting that Jacob has now become Esau. The *Or Ha-Ḥayim* suggests that since Jacob has bought his birthright from Esau, he has also acquired some essential attributes of his brother. The *Sefat Emet* suggests that when Jacob assumes the costume of Esau, he takes on what has been Esau's role. In assuming the clothes, smell, and character of his brother, Jacob actually becomes Esau.

For centuries, the Jewish people have identified with Jacob, "a mild man, who stayed in camp" (lit. "abiding in tents"). The Torah was our life and our refuge. We were pleased to abide in tents, to be secreted away from the impurities that were part of the society in which we were not welcome. We stayed apart from worldly affairs.

However, history has shown that there have been those who have invaded those tents and refused to allow us to dwell in them safely and securely. The greatest catastrophe that ever befell our people occurred relatively recently. The Shoah was the worst possible nightmare of the Jewish people. No place was safe to hide; no land was secure. We wanted to remain mild-mannered, abiding in tents, but were forced to recognize that we became the hunter's prey.

The year 1948 brought a new situation to the Jewish people. Through the visions of builders, the declaration of the United Nations, and the blood and sweat of soldiers and fighters, a new state was established. The Jewish people returned to our ancient homeland, and once more we were counted among the nations of the world. For 2,000 years, we never had to deal with power, and we were confined to tents, living apart from society. Then the situation changed, and a new ethos was presented to the Jewish people.

In an essay, "The Ethics of Jewish Power," Rabbi Irving Greenberg suggests that 1948 brought an entirely new scenario to the Jewish people, a scenario filled with challenges and, yet, great hope. We assumed power, and with that power came new responsibilities. Rabbi Greenberg suggests that it is better to assume that power with all of its tremendous challenges and paradoxes than to be powerless once more. He writes, "The creation of the State of Israel places the power in the hands of Jews to shape their own destiny and to affect and even control the lives of others. This is a revolutionary 180-degree turn in the moral situation. The dilemmas of power are far different from the temptations and problems of powerlessness."

The challenges of power have undergone many tests since 1948. A minority people dwells among those who live in the State of Israel. Demands for security are constant, and not a day passes without the possibility of terrorism or all-out war.

Many challenges confront Israel and the Jewish world at this juncture in our history. On the one hand, we cannot afford to be the simple, mild-mannered Jacob, and, on the other hand, we must not become Esau, the hunter. We need to live in the field, using power wisely and prudently, and in the tent, dedicating our lives to Torah values. We need to live in both places at the same time.

We possess the characteristics of both a Jacob and an Esau. We must use each judiciously for the betterment of our people and work toward a time of peace and security for all.

TOLEDOT
The Five Senses as a Source of Blessing

Some of us may remember the character of Charley Weaver who appeared on television in the 1960s and early 1970s. The actor, Clifford Arquette, was dressed in a squashed hat, little round glasses, ruffled shirt, broad tie, baggy pants, and suspenders. He had a corny sense of humor and read letters about the misadventures of his fictional family and townspeople. One day he was asked, "Which of your five senses tend to diminish as you get older?" As Charley Weaver, he replied, "My sense of decency."

While this may be true, schoolchildren are routinely taught that the five senses of sight, hearing, touch, smell, and taste—a classification first devised by Aristotle—are faculties by which outside stimuli are perceived.

All five senses play a significant role in *parashat Toledot*. We encounter the sense of taste a number of times in the *parashah*: "Isaac favored Esau because he had a taste for game" (Genesis 25:28). Then the text tells us that Jacob is cooking a stew. Esau comes in from the open field famished and sells his birthright to his younger brother, Jacob.

Later in the *parashah*, Isaac is blind and has lost his sense of sight. This fact allows Rebecca, his wife, to implore her son Jacob to trick Isaac into giving Jacob the blessing of the firstborn. When Jacob, dressed as Esau, brings food to his aged and sightless father, we find the confluence of three senses: "So Jacob drew close to his father Isaac, who felt him and wondered. 'The voice is the voice of Jacob, yet the hands are the hands of Esau'" (Genesis 27:22). The senses of touch and hearing confuse the conflicted Isaac as he prepares to offer the blessing. It is only when Isaac uses the sense of smell that he is fully convinced: "Then his father Isaac said to him, 'Come close and kiss me, my son'; and he went up and kissed him. And he smelled his clothes and he blessed him" (Genesis 27:26–27). When Isaac smells the odor of the fields, he is convinced that it is Esau and administers the blessing due the firstborn. All five senses play an important role in the blessing of Jacob.

A *midrash* in *Genesis Rabbah* 67:3 states: "Rabbi Levi said that six organs serve a man; over three he is master, and over three he is not. Over the eye, ear, and nose, he is not master, for he sees what he does not wish to see, hears and smells what he does not wish to hear and smell. Over the mouth, hand, and foot, he is master. If he desires, he studies the Torah, while if he wishes, he engages in slander, and if he wishes, he blasphemes and reviles. With the hand, he can dispense charity if he wishes, while he can rob and murder if he so desires. With his feet, he can go to the theaters and the circuses, while if he wishes, he can go to synagogues and houses of study."

The *midrash* understands some of the senses as involuntary faculties by which outside stimuli are perceived. We have no control over many of our senses. Yet, Jewish tradition wasn't prepared to allow these outside stimuli to be understood as completely involuntary. There is an entire set of blessings known as *birkhot ha-nehenin*, blessings over food, drink, and fragrance. Most of us are familiar with the blessings over food. But there are also blessings that involve the sense of smell for fragrant woods or barks, plants, fruits, spices, and even for fragrant oils.

Our liturgy also includes blessings recited for the sights and sounds of the wonders of nature. Special blessings exist for falling stars, lofty mountains, and great deserts. One is to recite a blessing on hearing thunder or seeing a rainbow in the sky. There are even blessings recited on seeing beautiful trees or animals and on seeing trees blossoming for the first time in a year. As one non-Jewish theologian states: "Natural phenomena move the pious Jew to praise, thanksgiving, and adoration. The realm of nature is to him nothing distant, strange, cold or uncanny; it is the workshop of the Almighty, and is ruled by His beneficent will."

Not everyone is blessed with the ability to use all five senses. People may be blind, deaf, or suffer hearing loss. There are others who, especially during times of illness, lose their sense of taste and touch. And there are still others whose sense of smell is not fully developed. Jewish tradition states that, for those of us who are blessed with the gift of these five senses, it is incumbent upon us to recognize that these are gifts, and we should recite blessings of gratitude when we use these gifts. As the Talmud states: "To enjoy this world without a benediction is like robbing the Holy One, blessed be He, and the community of Israel" (*Berakhot* 35b).

Yet while we may not have control over the outside stimuli, we do have control over how we use our senses and our faculties. We can use our mouth, hands, and feet for goodness, for kindness, for Torah study, and for charitable deeds, or we can engage in slander, thievery, and murder, and follow our inclinations into places of ill repute.

Perhaps if we take the concept of *birkhot ha-nehenin* seriously, if we appreciate the gifts around us, then maybe we will learn to make the right choices. Perhaps when we sense the beauty of nature, we will not want to destroy it. And if we appreciate the grandeur and wonder of nature and God's creative ability, why would we ever think of harming another human being created in the image of God?

It is possible to take this *midrash* and frame it as a cause and effect statement. If we follow our senses and attempt to use them appropriately by offering blessings and showing appreciation for the gifts that are ours, then, with our actions and words, we can attempt to enhance God's presence in our world and create a universe of beauty and meaning for all.

VA-YETSE
Eyes to See

The morning liturgy begins with the recitation of *Birkhot Hashaḥar*, the early morning blessings. We thank God for the gifts that are ours each and every day. One of the blessings, however, has always been somewhat problematic to me: "Praised are You, Lord our God, King of the universe who gives sight to the blind."

If I were visually handicapped, this statement would bother me. Does God give sight to the blind? What about those who are not granted that gift? The *Abudraham*, a commentary on the *siddur*, suggests that the blessing thanks God for arousing us from sleep. It is only when we open our eyes in the morning that we recognize the gift of sight. This explanation gives me greater comfort. However, another translation may be in order: "Praised are You, Lord our God, King of the universe who has granted us the capacity to see." This translation suggests that there are some people who are granted the blessing of sight but are not able to fully appreciate this marvelous gift.

In the Bible, the first mention of sight is evident in the story of the Garden of Eden. The snake convinces Eve, and then Eve convinces Adam to transgress God's command as they eat the fruit of the Tree of Knowledge. The Torah informs us of the result: "Then the eyes of both of them were opened and they perceived that they were naked" (Genesis 3:7). The ability to gain knowledge brought them the ability to perceive shame. Before eating of the fruit of the tree, they experienced Paradise. After they ate of the fruit, all they could see was their nakedness.

In a later story, the Torah describes the opening of the eyes of Hagar. Upon Sarah's bidding, Hagar and her young son Ishmael are banished from Abraham's house to the desert, and Hagar awaits certain death. An angel appears to Hagar and gives her hope in a brighter future: "Then God opened her eyes and she saw a well of water" (Genesis 21:19). Was this well newly-positioned in the desert, or had it been there all the time? Was Hagar so despondent that she was unable to see it, blinded by her tears and unable to see her salvation? When she opened her eyes and gazed upon her surroundings, she was able to see the life-giving source of water.

In *parashat Va-yetse*, Jacob gains new insight into the world around him. Upon fleeing from the wrath of his brother Esau, Jacob finds himself alone in the dark night. According to the text, he lies down to sleep and dreams of angels ascending and descending the ladder between heaven and earth. He wakes up to say: "Surely the Lord is present in this place, and I did not know it!" (Genesis 28:16). Is Jacob really sleeping or is he daydreaming, unable to perceive the world around him and God's presence in that world? Some commentators suggest that Jacob actually was asleep and upon awakening gained a new perception of the world. But Rabbi Levi Yitzhak of Berditchev interprets Jacob's mindset to be "as if he were asleep." Jacob wanders through life unsure of his future, living in a sleep-induced stupor. It is only when he truly is awakened that he can understand that God will be with him on his journeys.

A fourth example is evident in the story of Moses. Moses, the young Hebrew who was raised in Pharaoh's household, is forced to flee from the palace. He finds a home in Midian where he marries and tends the sheep of his father-in-law Jethro. One day, shepherding his flock, Moses "gazed, and there was a bush all aflame, yet the bush was not consumed" (Exodus 3:2). His ability to see that the bush was not consumed allowed him to be open to the presence of God and the possibility of leadership.

Which one of those Biblical personalities represents us? Does it take personal illness, an accident, or the death of someone close to us to perceive our own gift of life? Do we perceive the blessings that are ours each day or must some external stimulant wake us up to that reality? Perhaps we need to appreciate the blessing "Praised are You, Lord our God, King of the universe who has granted us the capacity to see."

So often we live our lives with blinders on. We rise in the morning, concerned for our own survival and do not possess peripheral vision. We don't see those sitting next to us around the family table, standing before us on the train downtown, working with us in our offices or our classrooms, or even seated next to us in synagogue. We stare forward unable, or perhaps unwilling, to avert our gaze. We walk around as if we were in Jacob's sleep-induced stupor.

The ability to see and perceive allows us to respond to the world around us. In Rabbi Lawrence Kushner's story, "Inaudible Screams," he writes:

> I once knew a man who was in psychoanalysis. His doctor's office was across the street from an old, red-brick, inner-city psychiatric hospital. One day, as he had regularly done for a few years, my friend walked down the street to his car in front of the hospital. Suddenly he heard a blood-chilling scream from the top floor that seemed to sound the deepest pain a soul could possibly feel. This unforgettable noise etched itself into his soul. The following day, back on the couch, he told his doctor of the scream from the top floor. To his astonishment, his therapist was surprised that he should mention it at all.
>
> "You mean you just now heard it?" asked the doctor. "After all these years? On the top floor across the street, that's where they put all the screamers." And from that day on, my friend said, he was able to hear the screams on the top floor almost every time. "The screams are all around us," he later mused, "waiting for our ears and eyes and hands."

Hopefully, we are fortunate to have been granted the capacity to see and perceive the world around us. Bearing this gift, we should never be blind to our responsibilities to those near and dear to us and to our fellow human beings. We need to open our eyes, look around us, appreciate our gifts, and respond to the needs of others so that we can say: "Surely the Lord is present in this place …" Once we attain that awareness, we can make a meaningful contribution to God's world here on earth.

VA-YETSE
The Dual Axis

Rabbi Kalonymous Kalman Shapira was the rebbe of the Warsaw Ghetto. Throughout his later adult years, Rabbi Shlomo Carlebach looked for a follower of Rabbi Shapira. One day, he met a hunchback sweeping the streets of Tel Aviv who told him he was one of Rabbi Shapira's children in the ghetto. Rabbi Carlebach asked him to tell a story about the rebbe. According to Rabbi Carlebach, the downtrodden man said:

> Reb Kalonymous would teach us, "children, precious children, remember, the greatest thing in the world is to do somebody else a favor."
>
> I came to Auschwitz. I knew my parents were dead. My whole family didn't exist anymore. I wanted to commit suicide. But, at the last moment, I heard the rebbe's voice say, "children, precious children, remember, the greatest thing in the world is to do somebody else a favor."
>
> Do you know how many favors you can do at Auschwitz at night?

Thankfully, most of us cannot fathom what this Tel Aviv street sweeper had to endure and what kindnesses he must have done for others. But the lesson taught to him by Rabbi Shapira can teach all of us how to make the world a better place.

Judaism teaches us that ritual observance and ethical conduct are both part of our religious tradition. Over and over, the prophets tell the Israelites that ritual observance alone is not enough to serve God. It is imperative to live a life based on justice, ethics, and moral behavior.

In *parashat Va-yetse*, Jacob is forced to flee from his parents' home out of fear of his brother Esau. One night, in the middle of his journey, he lies down to sleep and has this most fantastic dream. He sees a ladder with its bottom set on earth and its top reaching the heavens. He recognizes angelic beings ascending and descending on it in the presence of God.

When he awakens, he recognizes that this is a holy place, a *Bet El*, a House of God.

In *Genesis Rabbah* 69:3, Rabbi Ḥiyya and Rabbi Yannai engage in a theoretical argument over the meaning of the words: *ve-hinei adonai nitzav alav*. The commentary in the *Etz Hayim ḥumash* translates these words as: "And the Lord was standing beside him." However, this is not a literal translation. One midrashic commentator says that the image suggests that God is to be found on top of the ladder because the word *alav* means "on it." Another commentator, however, insists that *alav* means "on him," and the Torah is suggesting that God stands over Jacob, overseeing Jacob's aspirations and destiny. According to either interpretation, a vivid statement is being made against idolatry. There is a continual relationship between man and God, with God being the Ultimate Presence, and man, living on earth, in no way comparable to a Divine Being.

We can think of the relationship between man and God as a vertical axis, suggesting that man has a responsibility to serve God. Thus, Jacob and his future descendants are confronted with the challenge to act in relation to a God who is transcendent over all human beings.

In his book, *Conscience: The Duty to Obey and the Duty to Disobey*, Rabbi Harold Schulweis suggests that within the covenantal relationship between God and the Jewish people, there are two different religious temperaments that coexist within the same covenant. The vertical temperament favors a culture of assent and obedience to God's authority, while the horizontal temperament is open to a culture of dissent in which conversation and disagreement between God and the Jewish people are welcome. Schulweis maintains that while the vertical-unilateral aspect of the covenant conjures up metaphors of intimidation before God, the horizontal-bilateral aspect of the covenant "suggests a bridge that moves traffic in both directions. On this two-way thoroughfare, the commandment may be questioned in the name of conscience." Schulweis suggests that there are times when Judaism teaches that blind obedience is not always the proper approach. Instead, sometimes we must learn to resist authority, making way for courage and conscience, which will, in turn, allow justice, compassion, and moral sensibility to blossom.

Schulweis writes, "The duty to obey inclines toward a more stringent, absolutistic discipline that brooks no question of the divine commander ... The duty to disobey is more open to a reciprocal dialogue in which human conscience enjoys high status and encourages initiative and responsibility. Each perspective within the tradition engages the other with a temperamental and intellectual set of presuppositions that affect Jewish theology, ethics, and law. The character and power of each partner of the covenant are shaped by the two different versions of the covenant."

Schulweis suggests that the vertical and the horizontal axes of the covenant do not present an either-or conundrum; their options are shared. He writes that normative Judaism teaches that "everything and everyone is subject to evaluation. The pronouncements of divine commander and human rulings by priest and prophet, rabbinical and lay, are subjected to critical evaluation. The claims of no person, divine or human, are exempt from moral challenge."

Rabbi Ḥayim of Brisk once was asked to explain the function of the rabbi. He replied, "To redress the grievances of those who are abandoned and alone, to protect the dignity of the poor, and to save the oppressed from the hands of the oppressor." You will notice that he did not mention being an arbiter of ritual decisions or a teacher of the tradition. Instead, as Rabbi Joseph B. Soloveitchik points out, "Through the implementation of the principles of righteousness, man fulfills the task of creation imposed upon him ... No religious cult is of any worth if the laws and principles of righteousness are violated and trampled upon by the foot of pride."

There are both vertical and horizontal axes in the covenantal relationship between God and the Jewish people. There is a responsibility to recognize that God is above the ladder and that human beings must accept God's sovereignty through the external commands. But at the same time, the horizontal axis reminds us of our ongoing obligation to have a relationship with God through our internal moral imperatives. Both axes create an ongoing challenge to create a world of righteousness, justice, and morality under the Dominion of God.

VA-YISHLAḤ
Jacob's Encounter

Jacob's life was filled with struggles. Even before his birth, he was involved in a contest with his brother inside his mother's womb; he later fought repeatedly with Esau over the birthright, and, when he moved to Haran, his life was filled with constant conflict and difficulty.

Of all of Jacob's struggles, one encounter changed him forever and transformed him into a leader. Preparing to meet his brother Esau, Jacob transferred his family over the river and remained behind by himself, alone at night: "Jacob was left alone. And a man wrestled with him until the break of dawn" (Genesis 32:25).

Many interpretations have been suggested for this mysterious struggle. Some commentators suggest that a spiritual struggle occurred within Jacob. But one can also see the battle that occurred within Jacob as a purely human one. Until this point, Jacob's life was manipulated by others: his parents, Esau, Laban. Now he was on his own. He had to conquer his doubts and gain personal self-assurance before he could meet Esau.

Jacob was wrestling with his own projected image of himself. Did he have the courage to meet life's vicissitudes? Could he call upon the wellsprings of inner strength to meet the present crisis? Could the man who was party to the hoax that was played on his father and brother and who fought Laban's treachery with crafty schemes of his own rise to new levels of morality when called upon to be the leader of his family? Did Jacob have what it takes to follow in his father's and grandfather's footsteps? Could he possibly live up to their high ideals?

The text tells us that Jacob is victorious in his battle. He is able to overcome his fears and proceed to meet his brother Esau. But the story of his struggle is more than one single episode of a man fighting with his fears in the dead of night. It is the story of the victory of the human spirit. Able to overcome adversity and reach greater potential, Jacob learns that he can rise to new levels of inner strength and conquer his worst fears and doubts.

A writer interviewed a poor worker in his squalid home in Warsaw. When the subject of atomic energy came up, the worker said, "I don't think atomic energy is the greatest force on earth." "No," said the writer, "then what is?" The worker replied, "The greatest force on earth is the human being."

He was right. The greatest force on earth is the human being. I continue to be amazed by the resiliency of the human spirit, by the strength of character of human beings, and by the untold acts of personal courage that are displayed by individuals.

Human beings have within themselves the ability to go beyond normal limits and ascend great heights. We are the most imaginative, creative, and powerful force ever created, and we are able to call upon untold reserves of inner strength when necessary.

Visiting the sick is one of a rabbi's most difficult tasks. It is not easy to enter a hospital and spend time with individuals who are ill. It can be physically and emotionally draining, and it brings one to ponder one's own mortality. I once was asked to visit a young woman who was suffering from cancer. She was the daughter of one of my congregants, and her illness had reached an advanced stage. Visiting a young person with a serious illness was not something to which I looked forward. I was filled with trepidation.

The visit turned out to be one of the most enriching experiences of my life. I was entering her hospital room to enliven her spirits; she ended up picking up mine. Though she knew the severity of her sickness, she refused to let it vanquish her spirit, and, over the course of the next few months, we spent many hours together. I was amazed, not only by her indomitable will, but also by her ability to look beyond herself to help others afflicted with pain and sickness. Through her strength of character and strong will, she created an organization to help others stricken with cancer.

The triumph of the human spirit is revealed in countless ways. There are individuals who fight illness and personal tragedy, meet life's trials and tribulations, and rise to confront the challenges of the moment. There are times when despair threatens to get the better of us. It is exactly at these moments that we are able to call upon the reservoir of human spirit that is within us and win the battle. Let us never sell ourselves short. We can meet life's challenges with courage, strength, and faith.

This is the lesson that Jacob had to learn. He needed to know that within him there was a wellspring of physical, emotional, and spiritual prowess that could be called upon in times of need. This struggle was not an easy one. He was wounded in the battle and forced to limp on one leg. Now a changed person, he was blessed by his adversary. No longer was he Jacob; he was now Israel. With the personal knowledge that he could rise to life's challenges, Jacob could now lead others. With this transformation, he was prepared to meet Esau.

VA-YISHLAḤ
Deborah's Legacy

In the description of Jacob's travels in Canaan, the text includes a puzzling verse: "Deborah, Rebecca's nurse, died, and was buried under the oak below Bethel; so it was named Allon-bacuth ['the oak of the weeping']" (Genesis 35:8). This is the only time this Deborah is mentioned by name in the Torah. Who was this Deborah, and why did Jacob mourn her? What role did she have in his life that caused him to be taken so by her passing?

Let us examine the traditional Biblical commentators and see if we can ascertain answers to these most intriguing questions. Rashi asks the following question: "What is Deborah doing in Jacob's house?" After all, she was the nurse of his mother Rebecca. Rebecca had promised Jacob: "then I will fetch you from there" (Genesis 27:45), indicating that she would bring him back when it was safe for him to return without incurring Esau's wrath. Rebecca had sent Deborah to Jacob in Padan Aram to tell him to leave that place. Deborah died on the journey back to Jacob's home.

But Rashi does not solve the problem. Is this the same Deborah that was mentioned in Genesis 24:59: "So they sent off their sister Rebecca and her nurse along with Abraham's servant and his men"? If this is the same Deborah, then she was an extremely elderly person. One commentator suggests that she was 130 years old. If she had lived to such a ripe old age, why the tears? Perhaps Jacob had realized that this nurse had raised Rebecca and her children, and Jacob was very touched by her influence on his life. He and his family were overcome by emotion on her passing.

Nachmanides, the Ramban, disagrees. He suggests that this is another Deborah. Why then the great mourning? He follows the opinion of Rabbi Shmuel bar Naḥman in *Genesis Rabbah* 81:5 who states: "While he was mourning for Deborah, tidings reached him that his mother had died." Rebecca had an enormous impact on Jacob's life, and Jacob mourned her loss.

Rebecca's death is never mentioned in the text. The *midrash* suggests that she was buried secretly at night, for the family worried how Esau would react at her funeral. Thus, the death of Deborah is an allusion to the death of Rebecca. The name of the place is Allon-bacuth (Genesis 35:8), "weeping" (in the plural), and the *midrash* understands this as weeping for both Rebecca and Deborah.

The Spanish commentator, Don Isaac Abarbanel, suggests that this Deborah is indeed the same nurse. She was back in Ḥaran and was going with Jacob to see her beloved Rebecca. Unfortunately, she died on the way. Why the great mourning? "Because she was so close to them as their own mother, they mourned her greatly." She was a caregiver, a nurturer, and a member of the family. Her love had made a difference in Jacob's life.

The Italian commentator Samuel David Luzzatto, Shadal, takes it one step further and explicates the verse as follows: "to teach us an important lesson, to honor the nurse who cares for the young, even after one has grown up." Shadal suggests that Deborah had left her imprint and her influence upon the entire family, and her loss was greatly mourned by all. He informs us that those who nurture the young have a lasting influence upon them, a legacy that lasts a lifetime.

One last commentary, or to be more exact, translation, brings it all into focus. The *Targum Yerushalmi* states: "And Deborah, the pedagogue, the teacher of Rebecca, died." She may have been a nurse, but more important, she was Rebecca's teacher. Her influence was always with Rebecca, Jacob's mother.

Deborah made a difference, if not in Jacob's life personally, then by extension to the family. While she had taken care of his mother, Deborah was more than merely a nurse or a good day-care provider. She was a teacher, impressing on her young charges the important lessons of life. Thus, Jacob was greatly saddened when she died. He and his family would miss her.

In her book, *The Blessing of a Skinned Knee,* Dr. Wendy Mogel writes: "Children learn by our example. If your children are to develop genuine respect for you, they need to know what respect looks like in action … In Jewish theology, deed carries more weight than creed. This means that God is more interested in our actions than in pledges of faith, in how we treat others than in the quality of our prayer. The sages of the Talmud taught that God said, 'Better that my people should forsake me but observe my laws, than believe in me but not observe my laws.'"

This simple verse suggests a message of hope and an instruction for living. We often offer the blessing that a person may be an inspiration to others. When one has passed on, we recite: "may his or her memory be a blessing." It has been written that success in life is found in the fact that one may be a person "whose life was an inspiration, whose memory is a benediction." This was the legacy of Deborah, Rebecca's nurse and teacher. I pray that this phrase be our epitaph as well.

VA-YESHEV
Joseph's Core Values

People often discuss the dual influences of heredity and environment upon our personalities. While both factors shape personality, I believe that when it comes to spiritual concerns, environment takes precedence. We are not born with a regard and respect for the sacred; this sensibility must be learned, nurtured, and allowed to grow. Often, our first spiritual experiences emanate from our homes, our parents, and our upbringings. I believe these foundational experiences shape personal behavior as well.

In *parashat Va-yeshev*, Joseph emerges as a major character in the Genesis narrative. Loved by his father, envied by his brothers, he is sold to the Egyptian Potiphar to serve in his household. Potiphar's wife takes a liking to Joseph and attempts to seduce him. At first, Joseph resists her overtures, however: "One such day, he came into the house to do his work. None of the household being there inside ..." (Genesis 39:11).

The text suggests that Potiphar's wife made sexual advances to Joseph. Should he succumb or not? No one was there to observe the escapade. According to the interpretation expressed in *Sotah* 36b, Joseph's resistance had cracked: "At that moment his father's image came and appeared to him through the window." Joseph resisted her advances and eventually suffered because of his reticence to succumb to her wiles.

The Talmudic passage is a most revealing one. While one might be able to interpret the scene in a Freudian manner, it also can be understood in another fashion. Joseph had left his father's house, but his father's house had not left him. He continued to be influenced in his activities by what he had learned at home as a child. He was tempted but would not succumb to the temptation. The manner of personal conduct learned in his parents' house would stay with him for life.

Where do we learn the basis of our ethics and moral behavior? It begins at home, is nurtured in the family, and, hopefully, is buttressed and strengthened further in school and by peer groups. When conflicting values and variable norms of accepted behavior surface, something has got to give. And all too often, it is easier to give in to temptation than to resist it.

In order to have the strength to resist these temptations, one needs a belief in a strong moral and ethical code based on higher spiritual values. As Jews, our ethical conduct should be based on adherence to the fundamentals of the Torah and Jewish law.

Rabbi Walter Wurzburger, my family's rabbi for many years, in *Ethics of Responsibility*, suggests that *halakhah*, Jewish law, is not the only source of Jewish ethics. He also believes that a moral conscience plays a vital role in religious life, and, thus, one of the objectives of Jewish ethics is the cultivation of a spiritual vision and sensitivity to the needs of others. Ethical values are indispensable to the proper functioning of human society.

According to Rabbi Wurzburger, we gain that moral sensitivity through various means. We must first live our lives in accordance with the patterns of Jewish law and establish a standard of conduct that befits the concept of *Imitatio Dei*, emulating the Divine. But Rabbi Wurzburger does not stop there. Discussing the work of his teacher, Rabbi Joseph B. Soloveitchik, Rabbi Wurzburger writes that "one of the most basic requirements for the cultivation of moral sensitivity, according to Rabbi Soloveitchik, is the availability of appropriate role models. That is why, in his opinion, the Talmud declares that personal contact with scholars is more important than the mastery of their formal opinions."

This concept is expressed in the seduction scene between Joseph and Potiphar's wife. Joseph recalled his most important and influential model, his father. In seeing Jacob's visage, Joseph was forced to deal with the reality of his situation. Would he submit to the pleasures of the moment or abide by a proper ethical code of conduct taught to him in his parents' household? Because of his training, he chose the latter.

We need to understand the lesson well. As Rabbi Wurzburger suggests, we must find appropriate ethical role models in our society. Children must be presented with models of ethical behavior in their formative years, and these lessons need to be taught in our schools and communities. We must build a moral and ethical focus so that our children will have a firm foundation upon which to base their lives and their decisions. That task is incumbent upon all of us. To leave it to government, to schools, or even to our religious institutions, is not enough. Appropriate values begin at home and then permeate our lives.

Maimonides, in his *Mishneh Torah, Hilkhot Yesodei Torah* 5:10, codifies the law of *Kiddush Ha-Shem*, the sanctification of God's name. If one performs a deed or refuses to allow transgression to overwhelm him for no other reason than the fact that God wishes proper moral conduct, "he thereby sanctifies God's name." Rambam cites the story of Joseph's resistance to the advances of Potiphar's wife as an example of *Kiddush Ha-Shem*.

It is our task to establish homes filled with respect for God and for our fellow human beings. The conduct of the next generation is dependent upon our actions. Morality binds if it is grounded in God. We must endow our children with the respect for the sacred and establish ourselves as their appropriate models. I pray that we take this responsibility seriously, so we can make a profound impact upon generations to come.

VA-YESHEV
The Challenge of Good Fortune

A genie offered a poor woodsman three wishes. The woodsman rushed home to tell his wife of the good fortune. He walked into his house and without thinking, he said to his wife, "I wish I had a bowl of pudding." Immediately the food appeared, and the man related the good news. "You are a fool," said his wife. "You wasted a wish. I wish the pudding would stick to your face," and the pudding stuck to her husband's face. They tried to peel it off, but it was stuck. The woodsman and his wife had no alternative but to use the final wish to have the pudding removed.

All of us have wishes for our loved ones and ourselves. Many times we hope for good fortune to come our way. There are many people, for example, who play the lottery, thinking that winning money will solve their problems. Unfortunately, that is not always the case. There are no statistics on what happens to jackpot winners, but a body of evidence suggests that winning big often brings ruinous trouble.

In 1988, Mary Ellen Snipes won $31.5 million in Florida and split the prize with her sister. Mary Ellen spent the next three-and-a-half years in and out of court, fighting her ex-husband's claim to their fortune. He argued that he had picked the numbers and purchased the actual winning ticket. In 1981, Daisy Fernandez won $2.8 million in New York and was sued by her son's teenage friend whom she had asked to pray for her.

Instant fortune does not necessarily bring instant happiness. Many times, it brings troubles and sometimes even disaster. This is not a hard and fast rule, of course; some people have been successful and are truly happy winners. Studies show that these people tend to have close family ties and are sustained by strong religious faith and a solid sense of identity.

In 1990, Milt Laird, a financial analyst from California, won $27.5 million. He and his wife divided their winnings between investments and charitable donations for family, friends, and church groups. Also in 1990,

Lydia Neufeld and her husband won $17 million and used the winnings to buy a church and hire a pastor for their Spanish-speaking community.

It is natural for human beings to always wish for more than they have. In fact, the very act of wishing pushes us to strive with greater energy, effort, and sacrifice to succeed in our endeavors. However, when success comes too easily, we often don't know how to handle the results.

In *parashat Va-yeshev*, we read the saga of Joseph and his rise from rags to riches and back to rags again. From the pit into which his brothers had placed him, Joseph is sold into slavery and becomes the servant of Potiphar. After his aborted escapade with his master's wife, Joseph is thrown into prison and languishes there, only to interpret the dreams of the baker and the butler that eventually lead him into Pharaoh's court. Joseph's life is filled with peaks and valleys, moments of success and feelings of despair.

Yet the Torah tells us: "The Lord was with Joseph, and he was a successful man; and he stayed in the house of his Egyptian master" (Genesis 39:2). The word *va-yeḥi* appears three times in this verse. The Hasidic master Rabbi Mordechai of Chernobyl suggests that this repetition reveals a special attribute of Joseph's character and should be translated: "The Lord was with Joseph when he was a successful man and also when he stayed in the house of his Egyptian master."

Da'at Zekenim, a Torah commentary from the school of the Tosafists who lived in Northern France and Western Germany in the twelfth and thirteenth centuries, states that there are people who serve God only when they are poor. As soon as they grow wealthy, they forget God. Others serve the Lord as long as they lack for nothing, but as soon as they lose their wealth, they lose their perspective. But this does not apply to Joseph who clung to his God when "he was a successful man" and also "when he stayed in the house of the Egyptian master." He passed the tests of wealth and of poverty.

Rabbi Myer Kripke, a Conservative rabbi, profited from the success of Warren Buffet's Berkshire Hathaway company. Rabbi Kripke's wife, Dorothy, knew Mrs. Buffet and convinced her husband to invest modestly with Warren Buffet. As Rabbi Kripke served his community in Omaha, the fortune grew. After his retirement, Rabbi Kripke and his wife donated $7 million to the Jewish Theological Seminary to repair the library tower where a horrible fire had taken place in 1966. They lived modestly their entire lives, and their wealth became a gift bestowed upon a beloved institution.

Rabbi Hugo Gryn, a Reform rabbi who served at the West London Synagogue, told the following story about his time in Auschwitz:

> It was the cold winter of 1944 and although we had nothing like calendars, my father, who was my fellow prisoner there, took me and some of our friends to a corner in our barrack. He announced that it was the eve of Hanukkah, produced a curious-shaped clay bowl, and began to light a wick immersed in his precious, but now melted, margarine ration. Before he could recite the blessing, I protested at this waste of food. He looked at me—then at the lamp—and finally said: "You and I have seen that it is possible to live up to three weeks without food. We once lived almost three days without water, but you cannot live properly for three minutes without hope!"

Joseph recognizes that he possesses God-given talents and that he must use them appropriately. When he interprets Pharaoh's dreams, Joseph states: "Not I! God will see to Pharaoh's welfare" (Genesis 41:16). After Jacob's death, when Joseph's brothers express concern for their own welfare, Joseph tells them not to worry, for God has an intricate plan to ensure their survival.

In times of plentitude and in times of hardship, Joseph never lost his perspective. When he was successful and when he was a servant, when he was second to the Pharaoh and when he languished in prison, Joseph continued to serve God and fulfill his Divine purpose on earth. That is our role as well. Whether we are at the top of the crest or at the bottom of the valley, we have a role to fill. We must never lose faith in ourselves, in our abilities, and in our God.

MIKKETS
Joseph and Other Jewish Dreamers

Dreams occupy a very important place in Joseph's life. The entire Joseph narrative is framed by descriptions of his dreams and the dreams he interprets for others. The Midrash states: "Joseph was promoted through a dream [referring to those in prison and especially those of Pharaoh]" (*Genesis Rabbah* 84:6).

It is not at all surprising that dreams occupy such an integral part of Joseph's life story. In the Ancient Near East, dreams or visions of the night were believed to emanate from supernatural powers, and the content and interpretation of dreams were treated with great importance. Ancient Babylonians had implicit trust in dreams as a means of guidance, and on the eve of important decisions, leaders slept in temples hoping for dream counsel. Egyptians composed elaborate works devoted to dream interpretation, and even the Talmudic rabbis placed importance on individuals' dreams. They taught, "A dream is one-sixtieth part of prophecy" (*Berakhot* 57b).

The psychology of dreams has occupied both ancient and modern writers. Leo Oppenheim explains that there were three types of dream sequences in the Ancient Near East: dreams as revelations of the Deity, dreams that reflected the state of mind of the dreamer, and mantic dreams that prognosticated forthcoming events. All are evident in the Biblical record. In the modern world, Sigmund Freud wrote his great work, *The Interpretation of Dreams*, explaining the importance of dream interpretation. Freud viewed dreams as expressions of balked wishes or frustrated yearnings. In his view, dreams were the actual or attempted wish fulfillments of the dreamers.

Both ancient and modern writings posit that dreams suggest new directions, new possibilities, and various answers to important problems. Dreams are not simply a sequence of sensations, images, or thoughts passing through a sleeping person's mind; they reveal deep hopes and aspirations. In Jewish tradition, the dreamer has always occupied a central place. In the Book of Daniel, dreams and visions play an extremely important role. Not only is Daniel himself the recipient of visions, but the Babylonian king, Nebuchadnezzar, also has visions of the night. Daniel is described as unique: "Daniel had understanding of visions and dreams of all kinds" (Daniel 1:17).

In Jewish tradition, the dreamer is not only the one who is troubled at night but also the visionary who sees his unfulfilled wishes and dreams realized in some way. When his brothers see Joseph coming toward them, they say, "Here comes that dreamer!" (Genesis 37:19). This accusation caused Joseph's brothers to throw him into the pit and sell him into slavery, hoping to rid themselves of this bothersome character.

This very same accusation has been used against many people and has branded dreamers as people who are out of touch with reality. But where would we be without these dreamers?

The entire history of the Jewish people's return to Zion has been based on such a dream. In Psalms 126:1, the psalm that precedes the Grace After Meals on Shabbat and holidays, we recite: "When the Lord restores the fortunes of Zion—we see it as in a dream." Wherever we were in exile, we dreamed of Zion. Whether it was Yehuda Ha-Levi or Solomon ibn Gabirol, whether rich or poor, of high status or low, believers or non-believers, Jews never allowed the dream of returning to Zion to be forsaken.

Even modern-day political Zionism is based on a dream. Perhaps the greatest dreamer of all was Theodor Herzl. In his diary on September 3, 1897, Herzl writes, "At Basle I founded the Jewish State. If I were to say this today, I would be met with universal laughter. In five years, perhaps, and certainly in fifty, everyone will see it. The State is already founded in essence, in the will of the people for the State." In his book, *The Jewish State*, written over one hundred years ago, Herzl envisions an army, a flag, and the apparatus of a state. In his preface he asks, "Am I before my time? ... We shall see." History shows that fifty years later the State of Israel was born.

Chaim Weizmann and Ahad Ha'am were visionaries who saw the Jewish people returning to their homeland and to their cultural heritage. Eliezer ben Yehuda was an idealist who believed that the Hebrew language would be spoken on the streets of Jerusalem; in fact, the only language he allowed his children to learn and speak was Hebrew.

These individuals were dreamers who in their yet-to-be-fulfilled wishes rescued an entire people. They were visionaries who may have been out of touch with reality in their own time, but have proven to be prophets. When Reverend Martin Luther King, Jr. wished to frame his aspirations for the future, he cried out in Washington, D. C., "I have a dream," and an entire nation was moved. As the Talmud states: "Neither a good dream nor a bad dream is ever wholly fulfilled" (*Berakhot* 55a).

Joseph understood the importance of dreams, and he wisely knew that Pharaoh's dreams were foretelling the future. Using his God-given talent, Joseph could inform Pharaoh of what would unfold in the future for his nation and his country. Joseph realized that all dreams come from God. "God has revealed to Pharaoh what He is about to do ... As for Pharaoh having had the same dream twice, it means that the matter has been determined by God, and that God will soon carry it out" (Genesis 41:28, 32).

Dreams are an important part of the human psyche and of human history. Those who dream of the future may be castigated as being out of touch with reality, but sometimes we must all dream of better times. The Talmud tells us that if one has seen a dream and has not remembered it, let him offer the following prayer: "Sovereign of the universe, I am Thine and my dreams are Thine. I have dreamt a dream and do not know what it is ... if they are good dreams, confirm them and reinforce them like the dreams of Joseph ... so turn all my dreams into something good for me." (*Berakhot* 55b).

May our dreams be turned into good as we follow them to create a better day for all.

MIKKETS
Making a Difference

I am not a product of the civil resistance generation. I did not march for civil rights, nor was I involved in the anti-Vietnam war demonstrations. Born and raised in Toronto, these events were simply not part of my reality. Yet, when it came to one issue, I put on my marching shoes and made my protest known.

In the late 1960s, I read Elie Wiesel's book, *The Jews of Silence,* in which he wrote of the life of Soviet Jews and their difficulties behind the Iron Curtain. When I finished the book, I wasn't sure to whom the title was referring. Were the Jews of silence the Soviet Jews who, for many years, were not allowed to live as free Jews, or were they members of the Jewish community throughout the world who did not protest?

In the middle 1970s, the issue of Soviet Jewry was put on the worldwide agenda. We began to learn about the extreme hardships to which our brothers and sisters had been subjected for so many decades. As a young rabbi entering the rabbinate in the late 1970s, this became one of my key issues.

In June 1983, I traveled to Moscow and Leningrad (St. Petersburg) with Rabbi Mordecai Simon. That trip represents the most meaningful ten days of my life, as we spent our time visiting with Refuseniks, teaching and speaking Hebrew with many of them, and conveying messages from our sponsor, Chicago Action for Soviet Jewry. We presented them with many contraband Jewish items, including a *sheḥita* knife, Hebrew books, *tefillin, tallitot,* as well as medicine and clothes. I returned from those ten days energized and committed to their cause.

On November 8, 1985, I was chairman of a rabbinic demonstration march for Soviet Jewry in downtown Chicago. It was truly an historic event. Arranged through the Chicago Board of Rabbis, over one hundred rabbis of all denominations marched from Spertus College to the

Kluczynski Federal Building. Dressed in *tallitot*, with many of us carrying *sifrei* Torah, we marched north on Michigan Avenue to Jackson, west to State, north to Adams, and west to Dearborn. We recited prayers, sang songs, and carried placards on behalf of our brothers and sisters. I presented a declaration to Congresswoman Cardiss Collins who carried a message to President Ronald Reagan to discuss the issue of Soviet Jewry with the leader of the Soviet Union.

And then, on December 6, 1987, I was present with 250,000 other Jews and non-Jews at a major national demonstration on the National Mall. On the eve of the Washington, D.C. summit between the Soviet Premier Mikhail Gorbachev and President Ronald Reagan, this broad-based mobilization sent an ardent message, demanding that Gorbachev extend his policy of Glasnost to Soviet Jews by allowing their emigration from the USSR.

Soon after that, the doors began to open. Since then, over one million Jews have left the former Soviet Union and are citizens of the State of Israel. Over 500,000 have come to these shores and over 250,000 to Germany. Today the former Soviet Union is a different place. While anti-Semitism still exists today, there are Jewish schools, synagogues, rabbis, and cultural programs.

When the KGB arrested the well-known Refusenik Natan Sharansky, they tried to mock him with a question: "Whom do you think is going to help you? Look who they are—a bunch of students and housewives. We are the KGB." I am pleased to note for history that this collection of students and housewives defeated the KGB. Nothing is impossible.

This relates to the Joseph story that occupies the latter part of the Book of Genesis. This brazen young man became a leader in Egypt and single-handedly saved the Egyptian people and his own family from famine with his plan for food conservation. Where would we be without Joseph and his strength of character as he resolved to make a difference in his world?

These stories convince me that we can make a difference. Students and housewives can stand up to the KGB and the Soviet Union, and one person can save a country.

This message is reiterated by Hillel in *Pirkei Avot* 2:6: "Where there are no worthy persons, strive to be a worthy person." Or, in another translation, "In a place where there are no leaders, strive to be a leader."

Each of us can be a person who makes a difference, and each of us can be a leader. While this needs to take place on the worldwide stage, we can also lead within our own communities. Whether it is on behalf of our brothers and sisters in Israel or throughout the world, whether it is for those suffering across the globe, whether it is in our own neighborhood for people who need assistance and support, we can make a difference.

I don't believe that I personally had a great deal to do with the exodus of Soviet Jewry. However, I would like to believe that I, along with hundreds of thousands, did make a difference. Because of my trip to the Soviet Union in 1983, my chairmanship of the protest march in Chicago in 1985, and my presence on the National Mall in December 1987, I played a part in making a difference. I am proud of that participation and hope to continue to make a difference in the future.

VA-YIGGASH
Responsible for One Another

Two characters stand out in *parashat Va-yiggash*. One, of course, is Joseph who finally reveals his identity to his brothers and is reunited with his father. The other is Judah, the fourth-born son of Jacob, who takes the lead among his brothers and assumes a most prominent position.

Of all the brothers, why was Judah picked to represent the besieged children of Jacob? Why does Judah's tribal inheritance, the portion of Judea, become so prominent when Solomon's kingdom is divided?

The Torah tells us that Judah is the one who saves his brother Joseph from certain death. He is the brother who gives counsel concerning the sale of Joseph to either the Midianites or the Ishmaelites. In the story of Judah and Tamar, where Judah's character is not seen as so exemplary, his word is his bond. When he finds out that Tamar is correct in her assessment of the situation, Judah states: "She is more in the right than I, inasmuch as I did not give her to my son Shelah" (Genesis 38:26).

Judah is the one who takes personal responsibility for Benjamin when the time comes for the children of Jacob to return to Egypt because the famine is so great in Canaan. He steps forth and states: "I myself will be surety for him; you may hold me responsible: if I do not bring him back to you and set him before you, I shall stand guilty before you forever" (Genesis 43:9). It is again Judah who pleads for Benjamin's life and asks Joseph to incarcerate him rather than his youngest brother, Benjamin.

Judah's word is his bond; he is willing to take responsibility for his words and his actions. His public persona becomes the standard by which all of the brothers are judged. As Jacob states in his final blessings to his sons: "You, O Judah, your brothers shall praise; Your hand shall be on the nape of your foes; Your father's sons shall bow low to you" (Genesis 49:8).

Judah stands as a paradigm not only for his brothers but also for all of Israel. When he steps forth to assume responsibility for his brother

Benjamin, he is following through on his promise to his father that he will serve as Benjamin's bond, his personal savior, his *arev*. According to the dictionary, the word *arev* has three possible meanings. The Lubavitcher Rebbe, Rabbi Menachem Mendel Schneerson, suggests that each of these dictionary definitions is included in Judah's act of responsibility. Each has an inherent lesson for the entire Jewish people.

The first definition of *arev* is to be a bondsman, a surety, a pledge. Judah was willing to place his own life in danger to secure the safety of his brother. A well-known Talmudic quote reads: *kol yisrael arevim zeh ba zeh*, "All Israel is responsible one for the other" (*Shevuot* 39a). To create an even stronger impression, we can translate the phrase: "All of Israel is a surety, a bondsman one for the other." We don't only bear responsibility for our fellow Jew; we are pledged to his or her welfare, and we are responsible for that pledge all the days of our lives.

We bear that responsibility each and every day. We are pledged to our brothers and sisters. When they hurt, we feel it; when they suffer, we nurse their wounds. When events in the State of Israel or around the Jewish world call forth for action, we must be there. We must respond to the needs of our brothers and sisters.

Another definition of the word *arev* is "sweet" or "pleasant." The Lubavitcher Rebbe states that we have the responsibility of rebuking our fellow Jews if it is found to be appropriate. As the Torah states: "Reprove your kinsman" (Leviticus 19:17). However, he states, we should do so with love, care, and abiding concern since "Israel is sweetness one to the other."

Rabbi Norman Lamm, past president of Yeshiva University, has said that all Jews are our brothers and sisters, and we have a responsibility toward them. Lamm suggests that while we must not compromise our principles, we must also act with *derekh eretz* toward them without being patronizing or condescending. I would concur with Lamm's views. We owe each other responsible criticism and careful dialogue about our differences. But we also owe one another love, respect, and support. The Lubavitcher Rebbe reminds us: "All of Israel is sweetness one to the other." If this were only the case.

The third definition of *arev* is a mixture. Thus, the phrase can be translated as "All Israel is a mixture, one amongst the other." In other words, we are part of each Jew, and each Jew is part of us. We all stood at Sinai, and each of our souls was united forever at that very moment. We are many, but we are one. We come from various backgrounds, geographic locations, and ethnicities. Yet, our roots, the foundations of our faith, and the very promise of our future bring us together as a unified whole. Our diversity makes us richer. On Sukkot the four species—*lulav, etrog, hadas,* and *arava*—are meant to represent four different types of Jews (*Leviticus Rabbah* 30:12). Only when they are held together can the *mitzvah* be fulfilled. We are Ashkenazic and Sephardic; Ethiopian and Yemenite; Litvak and Galicianer; Orthodox, Conservative, Reform, and Reconstructionist; religious and secular. We are all Jews.

When Judah stood before Joseph and pleaded for the life of Benjamin and used the words "Now your servant has pledged himself for the boy to my father" (Genesis 44:32), he was speaking for all of us. We continue to have the ongoing responsibility of being the bondsmen of our brothers and sisters, of expressing our love and care for each other, recognizing that we are only strong as a unified whole.

VA-YIGGASH
Jewish Identity

The denouement of the Joseph story is a magnificent literary composition. *Parashat Va-yiggash* focuses on Judah's plea to the viceroy of Egypt to save the youngest child, Benjamin.

At this point in the story, Joseph realizes that his brothers have changed. They are no longer the same people who sold him into slavery. He decides to unmask himself in front of his brothers, orders his Egyptian helpers to leave the room, and reveals his true identity to his brothers. He says, "You can see for yourselves, and my brother Benjamin for himself, that it is indeed I who am speaking to you" (Genesis 45:12).

How could he prove that he was, indeed, their long-lost brother, Joseph? Rashi, the Biblical commentator, states that Joseph showed them his identity: "that I am circumcised just like you." Joseph demonstrates that he is part of the covenant.

If we examine the words in the verse literally, the Hebrew should really be translated, "Your eyes can see that it is my mouth that speaks to you." In the words that have been popularized by modern day politicians, Joseph is really saying "read my lips." There is something special about the words emanating from his mouth.

Rashi, following the *midrash* in *Genesis Rabbah* 93:11, offers another explanation: "Look and see that the mouth that speaks to you speaks the holy tongue." In other words, Joseph is saying, "I am speaking your language, the Hebrew tongue." If you listen carefully, you will hear that your accent is the same as mine. The *midrash* is pointing out the connection between the Hebrew language and Jewish identity. For the Jew, language is the tie that binds him to a common heritage, tradition, and our people's sacred sources.

Lashon ha-kodesh, the holy language, is the key to our liturgy and our sacred texts and is now the language of our reborn homeland. With knowledge of Hebrew, one can find oneself feeling comfortable in any synagogue service anywhere in the world, for the Hebrew *siddur*, with some minor revisions, is common to all Jewish communities. The knowledge of Hebrew allows us to communicate with Hebrew-speaking Jews around the world.

Another commentator, Ha-rav Mordechai Ha-Cohen, suggests that Joseph proved his identity in another fashion: "He showed them his bookcase that was filled, not with the words of Egyptian magicians, but with the holy books written in the holy tongue." In effect, Joseph is saying, "If you want to learn my true identity, let your eyes gaze on my library. I am one of you, a member of the people of the book." We are called *am ha-sefer*, "the people of the book," because of the importance we place upon education and learning. We all know the need for continuing education, growth, and personal development, and, at least some of that comes from book learning. Joseph told his brothers: "You want to know who I am? Look at my bookshelves. I know the importance of the continual study of our sacred tradition."

Finally, another commentator, the Ramban, Nachmanides, following the Talmud in *Megillah* 16b, suggests that Joseph attempted to convince his brothers of his true identity by appealing to his personal character: "as my mouth, so is my heart." If you really want to know whether I speak the truth, look at me directly.

When the actor Charles Laughton was asked to entertain at a dinner party, he recited Psalm 23. When he finished the recitation, a thunder of applause greeted him. The crowd knew that they were in the presence of a master performer. The next speaker was an elderly preacher. He said, "I, too, would like to recite the same psalm." Turning his face upward, he closed his eyes and began. When he was through, all were silent. There was no applause, but neither was there a dry eye in the room. Later, a man approached the actor. "I don't understand it," he said. "You both said the same thing. Your presentation was letter perfect. Yet, when the preacher spoke in his own halting manner, people were moved too deeply for words. What made the difference?" "I know Psalm 23," replied the actor. "But he knows the Shepherd. That's the difference."

Joseph told his brothers that they should examine the conviction, the sincerity with which he spoke. Joseph knew that the manner in which we converse informs others whether our words are really sincere.

Joseph's brothers finally believed him. What was it that convinced them? I'm not sure. But I do know that if we take seriously the comments on this passage, we learn important lessons. If a Jew wants others to know his identity, there are a number of requirements he must fulfill. He must be a member of the covenant, learn the language of our people, and be involved in personal study. And he must also be a sincere, sensitive human being whose words reveal true feelings of sincerity and conviction.

YA-YEḤI
The Value of Tears

One of my favorite movie scenes occurs in the film *A League of Their Own*. Tom Hanks, the manager of a women's baseball team during the Second World War, peers out from the dugout, looks onto the field, and sees one of the players crying. The camera focuses on him as he asks the player, "Are you crying? Are you crying? There is no crying in baseball. There is no crying in baseball." The camera then pans to the young woman who has been admonished by her manager.

There may be no crying in baseball, but there is a great deal of crying in the Bible. In fact, Joseph seems to cry more than anyone else. He is frequently moved to tears. Each one of these occasions reveals something about his character and can be a lesson for us.

Joseph weeps first when he hears the words of mutual recrimination of his brothers standing accused and helpless before him. His brothers are suspected of being spies as they state: "Alas, we are being punished on account of our brother, because we looked on at his anguish, yet paid no heed as he pleaded with us." Reuven then reminds them: "Did I not tell you, 'Do no wrong to the boy'? But you paid no heed." The Torah then states that Joseph "turned away from them and wept" (Genesis 42:21–22, 24).

Joseph has learned that his brothers are beginning the process of reconciliation. Perhaps he weeps out of legitimate self-pity, recalling his agony and his sense of total abandonment.

Our present lives are intertwined with our past histories. It is impossible to remove from our consciousness or subconsciousness what has happened to us. Very often, we bear a grudge against those who have wronged us. Thus, the Torah tells us: "You shall not take vengeance or bear a grudge against your countrymen " (Leviticus 19:18). Rabbi Abraham Twerski reminds us that by forgoing or suppressing our grudge, we profit far more than the one who offended us. Rabbi Twerski recalls the words of a patient who said, "Carrying resentments is like letting someone whom you don't like live inside your head rent free." Rabbi Twerski asks, "Why would anyone allow that?"

As Joseph's brothers stand before him, they remind him of what has happened in the past and not only they, but he, is now tested. Will he continue to bear a grudge or will he be able to move on and begin a new relationship with his brothers?

Joseph weeps again when Benjamin is brought before him. The Torah tells us: "With that, Joseph hurried out, for he was overcome with feeling toward his brother and was on the verge of tears; he went into a room and wept there" (Genesis 43:30).

In this case, Joseph felt compassion for his brother. Feelings of tenderness and affection surfaced, finding relief only through tears. Benjamin was not part of the plot to do away with Joseph. The two of them had a unique relationship.

There are people who move us to tears. When we realize the depth of our love for them, we are overcome with emotion. Often, these individuals are members of our family whom we tend to take for granted. Other times, they are close friends and confidants, trusted advisors or mentors upon whom we rely. As we take but a moment to recognize how precious they are to us, tears may well up in our eyes.

Joseph cries a third time as Judah steps forth and makes an emotionally wrenching appeal on behalf of Benjamin. Joseph can no longer restrain himself. The Torah states: "Joseph could no longer control himself before all his attendants, and he cried out, 'Have everyone withdraw from me!' So there was no one else about when Joseph made himself known to his brothers. His sobs were so loud that the Egyptians could hear, and so the news reached Pharaoh's palace" (Genesis 45:1–2).

This scene marks the beginning of the formal reconciliation between Joseph and his brothers. Once the brothers understand that they are not in danger from Joseph's possible revenge, Joseph kisses his brothers and weeps (Genesis 45:15). As they are reunited, the tears flow. And later, when Joseph meets Jacob, he cries again: "He presented himself to him and, embracing him around the neck, he wept on his neck a good while" (Genesis 46:29). True reconciliation often brings forth tears.

The final description of Joseph's weeping occurs in *parashat Va-yehi*. After Jacob blesses all of his children and dies, "he was gathered to his people" (Genesis 49:33). The Torah states: "Joseph flung himself upon his father's face and wept over him and kissed him" (Genesis 50:1). Dr. Nahum Sarna comments that such a gesture is unique in the Bible. The Biblical text contains descriptions of one falling upon another's neck, but in this scene, Jacob lies in a prone position, and Joseph falls on his face and kisses him. After Jacob dies, Joseph begins the mourning period for his father.

In our society, Americans are taught to keep a stiff upper lip. Men especially are expected not to cry, but to appear strong under all conditions. Even at a time of loss, many men feel it is inappropriate to cry. However, a time of loss can often bring forth tears, sometimes of deep mourning, other times of unresolved guilt. There may be tears of relief at the loss of someone who has suffered greatly, or tears stemming from unfulfilled promises. These tears are real, deeply felt, and totally appropriate.

There may be no crying in baseball, but there is a great display of crying in the Bible. Joseph's tears reveal his sensitivity to others, his willingness to grow, his deep love of family, and his abiding concern and devotion for his father. Through these tears, Joseph shows his real character, and our understanding of these scenes can be cathartic for us as well. As the Talmud in *Baba Metzia* 59a states: "Yet though the gates of prayer are locked, the gates of tears are not." May our tears be tears of joy, love, and reconciliation all the days of our lives.

VA-YEḤI
The Secret of the Two *Yud*s

Rabbi Eleazar Ha-Kappar in *Pirkei Avot* 4:29 states: "It was not your will that formed you, nor was it your will that gave you birth; it is not your will that makes you live, and it is not your will that brings you death; nor is it your will that some day in the future you will have to give an accounting and a reckoning before the King of kings, the Holy One, praised-be-He."

Rabbi Eleazar is teaching us that we come into this world through no fault of our own, and we all know that we eventually leave this world. The question, of course, is what do we do with the intervening days? How do we spend them, and do we use our time wisely? Do we follow the Psalmist who wrote: "Teach us to count our days rightly, that we may obtain a wise heart" (Psalms 90:12)? Or, do we waste our time here on earth not taking advantage of the greatest gift of all, the ability to live life to its fullest?

I find an ironic connection between the two *parshiyot* in the Book of Genesis that refer to the lives of individuals. *Ḥayyei Sarah* refers to Sarah and *Va-yeḥi* refers to Jacob. It is interesting to note that these *parshiyot* do not really deal with the concept of life; instead they deal with the passing of an individual. In *Ḥayyei Sarah*, we are told that the span of Sarah's life was 127 years and that she died in Kiryat Arba, in Hebron. *Va-yeḥi* begins with the words: "Jacob lived seventeen years in the land of Egypt, so that the span of Jacob's life came to one hundred and forty-seven years. And when the time approached for Israel to die, he summoned his son Joseph" (Genesis 47:28–29). In other words, both the lives of Sarah and Jacob are coming to an end, and yet the *parshiyot* in which these events occur include the Hebrew word *ḥayim*, "life."

This suggests to me that, though everyone will die, it is our responsibility, indeed our privilege, to live life to its fullest, to hold on to every precious moment, to experience the gifts that have been presented to us, and to make a difference in our world.

John Wesley, the eighteenth-century Anglican minister who was an early leader in the Methodist movement, provided a maxim about life: "Do all the good you can, by all the means you can, in all the ways you can, in all the places you can, at all the times you can, to all the people you can, as long as ever you can."

Sometimes words themselves teach us a great deal. Look, for instance, at the English word "life" and its counterpart in Hebrew. The two middle letters of life are "if." The two middle letters of the Hebrew word, *ḥayim* (also transliterated "*ḥayyim*"), are *yud*. The first word reminds us of doubt, anxiety. What is life if there are no guarantees? Life is filled with worry about the future. The two instances of *yud* in Hebrew represent God's name, a concept of faith in the present and in the future. Life should not be lived with doubt, but embraced with faith and confidence that we can surmount whatever challenges may come our way.

How do we live our lives? Are we positive about our own deeds, our relationships, our contributions to our family and society? Or do we live with an element of doubt, worried about what life will bring us and whether we will be able to withstand its challenges and difficulties? Are we prepared to give and receive love? Are we ready to share ourselves, our souls, our hearts, our dreams, and our vision with others? Or are we so frightened by the future that we are unable to bestow the love that we carry in our hearts? Are we prepared to make a difference in the lives of those around us and in our greater society? Or are we so confused that we are unable or unwilling to share our gifts with others?

I'd like to believe that the *parshiyot* of *Ḥayyei Sarah* and *Va-yeḥi* are specifically called by those names so that we recognize that, though they deal with the deaths of our matriarch Sarah and our patriarch Jacob, we are to concentrate on what they accomplished during their lifetimes. Sarah, after all, is the mother of the Israelite people. She gave birth to Isaac who carried on the lineage of his family. According to the Bible and Rabbinic legends, she was a true partner to Abraham from the moment he left Ḥaran until he decided, on his own, to take his son Isaac to Mount Moriah.

Jacob was a patriarch of our people. Though he did not start out as the most heroic of individuals, after wrestling with the "man" in the midst of night and reconciling with Esau, he assumed the mantle of leadership and became Israel, the man who strove with God and prevailed (Genesis 32:29). Through him, all of the tribes were born, and his sojourn into Egypt eventually led to the exodus of our people from slavery to Mount Sinai and, eventually, to the Land of Canaan. Where would we be without Sarah and Jacob?

The advice columnist Ann Landers shared the words sent to her by a reader who found them written in longhand in her grandmother's Bible: "What is life? Life is a challenge; meet it. Life is a gift; accept it. Life is an adventure; bear it. Life is a game; play it. Life is a mystery; unfold it. Life is a song; sing it. Life is an opportunity; take it. Life is a journey; complete it. Life is a promise; fulfill it. Life is a beauty; praise it. Life is a struggle; fight it. Life is a goal; achieve it. Life is a puzzle; solve it."

We should live life not with the "ifs," but with the double *yud*, not with doubt, but with faith. If we can live life this way, we will be remembered for the blessings we provided to our families, our communities, our people, and the world.

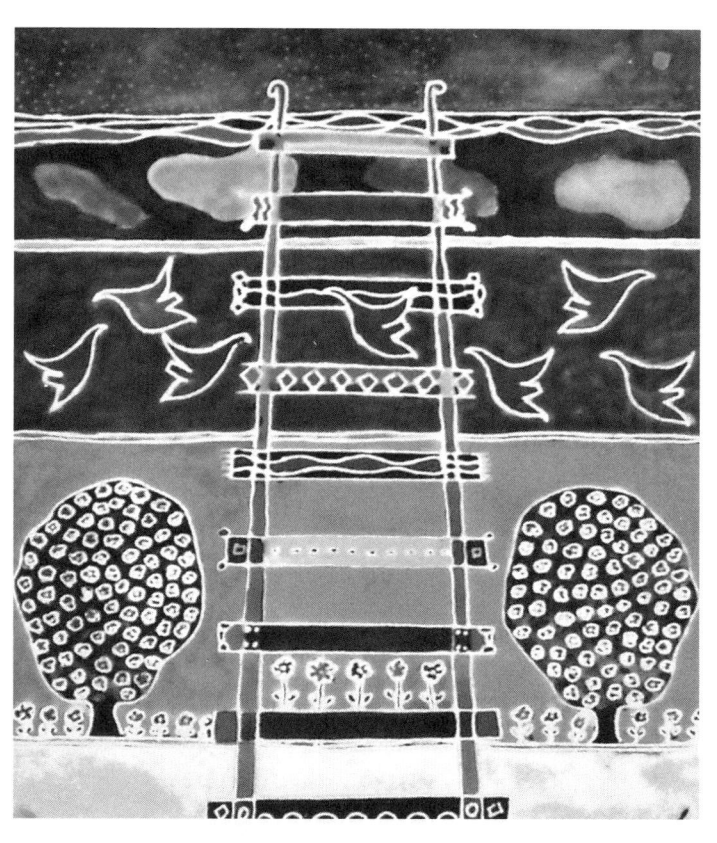

EXODUS
שמות
SHEMOT

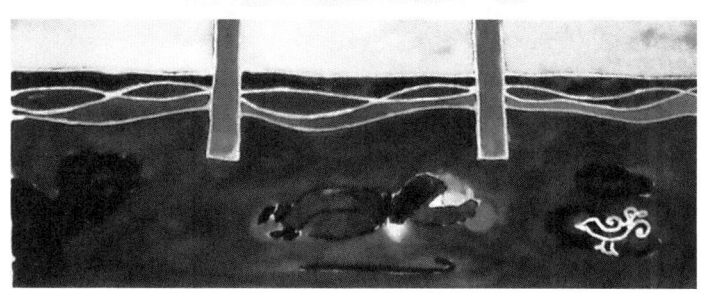

SHEMOT
Yihiye Tov—"It Will Be Good"

"A certain man of the house of Levi went and married a Levite woman" (Exodus 2:1). So begins the second chapter of the Book of Exodus, the story of Moses and the Exodus of the Children of Israel from the bondage of Egypt. The next verse in the chapter tells us that the Levite woman conceived and bore a son. Later, he is given the name Moses.

This verse presents us with certain problems. The Torah, usually so concerned with giving detailed information, omits the names of the Levite woman and man. One would think this to be rather important. More starkly, if they are the parents of Moses, why is there no mention of Moses' older siblings? We do know that Aaron and Miriam were born before their younger brother, and yet, their births are not mentioned.

We can understand the *peshat*, the simple meaning of the text, and explain that since the focus of the story is Moses' leadership, both Aaron and Miriam are secondary characters. The Midrash, however, offers a totally different scenario. Basing its explanation on the words "and he went, and he took" in the Biblical verse, Rabbi Judah ben Zebina, quoted in *Sotah* 12a, states: "He went in the counsel of his daughter." The following story is then recorded:

> Amram was the greatest man of his generation; when he saw that the wicked Pharaoh had decreed that all males born of the Israelites shall be thrown into the river, he said, "In vain do we labor." He arose and divorced his wife [so that no further children might be endangered]. All [the Israelites] thereupon arose and divorced their wives. His daughter said to him, "Father, your decree is more severe than Pharaoh's, because Pharaoh decreed only against the males whereas you have decreed against the males and females … In the case of the wicked Pharaoh, there is doubt whether his decree will be fulfilled or not, whereas in your case, since you are righteous, it is certain that your decree will be fulfilled." Amram was

convinced that his daughter was correct. He arose and took his wife back; and they all arose and took their wives back.

What a remarkable story! Amram, despairing of the future, could have decreed an end to Israelite existence. Without the wise words of Miriam, according to this *midrash*, Moses would not have been born, and Jewish history would have been very different. The message, I am sure, was critical for the days of Rabbi Judah ben Zebina, a third-generation Talmudic rabbi in Israel, when Roman persecution made life difficult for the Jewish community in Palestine. And this message has remained critical throughout Jewish history. Personal decisions have national implications. Never despair; never give up hope. As bad as things seem to be, believe that the future will be better and act to make it so. As the popular Israeli song states: *Yihiye Tov*. This is translated by songwriter David Broza as "Things Will Get Better"; the Hebrew translates more literally as "It Will Be Good."

In his book, *Moses and Monotheism*, Sigmund Freud wrote of the Jews: "They are animated by a special trust in life, such as is bestowed by the secret possession of a precious gift; it is a kind of optimism. Religious people would call it trust in God." I don't believe that Freud was usually correct in his assessment of Jews and Judaism, but in this case, he was. Jews have an innate optimism, a great sense of trust and faith, and a general sense that "it will be good."

As we look around the Jewish world, we can always find points of anxiety and crisis. Many are familiar with the anecdote in which a master of ceremonies at a big Jewish event starts the meeting with the words: "I have just received a message—start worrying, details to follow." There are moments of pessimism and cynicism. But like Miriam, I believe that one cannot be despondent. Miriam convinced her father that faith in the future is integral to Jewish life. One cannot be a Jew and despair. We have survived too much already in our history to give up hope in the future destiny of the Jewish people.

Emmanuel Ringelblum's diary depicts life in the Warsaw Ghetto during the Nazi occupation. He writes, "In the prayer house of the Ḥasidim of Bratslav, there is a large sign, 'Jews, never despair.' Know that the world is like a narrow bridge, and that man has to cross that narrow bridge. But what matters, above all, is not to be afraid as one walks over it." This was the message of the Bratslaver Ḥasidim to the people of the Warsaw Ghetto under the worst possible conditions; it is an echo of Miriam's message to her father, as told in the story of Rabbi Judah ben Zebina: "Jews, never despair, never give up hope." Even when all seems to be crumbling around you, persevere, go forward, have faith in yourself, your people, and your God. While a particular moment may seem dire and filled with great anxiety, it is our task to plan and build for the future.

A *New York Times* editorial from January 1, 1991, states: "Three hundred and sixty-five days lie ahead, each one a blank, beautiful page. No turned-down corners, no coffee stains, no scribbles. These pages are pristine, and there's no way to know what will appear on them eventually. No way at all." Let us have hope, faith, and trust that the days ahead will be filled with happiness and health, and let us work together to bring good tidings for our people and the entire world.

SHEMOT
The Book of Names

The second book of the Bible is commonly known as the Book of Exodus, based on its Greek translation. This title focuses on the Exodus of the Children of Israel from the bondage of Egypt. However, in Hebrew, the second book of the Bible is known as *Sefer Shemot*, literally, the Book of Names, based on the first verse: "These are the names of the sons of Israel who came to Egypt with Jacob" (Exodus 1:1). The Rabbis offer many reflections on why the focus on names is so important. The Ba'al Shem Tov, the founder of Ḥasidism, suggests that names tell the very essence of who we are from a spiritual point of view. When one is given a name, the name marks that person's distinctness and points to his or her spiritual soul that is part of the physical flesh.

Adam understands this lesson. When all of the animals are brought before Adam, he assigns names "to all the cattle and to the birds of the sky and to all the wild beasts" (Genesis 2:20). By naming the creatures, Adam understands the very essence of each of these animals.

Moses, too, understands this lesson. When he meets God at the burning bush, Moses offers various excuses for not accepting the mantle of leadership. Most significantly, he asks, "When I come to the Israelites and say to them, 'The God of your fathers has sent me to you' and they ask me, 'What is His name?' what shall I say to them?" (Exodus 3:13). Moses recognizes that he cannot rely on a past relationship with God; he must instill hope in the present by explaining to the Israelites the very essence of the God who has sent him to deliver the message.

It is for that reason, I believe, that *Leviticus Rabbah* 32:5 states: "Because of four things the Children of Israel were redeemed from Egypt: they did not change their names, they did not change their language, they did not go tale-bearing, and none of them was found to have been immoral." The fact that the Israelites did not change their names suggests that they understood their identities very well. They knew they were different from their Egyptian masters, and their very spiritual essence was defined by the fact that they remained true to themselves and to their ancestral tradition.

Our names tell much about us. In many cases we are tied to specific deceased members of our family who are remembered through us. As bearers of their names, we often carry on their spiritual essence in a meaningful fashion. The ancients believed that one's essence was inextricably bound to one's name. If you changed your name, you were, in effect, changing your basic identity. I believe it is essential that Jews remember their Hebrew names and know the background of those names.

In his book, *Inside, Outside*, Herman Wouk writes, "Every Jew who has ever stepped into a synagogue or temple knows that we have two names: the outside name with which we go through life, and the inside name, the Jewish name, used in blessings and Torah call-ups, marriage and divorce ceremonies, and on tombstones … It is a far-drifted Jew who has forgotten his or her inside name."

While I would like to believe that Wouk's observation is correct, I know it is not. Today, many Jews have forgotten their inside names. This suggests they have lost more than the name itself—they have lost their spiritual essence.

When our names are lost, we lose the very essence of being. While we don't want the entire world to know too much about us, I think anonymity scares us even more. In the TV show *Cheers*, everybody likes visiting the bar because it is a place where "everybody knows your name." We want to be known, and we want to be recognized by our names.

Our names do more than simply identify us to others; our names reveal something about our very essence. A passage from *Tanḥuma Va-yakhel* 1 states: "One finds that a person is called by three names: one that his father and mother call him, one that other people call him, and one that he acquires for himself. Best of all is the one he acquires for himself." We have no authority over the first name. When we come into this world, our parents give us a name. This name signifies their responsibility toward us and the hope that we will live up to this name. Over the second name, we have some control. The roles and responsibilities we take on in our lives are generally the product of some degree of choice. But we have almost total control over the third name. This is the name we acquire for ourselves in the land of the living. This name is earned by deeds of generosity and kindness. It is the name that tells the spiritual essence of who we are and what values we represent.

In Israeli poet Zelda's famous poem, "Each of Us Has a Name," she outlines how each person has a name given to him by his parents, his neighbors, his love and his enemies, his celebrations and his work, and his smile. "Each of us has a name given by the sea and given by our death."

The Children of Israel were redeemed from the exile of Egypt because they didn't change their names. They went down to Egypt as Reuven and Shimon, and they left Egypt as Reuven and Shimon—if not individually, then through the families that they created. They passed on the very essence of their spiritual beings to others, and this legacy merited their liberation.

May we hold fast to those same ideals, recognizing that our names carry our stories—both the names we acquire for ourselves during our lifetimes and the names we pass down in our legacy to future generations.

VA-ERA
The Four Cups of Wine

While most of us are familiar with the ritual of drinking four cups of wine at the Passover Seder, some may not be familiar with the rationale for that practice. The Biblical support for this particular custom derives from the first part of *parashat Va-era*, in which Moses and Aaron are disheartened after they are rejected both by Pharaoh and by the elders of Israel. They return to God who reassures them that their mission will be successful.

In the phrases known as "the four expressions of redemption," God reaffirms His vow to redeem the Israelite people from slavery. These four expressions: "I will free you from the labors of the Egyptians and deliver you from their bondage. I will redeem you with an outstretched arm and through extraordinary chastisements. And I will take you to be My people, and I will be your God" (Exodus 6:6–7) represent the rationale for drinking four glasses of wine at the Passover Seder. Each of the expressions is necessary for true redemption to take place and for God to fulfill His promise to the Israelite people.

The order of the four expressions is significant and should not be taken lightly. God first tells the Children of Israel that they will be freed from Egyptian slavery, and then they will be rescued. This notion represents liberation or "freedom from oppression." The Israelites have been enslaved by the Egyptians and are thoroughly depressed by their bondage. A savior must rescue them. God is that savior, and Moses is His messenger. The Israelites must be liberated from Egyptian bondage in order for them to recognize that the God of their ancestors is their true savior.

The specific order of these two initial phrases suggests an extremely important message. Rabbi Uziel suggests that a more perfect order would have the Israelites rescued before God takes them out of Egypt. After all, the act of rescue itself occurs on the night on which God slew the firstborn of the Egyptians. In each Israelite household that had been marked by blood on its doorpost, the firstborn son is saved. Is that not enough to suggest that rescue came even before the Exodus itself?

Rabbi Uziel responds by suggesting that the concept of salvation or deliverance is not individual but collective. The Israelites had been slaves for over 400 years and had no idea what true freedom, rescue, and salvation meant. They had to experience a taste of freedom before they understood its authentic meaning. Not only did the Israelites have to be taken out of Egypt, Egypt had to be taken out of the Israelites.

The second set of redemptive verbs suggests "freedom for." God will redeem the Children of Israel so that they shall see evidence of His saving acts. In this way, God will make them His people. This is one of the major challenges of American Judaism. We are freer than any Jewish community in history, and yet, what does that freedom mean? Does it allow us to simply run away from the past, negate our background, and assimilate? Or does our freedom allow us to be productive members of this society even as we practice and profess our Judaism in stronger patterns than those of our ancestors? Our tradition follows the teaching of Rabbi Joshua ben Levi who offers in *Pirkei Avot* 6:2 a comment on the words of Exodus 32:16: "No person is free except one who engages in the study of Torah." This is the purpose of liberty and freedom.

It is necessary to read these four expressions of redemption as one continuous act. And in a fifth expression, God tells Moses, "I will bring you into the land which I swore to give to Abraham, Isaac, and Jacob, and I will give it to you for a possession" (Exodus 6:8). This fifth expression of redemption is solemnized at our Seder by the cup of Elijah. This cup represents the final redemption, and each time we invite Elijah into our homes, we pray that redemption may come soon.

Today, we have been brought back to our land. In the prayer for the State of Israel, we describe the State as "the beginning of the flowering of our redemption." Israel is in its own way a Divine miracle and, with the ingathering of the exiles, our people have once more returned to the Promised Land. But even as Israel strives for peace, many burdens and challenges remain. In order to bring redemption to our people in the Land of Israel, we face not only the challenge of physical security, safety, and freedom, we also face the challenge of spiritual freedom. All must be allowed to live in dignity with freedom to practice their own spiritual beliefs.

The "four expressions of redemption" and the additional promise continue to challenge us in our own day. What is freedom, and how do we celebrate it? Are we truthful to our tradition, and are we willing to allow it to touch our everyday lives? These are the questions that we must ponder, not only at the Passover Seder and not only when we read *parashat Va-era*, but each and every day, for the answers that we give will set the stage for the future destiny of the Jewish people.

VA-ERA
A People Who Dwell Apart

What was the great miracle of the plagues? One could suggest that simply their appearance was miracle enough. However, I think the true miracle is that the Israelites living in Goshen, in close proximity to the Egyptian population, were not afflicted by the plagues.

When the fourth plague is recounted, God tells Moses to go to Pharaoh and warn him of the coming of swarms of insects upon the Egyptians. "But on that day I will set apart the region of Goshen, where My people dwell, so that no swarms of insects shall be there, that you may know that I the Lord am in the midst of the land. And I will make a distinction between My people and your people. Tomorrow this sign shall come to pass" (Exodus 8:18–19).

This is not the only time during the description of the plagues that a separation is made between the Children of Israel and the Egyptians, but it is the first and represents the awesome power of the God of the Israelites. The magicians' power cannot compare, Pharaoh's power cannot compare, and only the God of Israel is supreme over all.

In truth, separateness has been our destiny throughout Jewish history. In this case, separateness was for the good of the Israelite nation. But there have been times throughout history when being apart from the dominant culture forced us to be on the defensive as our uniqueness has been attacked, and our people have been persecuted.

The heathen prophet, Bilaam, uttered these words: "There is a people that dwells apart, not reckoned among the nations" (Numbers 23:9). For some commentators, this remark did not express a blessing, but a curse that has lasted throughout much of Jewish history. At its worst, the setting apart of the Jew has meant ghettoization, disenfranchisement, anti-Semitism, and finally, at its very worst, the Holocaust.

In their book, *Why The Jews? The Reason for Antisemitism,* Dennis Prager and Joseph Telushkin write that "the ultimate cause of anti-Semitism is that which has made Jews Jewish—Judaism." The authors contend that many non-Jews have regarded the mere existence of Jews, no matter how few, as terribly threatening. The presence of Jews, with their different values and allegiances, constitutes a threat to the prevailing order. Taking this further, they suggest that anti-Semites believe Jews must either convert, be expelled, or be murdered. As the authors examine possible reasons for anti-Semitism, they argue that this notion is at its core. With no rational reason for Jew-hatred throughout the ages, the notion of Jewish distinctiveness and separateness presents a challenge to outside society and leads to anti-Semitism.

I do not know if Prager and Telushkin are correct, but I do know that anti-Semitism still exists in the world in which we live. We need only think of the diatribes of the president of Iran. Unfortunately, we are not free of the abuses of Jew-hatred.

Yet we can consider our distinctiveness and our separateness in another way. Rabbi Gunther Plaut explains that chosenness has been a core factor of Jewish life for thousands of years. In times of stress, this belief has served as a source of hope and reassurance. The conviction that Israel is indeed God's beloved has played a role in Jewish survival. This explanation follows the teachings of the prophet Amos who stated that we were chosen by God not for special rewards: "You alone have I singled out of all the families of the earth—that is why I will call you to account for all your iniquities" (Amos 3:2). Extra burdens, special obligations, and responsibilities are placed on our communal shoulders.

We are asked to be distinctive and unique. The Torah tells us *kedoshim tihiyu,* "You shall be holy" (Leviticus 19:2), which Rashi understands as *perushim tihiyu,* "You shall be separate." *Kashrut* teaches us that our diet must be based upon a level of holiness. Shabbat instructs us that one day a week we dedicate ourselves to God and sacred time. Our value system leads us in moral and ethical ways so that we can, in Isaiah's words, become witnesses for God (Isaiah 43:10).

If we cannot comprehend the reasons for anti-Semitism and the isolation that it has created for us, we may also not be able to understand why our people were designated for a sacred purpose. Moses' long discourse to the Israelite people in the Book of Deuteronomy raises the issue: "It is not because you are the most numerous of peoples that the Lord set His heart on you and chose you—indeed, you are the smallest of peoples; but it was because the Lord favored you and kept the oath He made to your fathers that the Lord freed you with a mighty hand and rescued you from the house of bondage, from the power of Pharaoh, king of Egypt" (Deuteronomy 7:7–8).

This dilemma of being a people set apart has been our lot from the very beginning of our history. Abraham was known as "the Hebrew" (*ivri*) because, according to the Rabbis, he stood on one side (*ever*) of the bank of the river as everyone else stood on the other (*Genesis Rabbah* 42:8). He taught the world the monotheistic approach and the value system that emanates from it. If Prager and Telushkin are correct, this role is at the core of why the Jewish people have endured such hatred. Our separateness is at the heart of what it means to be a Jew in today's world.

Let us bear our distinctiveness and our uniqueness with pride. And let us hope and pray for the day when individuals and the nations of the world who have singled us out for hatred and enmity will join with us to create a universe of peace and harmony for all.

BO
Beyond Remembering

Americans are familiar with patriotic mottos that begin with the word "remember": "Remember the Alamo," "Remember the Maine," and "Remember Pearl Harbor." For Sephardic Jews, a rallying cry for the past 500 years has been "Remember the expulsion from Spain and Portugal." In modern times, Jews have added the motto "Remember the Holocaust."

As Jews, we are bidden to recall the events of our liberation from Egypt: "Remember the Exodus from Egypt." This is, of course, the main theme of the Passover festival. It is also one of the two major themes of Shabbat observance, the other being recognition of God's creation of the universe.

In *parashat Bo,* we read, "Remember this day, on which you went free from Egypt, the house of bondage, how the Lord freed you from it with a mighty hand: no leavened bread shall be eaten" (Exodus 13:3). Maimonides suggests that there is a commandment to recall the liberation from Egypt both by day and by night. And in our liturgy, we recall the Exodus from Egypt in our morning and evening prayers. We are to recall this framing event of our people not only when we read the story in the Book of Exodus, not only at the Seder when we celebrate the Festival of Freedom, but each and every day. The Exodus from Egypt is at the core of our peoplehood, and we are urged to understand its message.

Rabbi Abraham Joshua Heschel writes, "When the Voice of God spoke at Sinai, it did not begin by saying, 'I am the Lord your God Who created heaven and earth.' It began by saying, 'I am the Lord your God Who brought you out of the land of Egypt, out of the house of bondage.' … The most commanding idea that Judaism dares to think is that freedom, not necessity, is the source of all being. The universe was not caused, but created. Behind mind and matter, order and relations, the freedom of God obtains."

The Torah reading informs us that one of the modes of remembering is an intellectual exercise: "And when, in time to come, your son asks you, saying, 'What does this mean?' you shall say to him, 'It was with a mighty hand that the Lord brought us out from Egypt, the house of bondage'" (Exodus 13:14). The story is to be told from generation to generation, from parent to child, from teacher to student, from the elders to the young. We are taught that it is our duty to teach our children the story of the Exodus from Egypt.

But remembering is not only an intellectual exercise. Maimonides associates the verse "Remember this day when you left Egypt" with the verse "Remember the Sabbath Day and keep it holy" (Exodus 20:8). On Shabbat, we fulfill the *mitzvah* of remembering through the acts of reciting *Kiddush*, reciting the blessing over the lighting of the candles, and through the experience of imitating our God who abstained from creative physical activity on the seventh day of creation.

Similarly, the ritual of the Passover Seder, at which we remember the Exodus, obligates us not only to relate verbally the events of the story but to relive experientially that momentous time. Symbolism abounds: we eat the food that reminds us of our ancestors' bitterness, we taste the matzah that the Israelites baked on their hurried exit from the land of Egypt, and we sing the psalms of joy they sang at the moment of their deliverance. We teach not only through the mind but through our senses.

No people understands freedom like the Jewish people. Heinrich Heine said that "freedom has always spoken with a Hebrew accent." The Jewish people have understood what it means to be enslaved intellectually, physically, and spiritually. We, therefore, must be more sensitive than any other nation to those who are presently in that condition. Thus, it is our task to worry about those who are not as privileged as we, and to respond by feeding the hungry, sheltering the homeless, and clothing the naked. It is our task to break the patterns of racism, prejudice, bias, and bigotry. When any minority is enslaved by others, whether it be because of race, ethnicity, religion, or gender, Jews are obligated to rise up and protest. We were slaves in the land of Egypt, and we are to recall that degradation each and every day. We were fortunate to have been redeemed, and we are to teach others by our example.

It is our duty to teach our children through our actions and through our use of language, resources, and energy. We must be models to those who will follow us. In this way, our descendants will learn that the paradigm of remembering is not merely an intellectual exercise reserved for one or two nights a year but that it also determines our daily actions and responses. Just as the remembering of God's cessation from creative activity on the seventh day of creation serves as a model for us to rest every seventh day of the week and make that day holy, so the Exodus bids us to model our behavior after God and work to attain freedom for all people.

Each time we are asked to remember, whether it be the Exodus from Egypt, the holiness of the Sabbath, or even the evil deeds of Amalek, we are asked to respond in a way in which we use the intellectual exercise of remembering to inform our actions and teach the importance of living lives of holiness, serving as witnesses for God. Our tradition informs us: "Memory leads to action" (*Halakhot Ketanot of the Rosh, Tzitzit* 20). May we use the prototype of our liberation experience to appreciate our liberation from bondage and share the message of the Exodus with all people.

BO
The Challenge of Darkness

Parashat Bo commences with the plagues continuing to descend upon the Egyptian people. Perhaps the most interesting plague is the ninth, the plague of darkness. The Torah tells us: "Moses held out his arm toward the sky and thick darkness descended upon all the land of Egypt for three days. People could not see one another, and for three days no one could get up from where he was; but all the Israelites enjoyed light in their dwellings" (Exodus 10:22–23).

The text indicates that the darkness was so all-encompassing it could actually be touched. Some Rabbinic commentators stated that this darkness existed on earth before light was created. Other Rabbinic commentators noted that the darkness was the equivalent of the darkness of *gehinnom*, hell, itself. Yet, the text states that the Children of Israel did not sense it, for there was light in their dwellings (*Exodus Rabbah* 14:2).

A very interesting and rather puzzling *midrash* suggests that this plague is the only one among the ten in which some Israelites suffered. *Exodus Rabbah* suggests that darkness fell upon some Israelites as well. These were individuals who had Egyptian patrons and lived in affluence and honor and were unwilling to leave. The *midrash* states that God said, "If I bring upon them publicly a plague from which they will die, the Egyptians will say, 'Just as it has passed over us so it has passed over them'" (*Exodus Rabbah* 14:3). Therefore, God brought darkness upon the Egyptians for three days so that the Israelites should bury their dead without their enemies seeing them and for this they should praise God.

This is a very puzzling *midrash*, and it seems to counter the Biblical text. Yet, I believe this *midrash* is designed to convey an important lesson. Sometimes it is only when darkness occurs that we see the light. The light may be around us at all times, but it takes a plague of darkness for us to truly appreciate the light that is within our grasp.

Every year on January 15th, many people celebrate a significant anniversary. On that day in 2009, the passengers of U.S. Airways Flight #1549 were saved after their plane hit a flock of geese and lost power in both engines. Captain Chesley "Sully" Sullenberger became an instant hero as he guided the plane to a smooth water landing in the Hudson, saving all of the passengers. So close to death, to ultimate darkness, many of these passengers talked about "seeing the light."

In interviews with those who were saved, many returned from that experience with the desire to see their lives anew. They recognized that they had been granted extra time on earth, made significant changes in their lifestyles, and would not take for granted another minute with their loved ones.

As just one example, Maryanne Bruce, a mutual fund investor in Charlotte, North Carolina, decided that whenever she has the opportunity, she tries to do things a little differently. She remarked, "Why does everybody rush to a funeral? It's too late." Ms. Bruce told a former colleague how much she enjoyed working with her and how proud she was of her colleague's recent promotion. "She cried," Ms. Bruce said. "She had always looked up to me, and she didn't realize how much I meant to her."

Many of the survivors now try to spend more time with those who are closest to them. Having had a near-death experience, they recognize that the light almost went out for them, and there is so much left to be said and experienced.

Human nature doesn't allow us to see the goodness that is around us at all times. Rather than seeing the light, appreciating it, experiencing it, and sharing it with others, we sometimes only see darkness and lose ourselves in its blackness. Sometimes, we need an external event, an illness, the loss of someone close to us, or a life-threatening experience to wake us up. Perhaps these Israelites didn't appreciate the light that was always around them. They became so engulfed in the darkness that it seemed as if, like the Egyptians, they were dead.

There may be another possible interpretation of this difficult *midrash*. The Israelites who were engulfed in this Egyptian plague perhaps embodied the very same characteristics of the Egyptian masters who cared not for others, but only for themselves. The text seems to suggest that the Egyptians were enveloped in darkness as a punishment for the fact that they couldn't truly see those around them, feel their pain, and recognize the dignity of their afflicted neighbors. The text states: "People could not see one another" (Exodus 10:23). While they could not see one another for only three days, there was an element of darkness that characterized the Egyptians for a longer period of time. They did not recognize that, in their own country, a nation was subjected to slavery.

This explanation suggests that the Israelites had light in their dwellings, feelings of common concern and responsibility, even under the most extraordinary of circumstances. Unfortunately, according to the *midrash*, not all Israelites felt the same. Some were only concerned for their individual well-being and cared little, if at all, for the welfare of others.

How easy it is to live our individual lives without caring about others. How simple it is not to open our eyes to the suffering that is all around us. The text teaches us that there are some who are willing to open their eyes and some who are not. There are those able to experience the light, those who do not live in darkness.

The story of the darkness that enveloped Egypt and this difficult *midrash* force us to think about how we live our lives. Do we appreciate our gifts? Are we prepared to reach out to others in need? Our response to these questions will dictate how we live and the legacy we leave for others.

BE-SHALLAḤ—SHABBAT SHIRA
The Ultimate Song

This is the Sabbath of the great song. In the Torah reading, we read *Shirat Ha-yam*, the great song of triumph that Moses and the Israelites sang at the Sea of Reeds. The song is a magnificent poem whose imagery and beauty has resonated throughout the ages.

An incredible event moved the people to utter this song. As the Israelites were fleeing the Egyptian armies, they came to *Yam Suf*, commonly referred to as the Red Sea, but most probably the Sea of Reeds. There, in front of them was the water, in back of them were the advancing soldiers of Egypt. Suddenly, as Moses implored God for help, the sea split apart, and the Israelites walked through on dry land. But God was not finished. After the Israelites reached the other side, they looked behind them and saw the Egyptians setting out on the same path. Suddenly, the sea returned to its original form, and all the Egyptian soldiers, horses, and chariots perished in the midst of the sea. The people sensed that they were experiencing a saving miracle. For the first time they realized they were finished with Egyptian bondage.

The Midrash (*Mekhilta Be-shallah Shirata* 3:3) suggests that this was a very special event in the life of the Israelite people. Rabbi Eliezer wrote, "What a maidservant saw at the Sea of Reeds, Isaiah and Ezekiel and all the other prophets never saw." What had the Israelites seen? They were personal witnesses to God's saving acts in history. Their spontaneous reaction was expressed in song: "Then Moses and the Israelites sang this song to the Lord" (Exodus 15:1).

It must have been a magnificent occasion for all the Israelites: men, women, and children, the old and the young, the healthy and the sick—every individual experienced God's power. The Midrash (*Exodus Rabbah* 23:4) tells us that from the day that God created the world until this moment in human history, no one had offered a song unto the Lord—not

Adam, Abraham, Isaac, or Jacob. But when the people of Israel came to the sea and experienced the great miracle, they responded with this great song of thanksgiving and praise.

This passage from the Book of Exodus has become part of our daily liturgy. Each morning before we reach *Bar'khu*, the call to worship, we rise and recite this great ode of triumph to God. Why was this included in the liturgy? I believe it is part of the liturgical canon because the text wants to remind us of that moment almost 3,000 years ago when our ancestors recognized God's presence in history and responded with spontaneous song.

This is what prayer is all about. Prayer is not only petition and demands. When we come to the synagogue, we should not simply bring a shopping bag full of wishes to present before God. We also should come to the synagogue to offer praises onto God for the gifts presented to us. Examine the psalms chosen for the Preliminary Service, the *P'sukei D'zimra*. They commence and conclude with the word *Halleluyah*, "Praise the Lord." The psalms extol God's greatness in nature, God's mastery over the entire world. The Psalmist tells us to come before the Lord in song: "Sing to the Lord a new song … Let them praise His name in dance; with timbrel and lyre let them chant His praises" (Psalms 149:1, 3). When one comes before God, one offers songs of praise and joy for the great wonders of the world. The song of Moses fits right into this pattern. The Ḥafetz Ḥayim suggests that this song should be recited with great joy, as one should place oneself in the shoes of the Israelites and recite the song with the same joyous celebration.

A legend tells us that after God created the world, He called the angels to Him and asked what they thought of His creation. One of the angels responded, "One thing is lacking: the sound of praise to the Creator." God then created music, which is heard in the whisper of the wind, the song of the birds, and the human voice in song. The song of our souls is prayer.

But one is required to do more than just testify to God's presence in this world. When Moses and the Children of Israel reached the edge of the sea, the Talmud tells us that Moses was engaged for a long while in prayer, and the Holy One, Blessed be He, said to him, "My beloved ones are drowning in the sea and you prolong your prayer before Me? Speak unto the Children of Israel that they go forward" (*Sotah* 37a).

Prayer alone was not adequate then, nor is it enough now. Our tradition has always believed that it is the act, the deed, and the mode of behavior that must take precedence. To sing a song unto the Lord, therefore, is not only done with our mouths and our souls, but also with our hands, our feet, and our hearts. Abraham Joshua Heschel taught us that we attain faith through deeds; we perceive in doing. In our actions we give evidence to our faith in God.

We sing a song unto the Lord when we emulate God's deeds and bring goodness and righteousness to the world. When we clothe the naked, feed the hungry, shelter the homeless, we sing a song unto the Lord. When we spread kindness in our world, care and concern for our neighbor, we praise God with our deeds. When we display thoughtfulness to our friend, love to our family, we address God in our everyday lives. The music we play, the song we sing is not merely expressed through words; we also transmit our praise through deeds and actions.

BE-SHALLAḤ—SHABBAT SHIRA
Embodying Faith in Life

Most of the emphasis of *parashat Be-shallaḥ* concerns the great song that Moses and the Children of Israel sing at the Sea of Reeds. But there is another interesting section found at the end of the *parashah*. The Torah tells us that the Amalekites attacked the Israelites as they traveled in the desert. Moses instructs Joshua to find able-bodied men and meet the Amalekites in battle. Moses leaves the military maneuvers to Joshua, while he, Aaron, and Ḥur ascend to the top of a hill. The Torah then states: "Then, whenever Moses held up his hand, Israel prevailed; but whenever he let down his hand, Amalek prevailed" (Exodus 17:11). Then the Torah adds an interesting observation. Moses, the great leader and prophet, is only human after all. He grows tired sitting up on the hill and needs help keeping his hands in the air. "But Moses' hands grew heavy; so they took a stone and put it under him and he sat on it, while Aaron and Ḥur, one on each side, supported his hands; thus his hands remained steady until the sun set" (Exodus 17:12).

This verse teaches a number of very important lessons concerning human life. The text tells us that Moses sat on a stone as he watched the battle and rallied the troops. The Talmud in *Ta'anit* 11a asks: "Did not then Moses have a bolster or a cushion to sit on?" Why did he sit upon a stone? The Talmud offers this answer: "Moses said, 'As Israel is in distress, I too will share with them. He who shares in the distress of the community will merit to behold its consolation.'"

This commentary informs us that being sympathetic to another individual's troubles and sorrows is not enough. One must exhibit feelings of empathy, join others in their sorrow, participate in their hurt, and feel their sense of pain. Moses could not feel comfortable while the Israelites were doing battle with the Amalekites. He may not have been down on the battlefield himself, but he wanted them to know that he was participating with them in their travails.

A Native American prayer states: "Great Spirit, grant that I may not criticize my neighbor until I have walked a mile in his moccasins." The Jewish equivalent is found in *Pirkei Avot* 2:5: "Do not judge your fellow human being till you stand in his situation." Each of these statements suggests that if you really want to understand the predicament of another, it is not sufficient to judge or criticize from afar; it is essential to place yourself in his particular situation. Only then can you truly understand his feelings and his actions.

However sensitive he may be to the needs of others, Moses needs help in order to accomplish his mission and bear the burden of leadership. His brother Aaron and his brother-in-law or nephew Hur respond. They stand with Moses, holding up his hands so that the people can rally and win their battle. Moses needs the support of others to accomplish his mission.

Like Moses, each of us periodically becomes tired of life's travails. Doubts, fears, and anxieties are a part of all of us. There is no one alive who does not feel these emotions at some moment in life. Each of us needs others to be present with us to respond to our physical and emotional needs.

We need to build those types of relationships and communities in which we feel secure enough to trust others, share our fears and anxieties, our joys and sorrows, and know that there will be others who will be present for us when we need them. The Torah tells us that Aaron and Hur recognized Moses' silent cry for help and responded. They held his hands up high so that he could complete his task.

They were successful in their endeavors, for "his hands remained steady until the sun set" (Exodus 17:12). *Onkelos*, the Aramaic translation of the Hebrew text, suggests that his hands were outstretched in prayer. Moses recognized that he could not simply rely on the military prowess of Joshua or his own display of leadership—he needed to ask for God's help in the battle.

There is nothing more difficult for the modern person than prayer. With our vast scientific and medical knowledge, sometimes we think we have all the answers and only turn to God when we need to fill our desires.

But prayer is more than bargaining with God and attempting to get the best deal. Rabbi Naḥman of Bratslav, the great Ḥasidic teacher, suggests that Moses' hands were steady and they represented *emunah*, or faith. There is a faith that is felt only in the heart, and that kind of faith is not enough. Faith must pervade the whole body as it did for Moses whose hands were faith. We learn that prayer does not change God; it changes the person who prays. Abraham Joshua Heschel writes that "prayer teaches us what to aspire for … Prayer implants in us the ideals we ought to cherish." Thoughts of redemption, purity of mind and tongue, or a willingness to help others may hover as ideas, but when we pray, our ideas become genuine longings and goals toward which we strive. This was Moses' prayer. It was a statement of faith expressed with his entire body; it was his commitment to live his life in the service of the Lord.

As we read of Moses' leadership during the battle with Amalek, let us learn from his example by being people of faith who recognize the presence of the Almighty in our lives. Let us be supportive of family and friends alike, and let us respond to cries for help from the people of our community with a sense of love and responsibility.

YITRO
To Listen and To Hear

Someone once asked a psychiatrist, "How can you listen, hour after hour, day after day, to people pouring out their distresses and troubles?" The psychiatrist calmly shrugged his shoulders and responded, "Who listens?"

Parashat Yitro has a common thread which connects the three major episodes described by the text. The key word in each episode is *lishmoa* ("to hear"). In each of the three cases, this word leads to greater insights.

The *parashah* begins with the words: "Jethro priest of Midian, Moses' father-in-law, heard all that God had done for Moses and for Israel His people" (Exodus 18:1). Jethro was so impressed by what he had heard that he traveled from Midian to the Sinai wilderness to search out Moses and the Israelite people.

What was it that so impressed him? The Talmud in *Zevakhim* 116a offers three possibilities: Rabbi Joshua says, "He heard about the battle with the Amalekites." Rabbi Elazar Ha-Modai suggests that this passage should be placed after the revelation at Sinai as that was the event that so moved Jethro to travel to see his son-in-law. Rabbi Eliezer says, "He heard about the dividing of the Sea of Reeds."

These three suggestions bear a common theme and each one represents a significant aspect of Jewish life. Amalek is representative of the enemies of the Jewish people throughout history. Though persecuted by others, we have survived all vicissitudes. The Torah—its laws, teachings, and ordinances—has been our inheritance from the days of Moses and is the lifeblood of our existence. The traversing of the Sea of Reeds signifies God's saving grace, God's presence in history.

These three events are prototypes for Jewish survival as they describe us as a nation, a people, and a faith community. This section of Talmud is prefaced by the comment that "Jethro heard what had befallen the

Israelites and converted," or, at least, identified with the Israelite people and their God. In other words, it took a non-Israelite to listen carefully to Israelite experiences and appreciate their importance and meaning. We should follow Jethro's example.

Another episode involves Jethro as he observes Moses judge the people from morning until evening. A concerned father-in-law, Jethro recognizes that Moses' burden is too great; he cannot bear the responsibility completely by himself. "Now listen to me," says Jethro, "I will give you counsel, and God be with you!" (Exodus 18:19). He then instructs Moses to choose able men to help him administer the justice system.

Does Moses accept his father-in-law's advice? He is, after all, the leader of the Israelite people, the man who experienced God at the burning bush, who confronted Pharaoh in his palace, a man of considerable power and prestige. And here comes his father-in-law, an outsider, telling him how to manage his own affairs. Moses is bright enough and humble enough to realize that he has heard sound advice. "Moses heeded his father-in-law and did just as he had said" (Exodus 18:24). This is emblematic of Moses' greatness. He could listen to criticism and respond to positive suggestions.

Most of us find it difficult to respond to criticism. We tend to become defensive and often react negatively, even to positive suggestions. Yes, it depends on the manner in which the advice is offered to us. However, we must be prepared to be humble enough to recognize our own imperfections and respond to the criticism and not to the critic.

Statesman and philanthropist Bernard Baruch earned his first million dollars at the age of twenty. When he told his father that he had become a millionaire, his father didn't seem impressed. He remarked, "What are you going to do with it?" Baruch later commented, "I have spent a lifetime trying to answer that question."

Jethro asked Moses to hearken to his words. Moses willingly accepted his father-in-law's advice, thereby improving the justice system of the Israelite people.

The third instance of *lishmoa* ("to hear") is found in the prelude to the revelation, the giving of the Ten Commandments. God tells Moses to speak to the Children of Israel: "Now then, if you will obey [listen to] Me faithfully and keep My covenant, you shall be My treasured possession among all the peoples. Indeed, all the earth is Mine, but you shall be to Me a kingdom of priests and a holy nation" (Exodus 19:5–6).

This is the central motif and rationale for the revelation. The Israelites and their descendants were given a conditional covenant. If they hearkened to God's voice and obeyed the commandments, they would merit being a treasured people, the chosen nation. We, today, cannot absolve ourselves of that obligation, as the Torah tells us that all of us stood at the foot of Mount Sinai and were involved in the covenantal process.

A man who was notorious for ruthlessness in business once announced to Mark Twain: "Before I die, I mean to make a pilgrimage to the Holy Land. I will climb Mount Sinai and read the Ten Commandments aloud at the top." "I have a better idea," said Twain. "You could stay home in Boston and keep them." Listening to the Divine imperatives and responding to their dictates is our role in the covenant.

The common thread of *parashat Yitro*, the act of listening, teaches us many lessons. Like Jethro, we must listen to the events of our Jewish past, recognize their significance, and respond to them; we should be flexible enough to listen to positive criticism and accept advice from others; and we must continuously hearken to the obligations of the covenant between God and our people.

Let us not respond like the psychiatrist with the retort, "Who listens?" but instead make use of our sense of hearing to become better human beings and more responsible and responsive Jews.

YITRO
The Tenth Commandment

Rabbi Nilton Bonder was born in Brazil and received his ordination at the Jewish Theological Seminary. He currently serves as rabbi of a Masorti congregation in Rio de Janeiro and has been the president of the Institute for Religious Studies, the largest forum for civil rights activities in Latin America. Most of his books were written originally in Portuguese, and many have been translated into English.

In his book, *The Kabbalah of Envy: Transforming Hatred, Anger, and Other Negative Emotions*, he argues that envy, jealousy, hatred, and anger are great motivating forces in our lives. Rabbi Bonder attempts to show that whether we are on the giving or receiving end of these unpleasant emotions, we can learn to transform them and live peacefully in the spirit of the Biblical commandment, "Love your neighbor as yourself" (Leviticus 19:18).

Parashat Yitro contains the Ten Commandments. The tenth commandment is one of the most difficult to comprehend in its fullest form. In the Book of Exodus we read: "You shall not covet your neighbor's house: you shall not covet your neighbor's wife, or his male or female slave, or his ox or his ass, or anything that is your neighbor's" (Exodus 20:14). In the Book of Deuteronomy, the words are slightly different: "You shall not covet your neighbor's wife. You shall not crave your neighbor's house, or his field, or his male or female slave, or his ox, or his ass, or anything that is your neighbor's" (Deuteronomy 5:18).

In his book, Rabbi Bonder quotes the Rabbi of Radvil who stated, "He who doesn't have the self-discipline to obey this prohibition of coveting should begin anew, starting with the first commandment: to love and recognize divine justice; because if such an individual really believed in God, he would not envy that which was allocated separately as part of the portion of his neighbor." Thus, there are commentators who believe that this concluding commandment is the basis for all the others, and whoever observes this law is considered as if he kept the entire Torah.

The opposite of coveting is *histapkut*, contentedness. When we are satisfied with our lot, we can appreciate our individual gifts, value ourselves, and learn to appreciate others. This is not an easy task, and sometimes we are our own worst enemies. However, if we learn to recognize the special talents we possess, then we can sense a measure of gratitude toward others as well.

Pirkei Avot 4:1 states: "Who is rich? One who is happy with his portion." The four letters of the Hebrew word *ashir*, a rich man, form an acrostic of the Hebrew words: *einayim* (eyes), *shenayim* (teeth), *yadayim* (hands), and *raglayim* (feet). When one has all of these parts of the body in working order, one is indeed wealthy. Too often, we only recognize what we have when we lose it.

In Leviticus chapter 19, the main principles of the Torah are detailed for us as part of the Holiness Code. Each of the Ten Commandments has a verse in the chapter that concretizes its basic principles. *Leviticus Rabbah* 24:5 states that the verse in *parashat Kedoshim* that expresses "You shall not covet" is "Love your neighbor as yourself." If we love ourselves, we can love our fellow human beings; we can avoid conflict and create a peaceful world.

An anonymous but apparently true story concerns two best friends, Angela and Charlotte.

> Angela knew that Charlotte, her best friend, was having a rough time. Charlotte was moody and depressed. She was withdrawn around everyone except for Angela … No one was on particularly good speaking terms with Charlotte that summer. For most of her friends, Charlotte had become too difficult … Their attempts to "be a friend" were met with angry accusations or depressed indifference.
>
> Angela was the only one who could reach her … Then a day came when Angela had to move. She was going just across town, but Charlotte would no longer be her neighbor, and they would be spending far less time together.

The first day in her new neighborhood, out playing with her new neighbors, Angela wondered how Charlotte was doing. When she got home, shortly before twilight, her mother told her that Charlotte had called.

Angela went to the phone to return the call. No answer. She left a message on Charlotte's machine. "Hi Charlotte, it's Angela. Call me back."

About half an hour later Charlotte called. "Angela, I have to tell you something. When you called, I was in the basement. I had a gun to my head. I was about to kill myself, but then I heard your voice on the machine upstairs … When I heard your voice I realized someone loves me, and I am so lucky that it is you. I'm going to go get help, because I love you too."

If you first love yourself, then you can reach out to love others.

In his book, *The Nine Commandments*, Professor David Noel Freedman writes that the tenth commandment does not name a specific violation because, unlike the previous nine, it deals with motivation. Coveting is expressed principally in two ways: greed for property and lust for persons. The commandment provides the underlying motivation for each of the criminal violations in numbers six through nine.

In the Torah commentary edited by Rabbi J. H. Hertz, it states that the tenth commandment "goes to the root of all evil actions—the unholy instincts and impulses of predatory desire which are the root of nearly every sin against a neighbor. The man who does not covet his neighbor's goods will not bear false witness against him; he will neither rob nor murder, nor will he commit adultery."

Rabbi Bonder goes one step further. He suggests that combating the excess of envy in the world is fundamental to the eradication of idolatry. From the tenth commandment, we go all the way back to the first. If we are satisfied with our lot, we learn to love ourselves; if we learn to love ourselves, then we can learn to love our fellow human being; if we can do that, then we appreciate our place in the Divine order to become partners with God in affecting the world in which we live. The bar is set very high for us. As Rabbi Bonder writes, "The decision to accept the notion of one God depends above all on a feeling of gratitude." May we live up to this high standard.

MISHPATIM
Home, Sanctuary, Community—The Threefold Cord

Parashat *Mishpatim* begins with the law of the Hebrew slave, the indentured servant. The Torah tells us that he may work for only six years—in the seventh year, he is to be freed. However, it is possible for the servant to remain in the employ of his master for a longer period of time. Under those conditions, the Torah states: "His master shall take him before God [or, more likely, before the judges]. He shall be brought to the door or the doorpost, and his master shall pierce his ear with an awl" (Exodus 21:6).

The immediate question, of course, is why the mark on the ear, and why have the piercing take place at the door or the *mezuzah*? The answers are quite interesting and teach us a great deal about Jewish thought and practice.

The best-known explanation for the ear piercing is the one quoted in the Torah commentary edited by Rabbi J. H. Hertz. Taken from *Tosefta Baba Kamma* 7:5 and *Kiddushin* 22b, it states: "Why was the ear singled out from all the other limbs of the body? The ear that heard the Divine utterance 'for unto Me, the Children of Israel are servants,' and, yet this man went and acquired a master for himself—let it be bored." It is an example of measure for measure.

An Italian Jewish Biblical commentator Shmuel David Luzzato, Shadal, suggests another reason for the boring of the ear. He suggests that the piercing of the ear was a custom seen by travelers in Persia and India and was a symbol of idol worship. This piercing was understood to be a sign for the eternal slave and was seen as a symbol of shame and was not extolled as a custom of legitimate worship.

Why, though, must the procedure occur near the door? Why is that a significant place? There are three different explanations that I wish to highlight. *Kiddushin* 22b states:

> R. Simeon b. Rabbi said, "In what respect are door and doorpost different from all other objects in the house that they should be singled out for this purpose?" God, in effect, said, "The door and the doorpost were witnesses in Egypt when I passed over the lintel and the doorposts, freeing Israel from slavery and proclaimed, 'For unto Me the Children of Israel are servants' (Leviticus 25:55); and not servants of servants, and, so I brought them forth from bondage to freedom, yet, this man went and acquired another master for himself—let him be bored in their presence."

In other words the door referred to here is the door of one's home. Each time we look at the doorpost, at the *mezuzah*, we should think of freedom and God's saving deliverance.

Dr. Nahum Sarna suggests a different locale for this door. Following the practice of the ancient Near East, and based on a similarity to the laws of Eshnunna, he interprets the doorpost to be that of the sanctuary. The act also had deep religious significance: the loss of freedom was not a private matter; it was a religious statement.

The third interpretation is taken from the medieval Biblical commentator, Abraham ibn Ezra: "It was customary for the judges to sit in the gate of the city which had a door and doorposts. Thus, he was brought before them for the procedure." Ibn Ezra sees this taking place in public, before the court and its presiding judges. It was not a private affair between master and slave alone, nor should it be conceived as taking place in religious surroundings; instead, it occurred in the seat of justice of the public domain, the gates of the city.

Home, sanctuary, and the public communal space: these three places are not selected by random choice. It is clear that the affairs of one affect the affairs of the others. *Parashat Mishpatim*, which outlines the laws for Israelite society, is comprised of decrees in all three arenas. It is impossible to have a just society without proper respect for the home and the family. If there is no respect for religious attitudes, then society itself cannot function, for there will be no adherence to laws of communal justice and public welfare. And if there is no stability in the home, then communal institutions become almost meaningless and devoid of purpose. As Ecclesiastes 4:12 states: "A threefold cord is not readily broken!"

This is one of the challenges of modern American life. How do we forge alliances between the home, the house of worship, and the community? Each stands to benefit from the values and principles of the other. It seems to me that this alliance can only be sustained in a land of freedom and that freedom is enhanced by this threefold cord. No totalitarian regime can adequately respond to that challenge; only a free society can learn to enhance the position of each.

Nowhere is this principle more important than in the teaching of values. What values are we teaching our children? Alliances must be established to reinforce traditional values that ennoble the lives of men and women. It is our task to teach that each person is created in the image of God and is deserving of respect. The home, the sanctuary, and the community are inextricably bound together and must enhance human life through proper respect for human beings who are to be treated with dignity.

In his Biblical commentary, Rabbi Samson Raphael Hirsch suggests that the door was chosen because the swinging door implies not only entrance and exit for the home dwellers, but a sense of belonging to the home. The same is true of the synagogue sanctuary and the community. Each is a significant space in the establishment of a system of proper values and standards. In the case of the Hebrew slave, we learn that freedom is gained and protected by the preservation and enhancement of home, synagogue, and community. So it is with other Torah values as well. May we strengthen the institutions as they also strengthen us and enhance our lives.

MISHPATIM
Derekh Eretz

During his stint in Moscow, United States Ambassador Averell Harriman was shadowed everywhere by the Soviet secret police. One weekend he was invited to visit a British diplomat at his country retreat. The house was accessible only by means of a four-wheel drive vehicle. A Soviet policeman attempted to follow him in his sedan, but it soon became bogged down in the snow. The policeman got out of the car and set off on foot to follow Harriman. The jeep slowed down to allow the policeman to keep up, and the Ambassador, concerned that the man would freeze to death before they reached their destination, offered him a ride. He promised he would tell no one of the incident, and so the two of them, the Ambassador and the policeman, rode together for the rest of the journey.

Harriman understood that common courtesy—concern for one's fellow human being—dictates a certain type of behavior. Every human being, no matter of what station, creed, religion, or color should expect to be treated with a sense of dignity worthy of being created in the image of God.

"These are the rules that you shall set before them" (Exodus 21:1). With these words, *parashat Mishpatim* outlines the laws and statutes that comprise a just and ethical society, as well as a community based on reverence for God and deep and abiding concern for humanity.

The Ḥasidic rabbi, Rabbi Simcha Bunim of Peshischa suggests that we look at the last word of this phrase, *lifneihem*, "before them." To whom does "them" refer? The simple answer, of course, is that it refers to the Israelites. However, Rabbi Bunim explains that the Torah teaches us that these laws which establish order between man and his fellow come before everything else, even before the commandments between man and God, for "proper conduct, *derekh eretz*, comes before the Torah" (*Leviticus Rabbah* 9:3).

What an amazing statement! Before the laws of ritual, of sacrifice, of tithes, of Shabbat and the festivals, of *kashrut*, come deeds of *derekh eretz*. For Rabbi Bunim, the ritual laws were secondary to *derekh eretz*. And what is *derekh eretz*? We define it as good behavior, courtesy, politeness, etiquette, and dignified conduct.

A *midrash* in *Leviticus Rabbah* 9:3 tells the story of Rav Yannai who invited a man to his home and offered him hospitality based on his impression that this man was a *talmid ḥakham*, a scholar. But he found the man to be ignorant of Jewish law and custom, whereupon Rav Yannai asked, "How have you merited to eat at my table?" The man responded, "Never in my life have I, after hearing evil talk, repeated it to the person spoken of, nor have I ever seen two persons quarrelling without making peace between them." Rav Yannai realized his error and apologized for his conduct, for he remembered the teaching of Rabbi Yishmael bar Rav Naḥman that "*derekh eretz* preceded the Torah."

Derekh eretz is an important component of Jewish life. A minor tractate of the Talmud, *Derekh Eretz Zuta*, is a collection of ethical teachings concerning proper rules of conduct. It urges gentleness, patience, respect for age, readiness to forgive, and the moral and social duties of a rabbinic scholar.

There is a proper way to treat another human being; there is a code of conduct that is expected of all of us. Unfortunately, we don't always heed the lesson. American society promotes competition, and in any competition, there is a winner and a loser. Sometimes, the ends justify the means. In order to achieve the goal of victory in business, athletics, or any human endeavor, we promote personal success at the expense of others. People become stepping-stones over which others must tread in order to reach their goals.

The principle of *derekh eretz* dictates that this behavior is inappropriate. All human beings are deserving of respect. In meetings, for example, serious discussion of issues is important. Even heated controversy can be tolerated. But ad hominem attacks on any individual cross the line of proper decency and *derekh eretz*.

The manner in which we treat our fellow human being says much about us. If we are insensitive to others, what should we expect in return? If we are inconsiderate of another's feelings, what does it show of our character? If we treat people as stepping-stones, as objects on our road to success, what can be said about our priorities and our values?

A little kindness goes a long way. The former president of the State of Israel, Yitzhak ben Zvi, found a sentry outside his dwelling on a cold night. "Won't you come in for a cup of tea?" he asked. "I cannot leave my post," said the sentry, "orders are orders." Ben Zvi then said to him, "you go in and have some tea, and I will stand outside with your gun and take your post."

Rabbi Menahem Mendl of Kotzk stated that, in the same way that you can learn from the introduction to a book about its contents, so it is with the *derekh eretz* of a person. From a person's conduct you learn about his attributes and characteristics, about his Torah and his faith—in fact, about his very essence as a human being.

Pirkei Avot 3:21 teaches us that there cannot be Torah without *derekh eretz*: proper conduct, courtesy, and good behavior. May we be people of Torah, and may we follow the prescription of Rabbi Simcha Bunim of Peshischa and place *derekh eretz* at the top of our priorities.

TERUMAH
It Depends on Us

Parashat Terumah offers a description of the realm of human creativity. God tells Moses to speak to the Children of Israel and to take from them donations so that he, his artisans, and his architects can fashion a Tabernacle, a portable sanctuary. God then describes for Moses how the Tabernacle is to be built, what vessels are to be placed inside the structure, and where they are to be situated.

What amazes me is that, after the instructions were delivered, the Children of Israel knew exactly what to do. Where did they get the knowledge to fashion this magnificent Tabernacle that was to represent for them the Glory of God? After all, this was a slave population. The story indicates that human creativity and Divine instruction can join together to form new vistas of human endeavor.

In *Pirkei Avot* 5:8 we are taught: "Ten things were created on the eve of the Sabbath (of Creation), at twilight." These ten things include, among others, the mouth of the earth (Numbers 16), the mouth of the well (Numbers 21:16), the manna (Exodus 16:4), the rod of Moses (Exodus 4:17), and the Tablets (Exodus 31:18). All of these things are mentioned in Biblical stories. Commentators suggest that they are associated with some special Divine activity different from the ordinary works of nature. Therefore, they were not regarded as being included in the classifications of things created in the six days as recorded in the Torah.

On the other hand, these things could not have been created after the sixth day, for the work of creation was finished. Therefore, according to this source, they must have been created at the last moment, just before the onset of the seventh day. What is even more interesting, though, is the final statement under the category of "And some say." According to this view, some say that one of the ten things created on the eve of the Sabbath was "the tongs made with tongs."

These tongs are not scriptural at all; they are a symbol of unexplained beginnings. If tongs are needed to make other tongs, how were the first tongs made? By including them in this list, the lesson is taught that all such unexplained beginnings were brought about by Divine action.

All of our modern inventions were not created during the six days of creation. They emanated from the mind of man who was created by God on the sixth day and who, with his intelligence, knowledge, and insight, is able to add to God's creation.

There is nothing more wonderful and nothing more evil than the human mind. We have the capacity to create new worlds and destroy others. After the first atomic explosion, one of the witnesses said, "This is the kind of flash the last man will see the last fraction of a second before the world ends." William L. Laurence, the *New York Times* science reporter who witnessed the explosion, said, "This is the kind of a flash when the Lord said 'Let there be Light.'" The atomic explosion brought forth both points of view. It was a new creation. For some, it was as if God was involved in the re-creation of light. Others recognized that with this new force, the entire world could be destroyed. Now that it was created, it was up to man alone to use it properly.

And so it is with every human invention. Too often we believe that all our problems can be solved instantly by the invention of new technological advances. At first glance, these new inventions look terrific. We tend to forget that what we do with our technologices is of the utmost importance. The Children of Israel were blessed with the creative ability to fashion things in gold, silver, and brass. They used that talent to create both a Tabernacle and a golden calf.

I believe that each of us is blessed with God-given talent. For some of us that talent is in our hands. For some of us that creativity is found in our voices. For some of us it is found in our athletic ability. There are some among us who are musically inclined and others who have great aptitude for fixing things around the house. There are some of us who have the gift of photographic memories, the ability to do intricate mathematical computations, and there are others who do not even know what to do with a computer. And there are some of us whose expertise is found in the heart: caring individuals who, through the force of their personalities, are able to make a difference in this world by reaching out to show compassion, love, generosity, and kindness. No matter what our gift, I believe we are all gifted.

It is our task to take our God-given talent and develop it over the course of our lifetimes. Like the tongs that must be made with tongs, there are new inventions, beginnings, creative resources that are all brought about by Divine inspiration and human endeavor. The first person that held the tongs in his hands could have stopped there and not have created new ones, but he or she continued to work, and we were privileged to gain a new human invention.

We must learn to use our creative abilities in appropriate manners so that others can benefit from our talents. Once we share them, we must learn to share them for good. Like the blast of the first atomic explosion, when a new invention is introduced into the world, when new human creativity rises above the surface, it is our task to allow it to benefit humanity and not destroy it.

TERUMAH
Bread on the Table

Parashat Terumah contains a very detailed explanation of the construction of the Tabernacle and the vessels that are placed therein. It is very difficult for us in the twenty-first century to picture exactly what all of the vessels looked like based on that description, and it is even more difficult for us to understand their uses. Yet, our synagogue *bima* contains many items that remind us of those vessels.

One of the more interesting items that was to be constructed was the table. Today we consider the table, the *shulḥan*, the place on which the Torah is read. In the Tabernacle, the table was constructed in a most deliberate fashion. It was made of acacia wood, overlaid with pure gold, with a gold crown all around it. It was supported by four wooden legs to which golden rings were attached. Poles were inserted into those rings when the table was to be transported. The function of the table was totally different from today's usage. It was to accommodate a very special display. The Torah states: "And on the table you shall set the bread of display, to be before Me always" (Exodus 25:30).

This bread, also known as shewbread, had a special purpose. In the pagan world, the gods needed food that had to be sacrificed to them at regular intervals. The Jewish God needed none of that. One of the medieval commentators, Don Isaac Abarbanel, suggests that, while the shewbread may be a remnant of an old practice, its use was very different. According to a later section of the Torah, in the Book of Leviticus, we are told that there were twelve loaves in all, perhaps to symbolize the Twelve Tribes of Israel. The loaves were set out on the table in two equal rows and remained there undisturbed for an entire week until the Sabbath when they were replaced by freshly-baked loaves. According to Leviticus 24:5–9, the old loaves were eaten by the *kohanim* in the sacred precincts.

No commentator is sure why the bread was called *leḥem panim*. The Biblical commentator Rashi suggests that it was called "bread of faces" because it had faces or surfaces looking in both directions toward both sides of the sanctuary. The bread was placed lengthwise across the breadth of the table with the sides standing up exactly in a line with the table edge. Another commentator, Abraham ibn Ezra, suggests that it was called *leḥem panim* because it was before God always, perpetually set out before the Lord and, thus, became known as "The Bread of the Presence." A third Biblical commentator, the Rashbam, suggests that it was a high caliber of bread worthy of dignitaries.

Though we are still unsure about its origins and uses, the bread may present us with a very interesting lesson if we delve a little bit behind its historical meaning and look instead for a metaphorical explanation. The Talmud (*Shabbat* 119a) relates that Rabbi Ḥiyya bar Abba was once staying with a wealthy man in Latakia. The servants brought before him a gold table that was so large that it took sixteen men to carry it. The table was decorated with silver chains and was filled with cups, trays, plates, pitchers, and jugs of gold containing the finest and most precious fruits and sweet meats in the world.

When the table was put down, everyone present would say, "The earth is the Lord's and all that it holds" (Psalms 24:1). When the table was removed, they said, "The heavens belong to the Lord, but the earth He gave over to man" (Psalms 115:16).

How is it possible that both verses are correct? Rabbi Abraham Isaac Kook, basing his argument on the Talmud (*Berakhot* 35a), suggests it was the responsibility of humanity to make the earth belong to God. In other words, one should work to create a heavenly kingdom here on earth whereby God's laws are observed and every human being is entitled to live in dignity.

The table in the Tabernacle on which the shewbread was placed suggested to a number of Ḥasidic rabbis an important responsibility of the Israelites. Reb Moshe Leib of Sassov suggests that the shewbread was perpetually set out on the table in the Tabernacle to remind the Israelites of their need to take care of the poor. It is suggested that the table in the Tabernacle represents the table that is found not only in the large sanctuary but in every small sanctuary as well. The small sanctuary is everyone's home. It is the responsibility of everyone to ensure that on the table of each person's small sanctuary bread is served, representing sustenance for all.

The *leḥem panim* reminds us of our ongoing responsibility to take care of our fellow human beings around the world. We recognize that, indeed, the heavens belong to God and the earth was given to us, but it is also our task to try to make this world a little more heavenly for all human beings, ensuring that they are supplied with their daily needs.

The Gerer Rebbe suggests that the shewbread that was placed in the Tabernacle allowed each person to see the reflection of his own face in it and examine his spiritual nature. The bread taught an individual to recognize God's gifts, and this would, in turn, motivate him to go out and provide for others.

The shewbread and the table on which it stood no longer exist. This remains a complex and difficult concept for us in the twenty-first century to understand. And yet, when we look at its symbolic meaning, it reminds us of our ongoing responsibilities to keep God's presence before us at all times, to ensure that everyone is treated with dignity and respect. May we keep the picture of the shewbread before us at all times and recognize our responsibilities to create God's kingdom here on earth as we uphold the dignity of every human being.

TETSAVVEH
Who Is a Leader?

What is effective religious leadership? In other words, who is a good religious leader? Two stories give us a clue.

During World War II, people remarked that, although Winston Churchill was a magnificent war leader, he failed to provide the country with the strong spiritual guidance some people felt was needed. Churchill responded to the accusations and said, "I would have you know that in the past year I have appointed no less than six bishops. If that is not spiritual inspiration, what is?"

The second story concerns a Hasidic master, Rabbi Judah Zvi of Stretin, who was asked how he could possibly remember and enumerate in his prayers all the names and specific petitions of the hundreds of people who flocked to him with their requests for his intercession on their behalf in his prayers. "I do not have to list them all, one by one," the great rebbe replied. "When a person comes to me and tells me of his troubles, I feel so much for him until his troubles carve a scar in my heart. When my time comes to stand before God in prayer, all I have to do is tear my heart open and cry out to our Father in Heaven, 'Look.' When God looks into my heart, He can read the scars engraved upon it and witness every detail of the woes of all the suffering people who shared their troubles with me."

What is the difference between the Churchillian view and that of Rabbi Judah Zvi? It is not that one is clergy—in this case, a rabbi—and the other is a lay person, in this case, a prime minister. Each viewed his role differently and saw religious leadership framed according to different models.

In *parashat Tetsavveh*, there is a detailed description of the priestly vestments, the clothing worn by Aaron and the *kohanim*. The commentators suggested that each of the garments conveyed a special meaning. One of the pieces of clothing was the *ephod*. This garment was a short, close-fitting coat worn by the *kohen*, and it bore two stones on which were written the names of the Tribes of Israel. The names were inscribed so that "Aaron shall carry the names of the sons of Israel on the breastpiece of decision over his heart" (Exodus 28:29).

Religious leadership bears with it responsibility. Aaron, symbolically, carried the names of the Tribes of Israel upon his shoulders and over his heart to stress the fact that he personally bore responsibility for their welfare. He could not run away and hide; leadership implied the burden was his.

There is another example of religious leadership described for us in *parashat Naso*. The Torah enumerates the duties of the families of the *levi'im* (Levites), the helpers of the *kohanim*. Each family had the responsibility of carrying sections of the portable Tabernacle from place to place. Some families had wagons on which to carry their load. "But to the Kohathites he did not give any; since theirs was the service of the [most] sacred objects, their porterage was by shoulder" (Numbers 7:9). It was unseemly that the holiest vessels should be placed on wagons instead of being personally carried by the sons of Kehat. The interpretation is that, if one is to be involved in holy work, one must shoulder responsibility, giving of one's own body, and sacrificing of oneself.

Lest we assume this only applies to the *kohanim* or the *levi'im* in the Tabernacle, let us recall that Israel is to be a "kingdom of priests and a holy nation" (Exodus 19:6). Rabbinic understanding of this phrase suggests that we all assumed the obligation of religious leadership of the *kohanim*. Each of us bears some measure of responsibility to God as a member of our people and our faith.

So, what is the difference between Churchill and Rabbi Judah Zvi in this case? One understood that the burdens of leadership meant personal accountability, and the other felt that it was enough to pass on the responsibility to others.

How do we define religious leadership? Religious leadership implies being out front on the religious issues of the day and offering solutions to societal ills. It implies involvement in the work of social action, *tikkun olam*. It implies taking courageous stands on issues of human rights in our society.

Being a member of a community means much more than just paying dues; one is challenged to be involved, interact with others, and strive for the heights that animate the spirit and move the soul. A religious community or, for that matter, any community is only as strong as its professional and lay leadership and the willingness of all to shoulder the burdens of responsibility to lead by example and deed. A community is only as healthy as the weakest link in its chain. A vibrant congregation is only as strong as the involvement of its least active member. It is the role of leadership—professional and lay—to invest all with a sense of purpose, challenge, and commitment. This is known as leading by example.

As a community, we all must be religious leaders who embody both the privileges and obligations of communal responsibility. We must be motivators who reach out to others in our community and invite them inside the circle of the committed and involved.

Aaron wore the *ephod* with its two stones over his shoulders and upon his heart; the children of Kehat carried the holy vessels on their shoulders to symbolize the realities of religious leadership. It is our task to fulfill the same functions in our role as links in that ancient chain. May the leaders of today be the models for tomorrow, and may the children of today become the leaders of the future.

TETSAVVEH
Using Knowledge for Good

In 1988, scientists at the Environmental Protection Agency (EPA), preparing a draft study on the toxic gas phosgene, discovered that data included in the report had come from Nazi experiments on concentration camp victims. The scientists wrote a letter to Lee Thomas, administrator of the EPA, asking whether it was ethical to use material gathered in this manner. Thomas decided to bar the inclusion of the information.

At about the same time that the EPA was struggling with this issue, Robert Pozos, a physiologist and renowned expert on hypothermia, then working at the University of Minnesota Medical School in Duluth, decided to use data gathered in what were known as "terminal experiments" conducted by Dr. Sigmund Rascher at the Dachau concentration camp. Believing the data had relevance to his work, Pozos asked the department of bioethics at the University of Minnesota in Minneapolis if there were any ethical guidelines concerning his use of this material. Members of the department had no readily available answers for him.

In May 1989, nearly 200 scientists, physicians, bioethicists, and members of the clergy attended "The Meaning of the Holocaust for Bioethics" conference in Minneapolis. They considered the ethics of using the Nazis' data for scientific purposes and could not come to a satisfactory conclusion. However, it is clear from the proceedings of the conference that most participants were not in favor of utilizing the data.

In the Fall 1991 issue of *Tradition* magazine, Rabbi J. David Bleich of Yeshiva University took up the same question as it relates to Jewish law. While Bleich clearly was uncomfortable with the use of the data from experiments that were very often administered under the most brutal conditions by Nazi promoters of pain and death, he came to an interesting conclusion. He wrote, "It may well be true that, in terms of human sensibilities, the atrocities of the Nazis should be so abhorrent that, left to our own inclinations, we should not consider using such data for even the most exemplary purposes. Nevertheless, Halakhah teaches that, difficult though it may be, when confronted with a matter of *pikuaḥ nefesh* [the saving of a human life], those inclinations must be transcended because 'my Father in Heaven has so decreed.'"

While *parashat Tetsavveh* contains elaborate descriptions of the clothing worn by the *kohanim* and especially the *kohen gadol* during their service in the Tabernacle in the desert, the end of the reading contains a description of the incense altar upon which incense was burned every morning and evening.

Yoma 38a states that during the Second Temple period: "The house of Abtinas were expert in preparing the incense but would not teach their art to others. The Sages sent for specialists from Alexandria of Egypt who knew how to compound incense as well as they but did not know how to make the smoke ascend as well as they." The Sages were then forced to invite the house of Abtinas to return to their position but not before they had to double their wages. "The Sages said to them, 'What reason did you have for not teaching your art?' They said, 'We knew in our father's house that this House is going to be destroyed. Perhaps an unworthy man will learn this art and will serve an idol therewith.'" For this, according to the teachers of the Mishnah, "the house of Abtinas was mentioned to their shame."

Education, creativity, learning, and scholarship are neither good nor evil in and of themselves. It depends what we do with the data, the knowledge, and the educational resources that are at our command. The fruits of our scholarship or research can be used to benefit humanity or perhaps destroy it.

Knowledge itself is neither good nor evil. It depends upon what we do with it. While we extol the creation of the beginnings of atomic energy, after the first atomic explosion, J. Robert Oppenheimer is reported to have said, "I have become Death, Destroyer of worlds." Knowledge used for positive purposes advances the world and man's role in it. When used for destructive purposes, it diminishes the world and God's Presence in it.

And when that knowledge is gained appropriately, it should be taught to others and shared with peers and disciples. In *Pirkei Avot* 4:6, Rabbi Yishmael, the son of Rabbi Yohanan ben Beroka says, "A person who studies so that he may teach is given the opportunity both to study and to teach." There is no greater *nachas*, no greater joy, than to have a disciple, a student, a child—your own or another's—learn from your example and attempt to emulate your good qualities.

Each of us bears great responsibility toward the next generation. We are its teachers, and we are those who will mold its future. It is incumbent upon us to recognize that the words we utter and the deeds we perform serve as lasting models for those who are our students. Our society must be concerned with education as its highest priority in order to properly train those who will follow us.

We have enough evidence of how knowledge has been used to harm, injure, destroy, and kill. The data from the Holocaust medical experiments is perhaps the most abhorrent, but we could also examine the origins of other weapons of war and mass destruction. Knowledge must be taught along with proper values and respect for humanity. And once gained, it should be shared properly for the benefit of humanity.

KI TISSA
Partners with God

When Moses was descending from the top of Mount Sinai, he saw the Israelite people cavorting around the golden calf. Enraged, he immediately reacted: "He hurled the tablets from his hands and shattered them at the foot of the mountain" (Exodus 32:19). What made Moses react in such a startling manner? Who gave him permission to smash the tablets carrying the word of God? Did he do the right thing, and what were the implications of his actions?

The Jerusalem Talmud, in a remarkable passage in *Ta'anit* 4:5, offers different explanations for Moses' actions. "Rabbi Ḥilkiah, in the name of Rabbi Aḥa, said Moses made the following interpretation: 'In the case of the Passover lamb, which is a single religious duty, no uncircumcised person shall eat of it; in the case of the entire Torah in which all religious duties are contained, these people, dancing around the golden calf, are unworthy to receive it.'" According to this opinion, Moses made the judgment on his own. His reasoning led him to react in such a manner.

Rabbi Ishmael disagrees. "The Holy One, blessed be He, told him to break them. And when Moses did so, God said to him, 'You did the right thing in breaking them.'" Rabbi Ishmael saw Moses as merely following orders from above; he needed to receive directions for his actions.

Rabbi Samuel bar Naḥman, in the name of Rabbi Jonathan, disagrees with these opinions. The tablets, he suggests, were very large, and both Moses and God were carrying them together. "When the Israelites did their deed, God wanted to grab the tablets out of the hands of Moses. But the hands of Moses were stronger and he seized them from God." This view suggests a tug of war ensued between Moses and God that caused the tablets to break apart.

Finally, Rabbi Ezra, in the name of Rabbi Judah ben Rabbi Simon, has his own point of view. "The tablets were very heavy and the writing on them enabled Moses to carry them. Upon seeing the golden calf, the writing flew off the tablets. When that happened, the tablets became very heavy in the hands of Moses and the tablets fell and were broken." Moses dropped the tablets unwittingly. He may not have meant to do so; it simply happened.

Each of these four explanations amplifies for us the dilemma of human life. How much is in our control, and how much is in the control of God? What happens when we feel out of control, and how do we handle those situations? When are we masters of our fate, and when are we not?

The first explanation, making Moses the chief decisor, corresponds to the times in our lives when we seem to be the masters of our own destiny. We feel most in control when things are going well. The Torah itself warns against this type of attitude: "And you [shall] say to yourselves, 'My own power and the might of my own hand have won this wealth for me'" (Deuteronomy 8:17). You may feel on top of the world, but, immediately, the Torah warns us, do not become too cocky; you do not control all matters in your own hands.

The second response reminds us that much is in the control of God. It instructs us that there is a God watching over us, but we cannot always comprehend His ways. It was God who told Moses to throw down the tablets. Illness, accidents, natural disasters, business problems, and difficult personal relationships are sometimes beyond our ability to control. A passage in *Megillah* 6b informs us: "In business dealings, you need God's help." In short, you need good luck and God's support in everything you do.

The third explication suggests a tug of war between man and God. There are times when we feel we are on the edge of an abyss. We attempt to maintain our equilibrium, and, yet, we feel the constant tension in our lives. We want to believe that God will protect us, but we are only human, and we have lingering doubts.

The final answer reminds us that there are times when the situation is simply too difficult for us to handle. We feel totally out of control. We have fallen into the abyss, and we see no way out. When the letters flew off the tablets, Moses must have felt as if God had abandoned him. "Out of the depths I call you, O Lord. O Lord, listen to my cry," writes the Psalmist (Psalms 130:1–2). In the world in which we live, this is the most dangerous of all the positions. Arthur Schopenhauer writes, "No rose without a thorn. But many a thorn without a rose." Too often we feel only the thorns and that sense of abandonment and isolation. We pray that we may not find ourselves in this situation.

This remarkable passage in the Talmud sets before us life as we know it. We want to find the best way to respond to our circumstances but cannot always do so. Jewish tradition teaches us that it is our task to be partners with God in all our endeavors. Life was challenging then; it is challenging today. May our faith in God and our willingness to be partners with the Divine Presence give us strength to meet our challenges, hope to conquer our fears, and trust that all will be well.

KI TISSA
Two Sets of Tablets

A story is told concerning the third president of the United States, Thomas Jefferson. On a bitter cold evening in northern Virginia, an old man was waiting for a ride across the river. Anxiously, he watched as several horsemen rounded the bend. He let the first one pass by, then another, then another. Finally, the last rider neared the spot where the old man sat. As this one drew near, the old man caught the rider's eye and said, "Sir, would you mind giving an old man a ride to the other side?"

Reining his horse, the rider replied, "Sure thing, hop aboard," and he helped the old man onto the horse. The horseman took the old man not just across the river but to his destination that was just a few miles away.

As they neared the tiny cottage, the horseman's curiosity caused him to inquire, "Sir, I noticed that you let several other riders pass by without making an effort to secure a ride. I am curious why, on such a bitter winter night, you would wait and ask the last rider. What if I had refused and left you there?"

The old man replied, "I have been around these here parts for some time and I know people pretty good. I looked into the eyes of the other riders and immediately saw there was no concern for my situation. It would have been useless to even ask them for a ride. But when I looked into your eyes, kindness and compassion were evident. I knew that your gentle spirit would welcome the opportunity to give me assistance in my time of need."

These comments touched the horseman deeply. "I am most grateful for what you have said," he told the old man. With that, Thomas Jefferson turned his horse around and made his way back to the White House.

Parashat Ki Tissa features the Golden Calf episode. As the Israelites lose patience waiting for Moses to descend the mountain, in desperation, they construct a calf and cavort around it. When Moses commences his return from the top of Mount Sinai to the encampment, he hears noise and boisterous music. When he sees his people straying from the laws that he has just received, he shatters the two tablets containing the commandments. Later in the story, Moses asks forgiveness from God for the sin of the people, and he retreats once more to Mount Sinai in order to receive another set of tablets. This time, however, the story is different. These tablets are placed inside of the ark to accompany the Israelites as they make their way to the Land of Canaan. What is the difference between these two sets of tablets?

Deuteronomy Rabbah 3:14 tells of a dialogue between God and Moses that takes place after the smashing of the tablets. God says to Moses, "You have vented your wrath on the tablets of the covenant. Do you desire that I should also vent My wrath? You will see that the world could not endure even one hour." Moses replies, "And what can I do?" God replies, "I will impose a fine on you—you have broken the tablets and you must replace them."

This may have started as a punishment upon Moses, but it ended up as a great gift to the people. With regard to the first tablets, the Torah tells us: "The tablets were God's work, and the writing was God's writing, incised upon the tablets" (Exodus 32:16). Moses seems to have had no role whatsoever. The second tablets, however, were different. In this case, "So Moses carved two tablets of stone, like the first" (Exodus 34:4). Moses now has a role, and this time, he is more careful for his own labor is involved. It may have started out as a punishment, but I believe it turned out to be a great opportunity for Moses to show his love and devotion to his God and to his people. Thus, he lovingly brought these tablets down the mountain and taught their content to his people.

Another *midrash* in *Exodus Rabbah* 46:1 states that Moses was despondent after he had destroyed the tablets, but God consoled him, telling him that the second tablets would be different: "Do not grieve about the first tablets. They only contained the Ten Commandments, but in the two tablets I am about to give you now, there will also be laws, *midrashim*, and *aggadot* [legends]."

Most scholars view this as a suggestion that the second tablets contained all possible understandings of Jewish life, law, and lore. I see it a bit differently. The first tablets contained only laws and, thus, represented strict judgment and severe justice. The second tablets contained more. In addition to the laws, they also contained *midrashim* and *aggadot*. They represented not only the law but also the aesthetics; not merely severe justice but lovingkindness, mercy, and grace.

These two *midrashim* suggest to me an appropriate and proper way to teach Judaism in our own time in order to make our heritage palpable and endearing to our fellow Jews. Moses invested himself in the second set of tablets, which made their teachings much more relevant to him and, therefore, to his people. He may have been a lawgiver, but in Jewish tradition, he is known as *Moshe Rabbeinu,* Moses our teacher. He lovingly taught the second set of tablets and all they contained to our people. They represented not only law but also the beauty of our tradition, the grandeur and the mystery of Jewish life.

In his essay, "*Halakhah* and *Aggadah*," the Hebrew poet Hayim Nahman Bialik suggests that both *halakhah* and *aggadah* are necessary in Jewish life. "*Halakhah* is the embodiment of the Attribute of Justice, iron-handed, rigorous and severe … *aggadah* is the embodiment of the Quality of Mercy, essentially lenient and indulgent, as mild as a dove … *Halakhah* represents the body, the actual deed; *aggadah* represents the soul, the content, the fervent motive." Both *halakhah* and *aggadah* are necessary to lovingly transmit our tradition from one generation to the next.

The old man in our story recognized the kindness and generosity of Thomas Jefferson and knew that he would respond with grace and kindness. The second tablets, I believe, conveyed that sense of grace and lovingkindness to the Israelites and were, therefore, assured of greater longevity than the first set. Moses had put himself into their creation and was personally invested in their endurance. It is our task to convey the beauty of our tradition to the next generation so that they lovingly accept it and make it their own.

VA-YAKHEL
The Beauty of Shabbat

"More than Israel has kept the Sabbath; the Sabbath has kept Israel." This famous dictum of Aḥad Ha'am reminds us to enhance the observance of Shabbat in our communities.

The concluding part of the Book of Exodus deals almost exclusively with the construction of the Tabernacle. We are given detailed and elaborate descriptions of the necessary materials, the actual construction, the design of the clothing to be worn by the ordinary *kohanim*, and, in particular, the vestments of the High Priest.

Dr. Nahum Sarna, in his commentary on *parashat Ki Tissa*, points out that the series of instructions for the components of the Tabernacle are made up of seven subsections. Six of them deal with creativity; the seventh features the observance of Shabbat.

Dr. Sarna states: "The Tabernacle enshrines the concept of the holiness of space; the Sabbath embodies the concept of the holiness of time. The latter takes precedence over the former, and the work of the Tabernacle must yield each week to the Sabbath rest." In our *parashah*, correspondingly, the resumption of the Tabernacle narrative commences with the observance of Shabbat.

The juxtaposition of these two commandments, Shabbat and the construction of the Tabernacle, highlights two important principles. The fact that Israel is to desist from involvement in the work of building this portable sanctuary sets the basic understanding for the concept of rest on Shabbat. One is to refrain from creating or participating in those types of work that went into the molding of this structure. There are, according to the Mishnah (*Shabbat* 7:2), thirty-nine categories of work prohibited on Shabbat. The juxtaposition also sets forth Sarna's idea borrowed from Abraham Joshua Heschel's description of Shabbat as a "Palace in Time." Sacred time, rather than sacred space, is crucial to Jewish life according to Heschel. Roland de Vaux, a Franciscan monk and Biblical scholar, explained that Shabbat is a Biblical attempt to encourage the Israelites to take a tithe on time and to share their gratitude for the gift given to them by God—the gift of time.

Shabbat is the cornerstone of the Jewish week, the foundation of Jewish living. In 1950, the Conservative movement enacted a program for the revitalization of Shabbat observance. The responsum of the Rabbinical Assembly's Committee on Jewish Law and Standards expressed dismay and distress at the widespread disintegration of the observance of Shabbat among our people. The report envisaged an entire program for the furtherance of Shabbat observance among Conservative Jews. Within that context, the committee accepted two major halakhic decisions. It stated: "In this spirit it is our consensus that riding [driving] to the synagogue on the Sabbath and the use of electric lights in the course of this journey or for other purposes are comprised in the general category of *oneg* Shabbat, the delight of the Sabbath." This learned responsum permitted riding on Shabbat, but only to the synagogue. It did not, nor did the Conservative movement, ever countenance riding for other purposes. Unfortunately, the permission concerning riding became the focus of the program, and the revitalization program of Shabbat observance was not implemented in the weekly life of most Conservative Jews.

Over sixty years have passed, and we are still in need of that revitalization program. Without Shabbat in the home and without synagogue attendance over the course of the day, this cornerstone of the Jewish week is bereft of meaning and significance. Shabbat merely becomes Saturday, a day like all the rest.

Rabbi Pinchas Peli writes, "The real purpose of life is not to conquer nature, but to conquer the self; not to fashion a city out of a forest, but to fashion a soul out of a human being; not to build bridges, but to build human kindness; … not to manufacture an ingenious technical civilization, but to be holy in the midst of unholiness … It is the Sabbath that comes to remind us of all this."

For the Jewish people, Shabbat does not solely encompass laws of what we can do and what we cannot do on the seventh day. It also embodies the aesthetics of the Shabbat table, the sanctity of the lighting of the candles, the *oneg* Shabbat, the joy of being with family in the home and community in the synagogue, and the joy of celebrating a day of rest, tranquility, and peace.

In his book, *The Gift of Rest*: *Rediscovering the Beauty of the Sabbath,* former Connecticut Senator Joseph Lieberman writes, "I love the Sabbath and believe it is a gift from God … When people ask me: 'How can you stop all your work as a senator to observe the Sabbath each week?' I answer: 'How can I do all my work as a senator if I did *not* stop to observe the Sabbath each week?'"

He takes us on a journey from the preparations of *erev* Shabbat through the rituals of *havdalah*. "Observing the Sabbath is a commandment I have embraced," he writes, "the fourth commandment, to be exact, which Moses received from God on Mount Sinai. Most of the time, it feels less like a commandment and more like a gift from God. It is a gift I received from my parents who, in turn, received it from their parents, who received it from generations of Jews before them in a line of transmission that goes back to Moses. For me, Sabbath observance is a gift because it is one of the deepest, purest pleasures in my life. It is a day of peace, rest, and sensual pleasure."

Genesis Rabbah 11:18 relates how Shabbat complained to God because every day of the week had a partner: Sunday goes with Monday, Tuesday with Wednesday, Thursday with Friday. "All have a partner," said Shabbat, "while I have no partner!" The Holy One, Blessed be He, replied, "The community of Israel is your partner."

We, the community of Israel, still have the privilege of experiencing and observing a day that expresses the Jewish themes of creation, revelation, and redemption. Even the work of the Tabernacle was to be stopped in honor of this holy day. Surely, we can invite Shabbat into our weekly routines. May our homes, our synagogues, and our communities be filled with the light, the joy, and the real essence of *oneg* Shabbat—delight in the observance of the Day of Rest.

PEKUDEI
The Ideal and the Real

We have reached the conclusion of the Book of Exodus. The *Mishkan*, the Tabernacle, is now standing, and it is time to lovingly place the holy vessels within the walls of the portable sanctuary: "He took the Pact and placed it in the ark" (Exodus 40:20). Rashi uses one simple word—*luḥot*—to explain that Moses placed the "tablets of the Law" into the ark.

This seems rather simple. At the center of the portable sanctuary stood the ark, and in the ark were placed the two tablets that Moses had brought down from Mount Sinai. However, a *midrash* in *Numbers Rabbah* 4:20 did not find this fact so self-evident: "The tablets and the broken fragments of the tablets were deposited in the ark." The pieces of tablets were those from the first set of stone commandments that Moses had shattered, the two tablets from his second ascent to the mountain.

This midrashic commentary is probably based on an Aramaic translation of the Biblical text. The *Targum Yerushalmi*, which dates no later than the seventh or eighth century and has been erroneously attributed to Jonathan ben Uzziel, gives the following free translation of these verses: "And Moses put these two tablets of stone that were given to him on Mount Ḥoreb, these tablets of the testimony and the pieces of the broken tablets in the ark."

Why, according to the *Targum* and the Midrash, did Moses keep the pieces of the broken stones and place them along with the complete set of commandments into the central spot of the Israelite sanctuary? One answer suggests that these were pieces of stone upon which were written holy words and, just as we do not throw away holy books after they are tattered and torn, so we might expect the same treatment to be given to the set of stone tablets containing God's commandments. Another *midrash* states,

"The broken tablets of the Law are still holy" (*Midrash Tanḥuma*, 7 *Vayakhel*).

I would also like to suggest a more human-centered approach to the question. Throughout our lives, we are motivated by a set of goals that are framed by our dreams. Daniel Levinson, in his book *The Seasons of a Man's Life,* suggests that each of us evolves through life's transitions. He explains how, in early adulthood, a person "has to form a Dream, create an initial structure in which the Dream can be lived out, and attain goals through which it is in some measure fulfilled. In middle adulthood his task is to modify or give up the Dream." Levinson's outline takes into consideration the entire span of a person's life. At each life stage, dreams need to be modified as one's circumstances change.

Each of us is the product of successful dreams and fractured wishes. We want to be successful in all of life's endeavors, but we know that no one is granted that desire. As a *midrash* in *Ecclesiastes Rabbah* 1:13 states, "No man dies with even half his wishes fulfilled." Our lives contain both the complete set of stone tablets and the shattered pieces of broken commandments.

The real test of human character occurs when we are forced to deal with our failures, recognize our shortcomings, and proceed with life. When tragedies occur, when we lose someone dear to us, when our health fails, when a loving relationship is torn asunder, or when a business setback occurs, all of our best-laid plans are shattered. It then takes a resolute will and a creative mind to move beyond that moment and build life once more. It is at those moments that one's true character emerges. Even if we are successful at overcoming difficulty, we are never completely the same. The shattered fragments remain alongside our new set of goals and desires.

For thirty years, Norman Cousins held the position of editor of the *Saturday Review,* expanding its readership from 15,000 to 650,000. Then, in 1964, he was struck with a serious illness. He had considerable difficulty moving his limbs, nodules appeared all over his body, and his jaws were almost locked. His world came crashing down around him when his doctor told him that he had one chance in five hundred for a full recovery.

It would have been easy to give up, but Cousins set himself the goal of recovering gradually from the illness. Together with his doctor, he devised a program that brought laughter into his life. He used the unlimited capacity of the human mind to raise himself back to health. He was eventually able to return to work and was appointed senior lecturer at the School of Medicine at UCLA.

Then, in December 1980, Cousins suffered a massive heart attack that almost killed him. Again, he was forced to fight for his life. Once more, in a slow, painful return to health, he was forced to reevaluate his dreams and goals. He would never be the same; the shattered pieces of his life, represented by the two life-threatening illnesses, would always be with him. But he possessed great personal courage and perseverance to surmount these episodes and get on with life.

Our lives are represented by the contents of that ark in the Tabernacle. Nobody lives a life without trials, tribulations, and travails. Even when we think we've got it made, we can be dealt a bad hand. The challenge is to surmount that moment, put our lives back together, reformulate our dreams, and get on with living.

The ark contained the shattered fragments of the first set of tablets and the second tablets that were whole. These two sets represent the story of our lives: the ideal and the real. Some dreams are fulfilled; others remain mere wishes.

May we have the courage to meet the difficult moments of our lives with courage, strength, creativity, and faith and be blessed, we pray, with wholeness.

LEVITICUS
ויקרא
VA-YIKRA

VA-YIKRA
Good Manners

Va-yikra, the name of third book of the Bible, has no relationship whatsoever to its content but is actually the first word of the book. The Hebrew word *Va-yikra* simply means "he called" and gives no hint of the book's subject. There must, therefore, be some sort of lesson attached to that word which permeates the entire book and maybe even all of Jewish life.

The Torah reading begins with the phrase, "The Lord called to Moses and spoke to him from the Tent of Meeting, saying ..." (Leviticus 1:1). A more literal way of translating this verse would suggest, "He called to Moses. God spoke to him from the Tent of Meeting saying ..." The phrases seem to be redundant. Why would God first call to Moses and then speak to him? The Talmud was especially sensitive to these nuances of language. In *Yoma* 4b, the Rabbis ask, "why does Scripture mention the call before the speech? The Torah teaches us *derekh eretz* [proper conduct]: a man should not address his neighbor without having first called him." The commentators on the Talmud seem to feel that God showed special sensitivity to Moses by first calling to him so that Moses would be ready to listen. Moses could train his ear to God's command, be prepared to listen to God's voice, and intently concentrate on the meaning of the message.

Rabbi Eliyahu Mordechai Ha-Cohen Mazah, in his book *Sefer Kol Mevaser*, suggests that the phrasing of the verse intimates more about Moses than it does about God. "The Torah says, 'He called to Moses.' This teaches that even though Moses had authority to enter, he did not enter until God called him." Though Moses could easily have walked into the Tent of Meeting, he refused to barge into God's habitation. He wanted a personal invitation before entering God's space. These two comments suggest a charming picture of both God and Moses observing appropriate amenities. The interaction between God and Moses sets a prototype for proper behavior; appropriate protocol and respect for personal dignity should form the basis of all our encounters.

In our day and age, we have lost the art of civil discourse. We don't talk to one another; we talk at one another. If you watch many of the talk shows on TV, you will notice that shouting has become an acceptable human activity. Calm discourse and civil language are rare. People seem to think that they can only get their way if they shout, scream, and protest. Unfortunately, they are sometimes correct. If you go to a sporting event and listen to the language in the stands, you will note that it is not the children who berate the players or call the referees and umpires names; it is the adults who engage in immature behavior. Is it any wonder that children then go back to their playgrounds and their basketball courts, their baseball diamonds and hockey rinks, and use the same language they've learned from adults to berate the players and officials?

Lest we think that it is only American society that has moved in this direction, all of you who have been in Israel know that the same problem is paramount in Israel. Have you ever watched a Knesset debate? It is not even organized chaos. Name-calling, shouting matches, and rude interruptions are tolerated, and time after time, individual members have to be thrown out of the hall. Shouting seems to be a natural Israeli activity. Rarely do you hear civil discourse in the shops, on the street, or anywhere else. Is it any wonder? What do Israelis hear from their politicians and leaders? If those are the models, I am not surprised at the results.

I attend many Jewish organizational meetings. I have observed behaviors at these meetings that would be totally unacceptable in my house and in yours. In his book, *Church Meetings That Matter*, Philip Anderson writes, "Three steps are necessary to complete an act of communication: expression, listening, and response. Unless all three steps are completed we cannot be certain that communication has taken place." Perhaps, even before a meeting begins, the members should draw up a contract outlining appropriate speech and behavior.

Derekh Eretz Zuta, a minor tractate, begins with the following statement: "The characteristics of a scholar are that he is meek, humble, alert, filled [with a desire for learning], modest, beloved by all, humble to the members of his household and sin-fearing. He judges a man [fairly] according to his deeds."

Every Jew can be a Torah sage. Unlike the priesthood, it is not reserved for a special class or family. Each of us is asked to model behavior of a certain fashion. We must learn to watch our words, consider our behavior, and recognize that whatever we do is being watched both by God and by other human beings. Appropriate etiquette is not merely reserved for fancy dinner parties. There is also an ethical dimension to good manners. We should behave in respectful and polite ways for the sake of our communities and society at large.

When we wish to teach our children the importance of being a mensch, what do we have in mind? What do we want our students to come away with but an understanding of how to act in an appropriate fashion in our society? What is it then that we expect from our leaders, scholars, athletes, actors, actresses, and politicians but that they are guided by the fact that there is always somebody watching what they do? The manner in which they wish to be respected is the manner in which they should respect and behave toward others. *Derekh Eretz Zuta* 5:1 states: "A person should always make a point of knowing with whom he is sitting or standing, with whom he is sitting at table, with whom he is conversing and who is a co-signatory to a deed."

I find it fascinating that the Book of Leviticus, the most technical of all of the Biblical books, begins in a manner which allows for the teaching of a moral lesson. Both God and Moses are sensitive to the needs of the other. Both God and Moses attempt to show that *derekh eretz* is appropriate in a Divine-human encounter. Both God and Moses recognize that in approaching the other, one needs to show respect in word and in deed. This lesson should not be lost on us.

VA-YIKRA
Taking Responsibility

The thirteenth-century scholar Bahya ben Asher wrote: "Just as the body is subject to health and sickness, so is the soul ... Just as physical illness is cured by its antithesis, so is the sick, sinful soul restored to health by its antithesis. What is the antithesis of sin? Repentance and good deeds."

The third book of the Bible is perhaps the most difficult of all the books. In Rabbinic Hebrew, Leviticus is known as *Torat Kohanim,* the book or the precepts of the *kohanim* (priests), for it describes the work of the *kohanim* and the sacrificial system.

The concept of sacrifice is difficult for moderns to understand. We are so far removed from that ancient world and mode of worship. Prayer has become our way of worshiping the Almighty, and the concept of sacrificing animals, sprinkling their blood, and offering their carcasses on an altar is not only foreign to us, but, in many ways, somewhat abhorrent. For the ancient Israelites this was the manner to approach God, and the concept of *korban,* normally translated as sacrifice, should be understood as coming from the word *lekarev,* to bring closer.

The Hebrew words *nefesh ki teheta* appear several times in this *parashah* (Leviticus 4:2; 5:1, 17, 20). In the *Etz Hayim* translation, these words are taken to mean "when a person incurs guilt." However, the Hebrew word *nefesh* should be translated as "soul." A wonderful *midrash* in *Leviticus Rabbah* 4:5 states that in the world to come, God will bring the soul of a person for judgment and ask it: "Why have you not observed all of the commandments?" And the soul will respond: "The body disobeyed your commands, not I." Then, God will bring the body to Him and ask the same question: "Why have you sinned?" And the body will respond: "The soul which You put in me did the sinning." What will God do? The *midrash* states that He will bring them both together and judge them as one unit.

The *midrash* suggests a parable: A king wanted to plant an orchard with grapes, dates, and pomegranates. He said to himself, "If I place a walking, sighted person to guard this place, then what will he do? He will eat from the beautiful fruits." Therefore, the king decided to place two guards over the orchard. One was blind and the other lame so that they could guard the orchard and not be tempted to eat of its fruits.

One day the lame said to the blind, "The fruit of the orchard I see is beautiful. Come, let me stand on your shoulders and take me closer so that we shall eat them." The lame person climbed upon the sightless one, and they ate of the fruit.

A number of days passed, and the king went to visit his orchard, but he could not find the fruit. He said to the lame guard, "Who ate them?" And the lame guard responded, "Do I have legs that I could walk into the orchard to eat the fruit?" The king then said to the sightless guard, "You must have eaten them." The blind person responded, "Have I eyes to be able to navigate all the trees and take the fruit from them?"

The king decided then to judge both the blind and the lame together and said, "In the same way that the two of you together stole the fruit, so you will be judged together." Thus, God will do the same. The *midrash* states that He will bring them both together and judge them as one unit.

Most of us tend to overlook our weaknesses and our own misdeeds. It is easier to blame someone else, just as our *midrash* relates how the body and soul or the lame and the blind guards did. We? Guilty? It must have been someone else. From the very beginning of the creation of humanity, we have followed that pattern. When Adam ate the fruit of the Tree of Knowledge, did he accept responsibility? No, he blamed Eve. Did Eve accept responsibility for her actions? No, she blamed the snake. And from that time onward, we have continued to place the blame on others, refusing to accept our own responsibility and guilt.

In his book, *The Abuse Excuse,* Alan Dershowitz laments the fact that individuals, especially through the assistance of the legal profession, do not accept responsibility for their own actions. He lists as examples some of the defenses that have been used for crimes that have been committed. They include the "battered persons syndrome," the "fetal alcohol syndrome," the "premenstrual stress syndrome defense," the "Stockholm syndrome," and the "Twinkie defense."

Dershowitz states: "Evasions of responsibility breach the social contract and rend the very fabric of democracy. We must stop making excuses and start taking responsibility. What is at stake is far more than the punishment of criminals and the deterrence of crime. It is the very nature of our experiment with democracy."

The Torah understood this long ago. One must claim one's guilt and trespasses. If one recognizes one's sin done in error, unwittingly, and without malice, then one can bring a *korban*, come close to God, and through repentance and good deeds move to become a better person. Our *parashah* outlines crimes against persons which, from the Torah's point of view, are also crimes against God. These include dealing deceitfully with another in a matter of a deposit or a pledge, or through robbery, defrauding another, or finding something lost and lying about it. Should that happen, one must recognize that in hurting another human being, one has hurt God's image found in that human being.

The sacrificial system may seem antiquated and even abhorrent to us. Yet, the lessons that emanate from its regulations and laws should continue to motivate us even if we have a different mode of worship. Dershowitz quotes George Bernard Shaw who said, "Liberty means responsibility. That's why most men dread it." Dershowitz continues, "Today, many men and women seem unwilling to take responsibility for their actions. Excuses abound in every sphere of life from the most public to the most private."

The sacrificial system explicated for us in *parashat Va-yikra* tells us that should not be the case. When we inevitably make mistakes, we must admit our failings and, with repentance and good deeds, make amends for our transgressions. It is a lesson all of us must learn.

TSAV
The Path of Judaism

A midrash in *Tanhuma Va-yikra* 3 states that Moses, in his humility, felt that his mission as a leader of the people ended with the erection of the Tabernacle because Israel could now satisfy all its spiritual needs without his aid. God, however, said to Moses, "As truly as you live, I have for you a far greater task than any that you have as yet accomplished, for you shall now instruct My children about 'clean and unclean' and shall teach them how to offer up offerings to Me." God thereupon called Moses to the Tabernacle to reveal the laws to him.

Moses was disconsolate at this point. All the miracles had been accomplished, the Tabernacle had been erected, and now he had no role to play. When God told him that his role was not completed, Moses resumed his task with great vigor. From this we learn that miracles are God's work, but the key role in the life of Moses, our teacher, is to instruct the Israelites how to worship God appropriately.

The Book of Leviticus is mainly concerned with these latter issues. The laws of cleanliness and uncleanliness, the sacrifices in the Tabernacle, the regulations of diet, dress, and ritual behavior are the main emphasis of the third book of the Torah. For many of us, these laws seem rather mundane and, in fact, not inspiring. Yet, for the Israelites of old, these laws represented the key to understanding their relationship with the Holy One, for it was the act of sacrifice and the ritual behavior surrounding it that brought the Israelites closer to God.

For us in the twenty-first century, that message is lost. There is no longer a Temple, we do not offer sacrifices, and many of the ritual behaviors described in the Book of Leviticus are obsolete. But we are not the first generation to have felt that way. Already with the destruction of the Temple, the ancient sages were concerned about connecting with the Divine Presence in this world. Without the Temple and its accompanying rituals, many of the Rabbis felt bereft of God's presence. It is to the credit of Rabbi Yohanan ben Zakkai and his school at Yavneh that we are still practicing Judaism. In the wake of the Temple's destruction, they redefined Judaism by emphasizing prayer rather than sacrifice, deeds of lovingkindness rather than Temple gifts, and Rabbinic scholarship instead of priestly leadership.

Rabbi Joseph Telushkin, in *A Code of Jewish Ethics*, offers illustrations from the Torah, the wisdom of our sages, and contemporary stories concerning how ethical teachings can affect our daily behavior.

> Rabbi Shalom Schwadron, the renowned Jerusalem *maggid* (inspiring lecturer) was known for his generosity to those in need. One afternoon, just before a holiday, a poor man came to his house for assistance, and Rabbi Schwadron's daughter was chagrined to see her father taking out a new and expensive shirt he had purchased on a trip to England. He opened the shirt, showed the man how beautiful it was, and then refolded and rewrapped it. "Take it! Take it!" he said. "You should have a new shirt. Good *Yom Tov* [Happy Holiday]."
>
> When the poor man left, Rabbi Schwadron's daughter, who was present along with her husband, was upset: "If you had to give him a shirt, why the special shirt from England, the shirt you had bought for your own holiday celebration? Why?"
>
> Rabbi Schwadron went over to his bookcase, took down Maimonides' code of Jewish law, and read aloud from it: "One who wishes to offer a sacrifice [at the Temple] for his own merit should suppress his evil inclination and bring of the best quality there is of the type he is offering. This is the law with everything. If one builds a House of Prayer, it should be more beautiful than his dwelling place. When feeding the hungry, he should give of the best and sweetest foods on his table. When dressing the naked, he should offer his finest clothing" ("Laws of *Issurei Mizbeach* [Things Prohibited for the Altar]" 7:11).

Telushkin contends that we serve God best when we bring God's presence into our daily activities through our ethical behavior. He begins his introduction with these words: "This book has a simple thesis: God's central demand of human beings is to act ethically." He reminds us, as do the prophets of old, that ritual observance is important, but not enough. Living an ethical life has a bearing on a person's level of religiosity and piety. Emulating God by performing deeds of lovingkindness is one way to bear witness to our relationship with God in whose image we have been created.

How do we begin the Passover Seder experience? We begin with the words *ha laḥma*, "Let all who are hungry come in and eat and all who are needy come in and make Passover." By the time we read these words, we are already sitting down to our Passover Seder, surrounded by relatives and guests. It would be highly unusual at this particular moment to have a new guest walk through our door and find a place at our table. This passage in the *Haggadah* teaches us that our concern for those who are hungry and needy should be expressed before the Passover Seder begins. Our intensive preparations for Passover must include providing support for those who are in need of our assistance. Thus, it is incumbent upon all of us to support our community's *maot ḥittim* program, which aids those members of our community who are in need.

We may not offer sacrifices any longer at the Temple, and the Book of Leviticus may sometimes seem outdated. Yet, ancient rabbis, medieval commentators, legal codifiers, and modern scholars have interpreted these practices for us, and we now understand the lessons behind them. It is our task to bring our lives closer to God and understand that, just as our prophets taught us, ritual behavior and ethical living together form the totality of Jewish life.

TSAV
Meaningful Effort

When I was a college student and living at home, as most Torontonian students did in those days, I learned that a synagogue in my area had invited a prominent guest to lecture on Shabbat morning. I decided to walk to the synagogue to hear Rabbi Bernard Mandelbaum who was at that time the president of the Jewish Theological Seminary. Rabbi Mandelbaum was known as an outstanding preacher, and he delivered a very powerful sermon. I don't recall the entire context and message of the sermon, but I have always remembered the text he quoted from *Megillah* 6b. "Rabbi Isaac said, 'If a man says to you, I have labored and not found, do not believe him. If he says, I have not labored but have still found, do not believe him. If he says, I have labored and found, you may believe him.'" This text has remained with me to this day and has motivated me to recognize that hard work is necessary in order to succeed.

I have always been extremely jealous of those who possess a photographic memory. While I have to labor long and hard to remember what I have read or heard, I have always envied those who have that instant recall. In both my schoolwork and my rabbinic scholarship, I have had to expend great effort in order to gain the knowledge that is necessary for religious leadership and personal observance. This text reminds me that nothing comes easily; it requires effort and enormous sacrifice. Hopefully, by the end of the journey, the work can be deemed appropriate and the effort worthwhile.

This lesson is especially important for our society, which is informed by a culture of "instants." We have instant communication, we look for instant satisfaction, and we possess instant knowledge at our fingertips. Google has revolutionized the research abilities for all of us. E-mail and cell phones have made us available at all times and in all places.

Sometimes we need to understand that gratification is not so instant and that effort, sacrifice, and hard work are necessary to achieve success.

This lesson is not lost on religious life. Anyone who has read Torah from the scroll knows that it takes a great deal of effort. No matter what your training may be, one must spend hours learning the trope and its accents and proper pronunciation of the text. There are no shortcuts. Prayer, too, is a skill. You can't expect to be turned on instantaneously by the words in the *siddur*. It takes almost a lifetime to feel comfortable with the words and the concepts in the prayer book and then add personal meaning to those words.

The same is true, of course, with any skill. Athletic skill takes years to perfect. We may see the results in athletic competition, but we don't see all the bumps and bruises, all the trials and errors, and the years of sacrifice that went into the making of these wonderful athletes. Any kind of good scholarship takes hours upon hours mulling over research documents. There are no "instants" in life. As Thomas Edison said, "genius is one percent inspiration and ninety-nine percent perspiration." We learn the hard way that what you put into something is what you ultimately get out of it. As *Pirkei Avot* 5:25 states: "The reward is proportionate to the suffering."

In *parashat Tsav*, after the introductory discussion concerning sacrifices, a long section details the initiation of the formal service in the Tabernacle. For seven days, the *kohanim* prepared with sacrifices and with water purification, with special vestments, and with anointing oil. Sacrifices were offered, and unique rituals and rites were implemented. It is only after all of these ceremonies took place that on the eighth day, the *kohanim* were inaugurated and could begin their holy work in the Tabernacle. It took a period of time for them to prepare physically and spiritually to assume the monumental task of serving on behalf of both the Children of Israel and God in this sacred endeavor.

The same truth is reflected on our religious calendar as we prepare for Passover. A few days after we read this *parashah,* we will all sit down at our Passover Seder and retell the story of our people's Exodus from Egypt.

No holiday takes more preparation than Passover. Our tradition tells us: "People must begin to inquire into the Passover laws thirty days before the festival" (*Sanhedrin* 12b).

And no holiday has more laws than the holiday of Passover. Not only do we have to thoroughly clean our homes, change our eating style, and implement an entirely new mode of behavior, but also for eight days, our lives are changed. It takes a great deal of effort, as well as economic and personal sacrifice and just old-fashioned hard work to prepare properly for Passover. We also need to prepare ourselves spiritually for the Seder experience. The ritual foods and meal are central to the Seder, of course, but the spiritual food that we share is also of great significance. Will we be touched by the Passover story and internalize it as we sit around our family tables? Will we instruct the next generation about the importance of the Passover holiday and its message for them and for subsequent generations? Will our children have meaningful memories of the *Sedarim* in which they participated as young people? It takes effort and hard work, physically and spiritually.

"The reward is proportionate to the suffering." May our effort be rewarded and, in the words of Rabbi Isaac, may we all be able to say, I have labored and found meaning in my religious practice.

SHEMINI
Swimming Upstream

This *parashah* contains a long list of the characteristics of animals, fish, and fowl that classify them as fit for eating. According to traditional Rabbinic practice, the animals and fowl must be slaughtered in accordance with specific rules in order to be considered kosher. Those classified as *nevelah,* animals or birds that die of natural causes or as a result of an improperly carried out act of ritual slaughter, and *terepha,* animals or birds suffering from a wound or illness that will cause them to die within twelve months, are not considered kosher and cannot be eaten.

The Talmud, in *Ḥullin* 51b, outlines a very interesting case: when a bird is thrown with force upon water, we are uncertain whether a serious injury has occurred which that render it non-kosher. Rav Judah in the name of Samuel was led to establish an objective criterion: "It is sufficient if it swam the length of its body. This is so, however, only if it swam upstream." If it simply floats with the tide, Rav Judah suggests, it may be mortally wounded and unfit for slaughter. However, in his view, should it be able to swim upstream, then the bird itself does not have a serious injury and may be ritually fit for slaughter.

Irving M. Bunim, in *Ethics from Sinai*, suggests that this law is applicable, not merely in the context of *kashrut*, but in all aspects of Jewish life. A Jew must be willing to swim upstream against the tide. If a Jew can withstand the countervailing forces, his or her Judaism will survive. If, however, a Jew is merely carried downstream by surrounding currents and takes the path of least resistance, that person's Judaism and Jewish identity will eventually fade away.

Alan Dershowitz, in his book *The Vanishing American Jew*, writes that being Jewish in America today is easy, at least in relation to external burdens. "Jews today assimilate not because Christianity or Islam is 'better' or 'easier,' but because Jewish life does not have a strong enough positive appeal to offset the inertial drift toward the common denominator. Jews do not convert to Christianity; they 'convert' to mainstream Americanism, which is the American 'religion' closest to Judaism." According to Dershowitz, "most Jews who assimilate do not feel that they are giving up anything by abandoning a Jewishness they know little about." It is very easy to assimilate when one is part of a minority. In fact, it takes very little action; all it takes is inertia. On the other hand, in order to maintain a Jewish identity and transmit that identity from one generation to the next, effort, energy, and great commitment are required. It is a challenge to be a Jew in the open society of America. But it is a challenge that we must willingly accept.

In 1988, the Conservative movement organized a task force to articulate the philosophy of Conservative Judaism and published their work in *Emet Ve-Emunah: Statement of Principles of Conservative Judaism*. While *Emet Ve-Emunah* was written to describe the Conservative movement and its ideals and beliefs, this standard of conduct, I would suggest, is a common vision for all Jews in America or for Jews living anywhere in the world.

The booklet suggests that there are three characteristics for which all Jews should strive. The first is that a person should be a willing Jew. This willingness involves not only a commitment to observe the *mitzvot* and to advance Jewish concerns, but to refract all aspects of life through the prism of one's own Jewishness. The second characteristic is that a person should be a learning Jew. Jewish learning is a lifelong quest through which we integrate Jewish and general knowledge for the sake of personal enrichment, group creativity, and world transformation. And the third characteristic is that a person should be a striving Jew. One should strive for greater heights in observance, piety, knowledge, and Jewish activity.

This ideal is a pattern of belief and conduct that would serve us well in defining our Jewish identity in the context of a broader America. While we may be a minority, we are the bearers of a proud tradition and a meaningful heritage. However, if our generation becomes apathetic to the tradition lovingly bequeathed to us, we will sever the link from past to future generations.

This is the time for us to learn to swim upstream, to buck the tide, and to stand up for our principles as proud, identifiable, and active Jews. Dershowitz warns us that unless we do so, we will indeed become "the Vanishing American Jew." It is imperative that we recognize our responsibility to past generations and our commitment to the Jewish future as we dedicate ourselves to becoming willing, learning, and striving Jews.

SHEMINI
Using Time Well

"On the eighth day Moses called Aaron and his sons, and the elders of Israel" (Leviticus 9:1). The Torah reading begins exactly where the last *parashah* concluded. Aaron and his sons prepare for their service in the Tabernacle for seven days as an elaborate ceremony takes place. This ritual includes the sacrificing of animals, the anointing with oil, and the sprinkling of blood. Only on the eighth day are Aaron and his sons ready to serve in the Tabernacle.

The eighth day is mentioned a number of times in the Biblical story to symbolize the turning of a page: the end of one phase of life and the beginning of the next. We are most familiar with the law of circumcision on the eighth day after birth: "And when his son Isaac was eight days old, Abraham circumcised him, as God had commanded him" (Genesis 21:4). Seven days have passed and a new phase of life is to begin. Isaac joins the covenanted people, as the *brit*, the covenant, becomes part of his flesh.

According to the Biblical law of the *metsora*, one who contracts a skin disease is sent outside the camp. Upon his return to health, a purification ceremony ensues. Again the eighth day is prominent. The Torah states: "On the eighth day he shall take two male lambs without blemish" (Leviticus 14:10), commencing an elaborate purification rite. After seven days of cleansing, he is now ready to resume his place in the Israelite camp.

Once more in the Book of Leviticus, the eighth day signals a new stage. We are instructed, "When an ox or a sheep or a goat is born, it shall stay seven days with its mother, and from the eighth day on it shall be acceptable as an offering by fire to the Lord" (Leviticus 22:27). The animal had time to be nursed by its mother. On the eighth day, it is permitted as a sacrifice to God.

I would suggest that a seven-day period is important because it reminds us of God's creative powers. The world, according to the Biblical tradition, was created in six days, as God rested on the seventh. However, Rashi and other Biblical commentators suggest that God also created something on the seventh day: God created rest. Before that time, rest did not appear in God's creative process. The world took seven days to be created and only on the eighth day did the second week begin.

Perhaps the Biblical association with a week, a seven-day period, harbors back to God's creative process. Thus, each time a week goes by, we become partners in that creative process, as we use six days to shape the world for human purposes and the seventh day to recognize God's ownership of the world and our borrowed authority to manipulate it. The Torah seems to suggest that a seven-day period is a very valuable measure of time. We dare not miss the opportunity of taking advantage of it, for if God could create the world in seven days, we must emulate God and use our personal capabilities during this period of time to create a better world for all.

In Herman Wouk's World War II novel, *The Caine Mutiny*, Willie, the central character, is serving in the Navy when he receives a letter from his father who is about to die from cancer. Reflecting upon his life's disappointments, his father cautions his son, "Remember this, if you can—there is nothing, nothing more precious than time. You probably feel you have a measureless supply of it, but you haven't. Wasted hours destroy your life just as surely at the beginning as at the end—only at the end it becomes more obvious."

We often use the expression "killing time." In Jewish thought there is a concept known as *bittul Torah*, literally, "the wasting of Torah." The term refers to the time one squanders that could have been better spent learning Torah. Since Jewish tradition regards Torah learning as among the most pious and worthwhile acts in which a person can engage, it regards wasting one's time on unnecessary matters as wrong or even sinful.

In truth, we are taught that time is divisible not only in weeks, not simply in days, but even in hours. *Avodah Zarah* 10b relates a story concerning Keti'ah ben Shalom. We are informed that there was a Caesar who hated Jews and one day said to a prominent member of the government, "If one has a wart on his foot, shall he cut it away and live in comfort or leave it on and suffer discomfort?" He replied that the wart should be cut away and one should live in comfort.

The king was referring to the Jewish people and intimating to his advisors that it was time to do away with the Jews. Keti'ah ben Shalom, one of his advisors, began to reason with him and said, "Just as the world cannot exist without winds, so the world cannot exist without Israel." The king replied, "You have spoken very well; however, he who contradicts the king is to be cast into a circular furnace." As he was being cast into the furnace, he said, "All my possessions are to go to Rabbi Akiba and his friends." A *bat kol*, a heavenly voice, then exclaimed, "Keti'ah ben Shalom is destined for eternal life in the world to come." Rabbi Judah the Prince, on hearing of it, wept, saying, "One may acquire eternity in a single hour, another may acquire it after many years."

The beginning of that statement is displayed on our living room clock, reminding us of the preciousness of time. Sometimes a single hour is all it takes to make a difference, to change a life, to ameliorate a situation. Once that hour is passed, it cannot be retrieved. If wasted, it is gone forever.

If a single hour can make a difference, then what can 168 hours do? Clearly a week is an important period of human life and human endeavor. In each of the cases mentioned by the Torah, a new stage begins on the eighth day. The seven previous ones are a prelude to it. One cannot reach the eighth day without having lived, experienced, or participated fully in every hour of the previous seven days.

May we build upon each hour of each day to create a lifetime of meaningful living.

TAZRIA
Ultimate Wonder

The Torah reading begins with the laws concerning the birth of a child. These laws deal with the concept of purity and impurity and are difficult to understand. However, if we examine them in light of Rabbinic thought, we can find insights relevant to our modern age.

The Talmud in *Berakhot* 10a brings together some statements that apply to the first verse of the Torah reading: "When a woman at childbirth bears a male" (Leviticus 12:2). This reminds us of the story concerning the birth of the prophet Samuel. Hannah, upon giving birth to Samuel, sings a song of glory unto the Lord. She states, "There is no rock [*tzur*] like our God" (1 Samuel 2:2). The Rabbis suggest that the reading of this particular verse can be rendered otherwise. "There is no artist [*tzyar*] like our God." By changing the letter *vav* to two *yuds*, the Rabbis attempt to teach us a very important lesson. "It is in the capacity of a human being to draw a figure on the wall, but he cannot invest it with breath and spirit, bowels, and intestines. But the Holy One, blessed be He, is not so; He shapes one form in the midst of another and invests it with breath and spirit, bowels and intestines."

The Rabbis may not have understood all of the biological stages of the fetus, but they certainly recognized the great miracle present in the birth of a human being. They were not party to all the scientific data that we possess today, but they could still be witnesses to God's great presence in the event.

How does the human artist work? He speaks, but the work of art cannot speak. He creates, but the creation cannot create. But the Holy One, blessed be He, makes a work of art that can speak, create, and praise the Creator. With this magnificent image, the Rabbis set the stage for one of the great miracles of life: the birth of a new human being.

Perhaps the wonder and majesty of birth can help explicate the categories of impurity and purity. According to the text of the Torah, while the child is born pure, the mother is considered to be impure for varying periods of time depending on the sex of the child. While the text is not explicit about the precise nature of the impurity sustained by the new mother during this initial period, at the conclusion of this period of time she brings an offering to signify the elimination of all impurity. The Kotzker Rebbe stated that God is involved in the opening of the womb. When God's presence moves on, it leaves a spiritual vacuum and the concept of impurity ensues.

Today, we see ourselves as more sophisticated than ancient man. We talk of progress and refer to the ancients as primitive. And yet, with all our sophistication and presumed knowledge, we may be truly naive, for we believe we have all of the answers to the mystery of being human. Science has replaced religion, and we often rely on its methodology and its language to understand the world. Yet, we often lose sight of the wonder and the mystery of the world around us. As Albert Einstein said, "The fairest thing we can experience is the mysterious." Without that sense of mystery, we lose our essence of humanity.

And there is nothing more mysterious and wondrous than the human body itself. A pious Jew recognizes this each time he or she leaves the bathroom and recites a special prayer that acknowledges the intricacies of the human body. The prayer states: "Praised are You, Lord our God, King of the universe, who with wisdom fashioned the human body, creating openings, arteries, glands and organs, marvelous in structure, intricate in design. Should but one of them, by being blocked or opened, fail to function, it would be impossible to exist. Praised are You, Lord, healer of all flesh who sustains our bodies in wondrous ways."

The fact that we understand more about the human body than our ancestors did should not diminish our sense of wonder. Likewise, the fact that we now comprehend the intricacies of birth in no way diminishes our sense of awe at that magnificent event.

Anyone who has been present in a delivery room when a baby is born will agree that birth is a great miracle. As the Rabbis state: "The child comes forth from the womb covered with mucus and blood and yet everyone praises and cherishes the infant" (*Midrash Aggadah Leviticus* 12:2). Having been present in the delivery room when each of my two daughters was born, I know exactly the wonder of which they speak and the great sense of mystery and privilege in being part of God's creation.

It is for this reason that I believe there is no real debate between evolutionism and creationism. We are not prevented from examining and learning from new theories about how the physical universe operates, and yet, we should see the hand of God present in it all. Even Charles Darwin, in his concluding remarks to *The Origin of the Species* writes, "There is grandeur in this view of life … having been originally breathed by the Creator into a few forms."

For the religious person, the wonder of the human body with its openings and closings, its heart and pulse, its blood vessels and arteries, ears, eyes, eyelashes, and fingernails is proof that God watches over His creations. How is it that we take for granted that our cuts will heal, that our blood will coagulate, and that we will not bleed to death? Why is it that we expect that our stomach aches will go away, that our fever will come down, that most of our sicknesses will cure themselves, and that our fractured bones will mend?

As the Rabbis looked at this very difficult text, they attempted to teach us about the very essence of being human. They understood that we might not comprehend the concepts of purity and impurity as our ancestors may have, but we could learn from the categories that they represent. Just as when one witnesses God's presence at the birth of a child, we should be thankful for all the many wonders that daily attend us and learn to appreciate our own creative abilities and the grandeur and mystery of God's presence in our world.

METSORA
Watching Our Words

The Industrial Revolution overwhelmed the world of the *shtetl*. It is told that the disciples in one *shtetl* asked their rabbi, "What can we learn from the invention of the train, the telegraph, and the telephone?" The rabbi answered, "From the train, you learn that, but for one moment, everything can be lost. Once the doors of the train are closed, you miss the great journey. Pay attention." "And what can you learn from the telegraph?" The rabbi answered, "From the telegraph you learn that every word counts. Guard your tongue." "And what can you learn from the telephone?" "From the telephone," the rabbi answered, "you learn that whatever you speak here is heard there. Words have consequences."

This story applies to this *parashah* and its complex amalgam of laws concerning purity and impurity, skin diseases, molds on fabrics and leather and on the walls of one's home, and the purification rites for all of these afflictions. The Rabbis attempted to understand the concept through a moral perspective and suggested that an infected person may have been stricken with a disease because of a serious transgression. Playing on the linguistic similarity of the Hebrew word *metsora* (leprosy) and the Hebrew for *motzi shem ra* (slander), the Rabbis considered the disease to be punishment for slander and malicious gossip.

Now, we further understand the *shtetl* rabbi's answers to his students. One can only presume how careful he would have told them to be if during his time words were transmitted through the Internet and social media.

Most of us understand the term *lashon ha-ra* as gossip, and we know that Judaism frowns upon it. There are always people hurt when gossip is told about another, and our Rabbis warned us about *shmirat ha-lashon*, guarding our tongue. But *lashon ha-ra* is not only gossip. According to the *Alkalai Dictionary*, it can also be translated as slander. Slander has not only a social connotation, but a legal one as well. It can be uttered against an individual, an ethnic group, a race, a nation—usually stereotyping them in a manner that will lead to hatred, enmity, and perhaps violence.

In *Arakhin* 16b, Rabbi Samuel ben Nadav asks of Rabbi Ḥanina: "Wherein is the leper different that the Torah said: 'Being impure, he shall dwell apart; his dwelling shall be outside the tent?'" The Rabbi wanted to know why this person was separated from the community unlike any other impure individual. From a medical point of view, we can understand that the separation was due to the contagious nature of an infectious disease, but the Rabbis wanted to go further, as they believed moral blight was the basis of physical affliction.

Rabbi Ḥanina responds to his student's question: "The leper separated a husband from his wife, a man from his neighbor; therefore, said the Torah, 'he shall dwell apart.'" Because of the moral blight of *lashon ha-ra*, he is to be isolated from everyone else. He has created hatred and enmity in his home, in his community, in his society. He therefore is to be banished from the community. He is to sit isolated until his infection is healed, until he understands that what he has done is improper, inappropriate, and hateful in the sight of God and humanity. Only then can he be examined by the priest, not as a doctor, but as a moral guide and teacher who will decide whether this person is now cured of his terrible sins.

This Torah reading presents us with the challenge of the proverb: "Death and life are in the power of the tongue" (Proverbs 18:21). With the tongue, we can bring words of comfort, reconciliation, hope, and healing. We can offer sentiments of love, understanding, and kindness. But the tongue can also offer words of gossip, tale-bearing, and malicious slander. It can voice words of hatred, enmity, and violence. The choice is ours. We cannot expect of others what we do not take seriously ourselves.

The Talmud talks about the fact that it is our task to speak in *lashon nekia*, in appropriate language, to stay away from gossip and tale-bearing and words of hatred and enmity. Let us remember that, at the end of every silent *Amidah*, three times a day, we recite the phrase: "My God, keep my tongue from evil, my lips from lies." This is not easy for us, and we therefore utter this request of God each and every day. It is our task to keep our words appropriate, our motives pure, and our language sincere and meaningful.

AHAREI MOT
Adding Meaning to Life

In his novel *Hakhnassat Kallah,* translated as *The Bridal Canopy,* the Nobel prize-winning Israeli author, Shmuel Yosef Agnon, relates a story about Mechel the *shamash* (beadle) and the wealthy widow Sarah Leah. The *shamash,* a poor widower, closes up the synagogue on the eve of Passover and begins trudging home to an empty room to make a Seder for himself with only the barest of necessities. While many people had invited him to celebrate the Passover feast with them, he felt he should celebrate it on his own as he did not wish to burden anyone.

On the way home the *shamash* noticed an open window. It was the window of the house of Sarah Leah, the widow. They wished each other a good *yontif.* Even though Sarah Leah had lost her husband, out of habit, she prepared the same marvelous Seder she had made while her husband was still alive. She had been invited to another's house and though she did not feel comfortable, she had decided to go but had not yet left her house.

As they each felt sorry for the other and for themselves, Sarah Leah said to the *shamash,* "Reb Mechel, don't stand out in the cold; winter may have gone but it's still chilly. Better come into the house and not stand about in the open." Mechel agreed and walked into a room with candles lit and every corner gleaming and shining for the festival. The table was set beautifully, and Sarah Leah asked him to recite *Kiddush* for her. Before he knew it, Reb Mechel proceeded to lead the entire Seder, explaining to Sarah Leah the meaning of each of the rituals and the significance of the Seder night.

Agnon concludes his story with the widow and the *shamash* reciting the Song of Songs together. There is hope that the two of them may no longer be lonely.

This delightful little story contains some very important truths. While we can understand Reb Mechel's sadness at having to celebrate the

Seder by himself with his poor offerings on the table, it is even sadder to learn the tale of Sarah Leah. Money does not seem to be a problem as she continues to set a beautiful table. However, there is no one with whom she can share her company. Her home may be ready for the festival, but her life is devoid of meaning as she pines away for someone to lead the Seder. Wealth was not her issue; loneliness was.

Our Torah reading begins with the words, "The Lord spoke to Moses after the death of the two sons of Aaron who died when they drew too close to the presence of the Lord" (Leviticus 16:1). This refers us back to the reading in *parashat Shemini* when we heard of the unfortunate deaths of Nadav and Avihu who were killed when they offered a strange fire before the Lord.

What is curious about that event is that Moses calls to Mishael and Elzaphan, the sons of Uzziel, the uncle of Aaron, and asks them to carry away these two individuals from the sanctuary to a place outside of the camp. Apparently, the bodies of the two *kohanim* were not completely consumed by God's fire. Rashi states: "Their souls were consumed; their bodies remained intact."

There are some people in this world who could be considered to be the living dead. Their bodies remain intact but their souls are no longer extant. They go about life without giving meaning to their days. They experience the world but refuse to be touched by it. This may have been the case of the widow Sarah Leah. She could prepare the feast for the Passover holiday and follow all of the rituals, but without someone to share it, there was no spirit present. Her body was involved in the preparations but not her soul.

The Talmud in *Berakhot* 18b states: "The wicked even in life are considered dead." They may seem to be surviving in this world but as the Talmud understands it, their lives are devoid of meaning and significance. It is as if their souls have been taken even as their bodies are intact.

The Psalmist writes: "Blessed is the Lord. Day by day He supports us" (Psalms 68:20). Every day can be meaningful and significant. We should not be merely consumers of life; we should live it to its fullest. The difference between an effective life and an ineffectual life is based on how we spend our time. Have we added goodness to the world? Have we made a difference? Have we used our God-given talents appropriately? Have we expanded our minds and taken advantage of the gifts of the world? Have we appreciated those around us and reached out to them with care and nurturing concern? Have we truly lived, or have we only existed?

Rabbi Sidney Greenberg wrote: "To live all the days of our lives means to keep our souls alive, to grow more responsive to the needs of others, more resistant to consuming greed, more nourishing of our craving for fellowship, more devoted to truth and integrity. To live all the days of our lives means to keep our spirits alive, to face the future with confidence, secure in the knowledge that we can meet every challenge with fortitude, emerge with honor and be enriched by every experience."

If we follow these words of Rabbi Greenberg, we will bring meaning into our lives. This is the challenge of daily living. The widow Sarah Leah could function in her life but needed companionship, friendship, and a sense of purpose in order to be fully alive. Nadav and Avihu, according to our scholarly texts, were left with their bodies intact but their souls destroyed. May we nurture both our bodies and our souls.

KEDOSHIM
The Holiness Code

Parashat Kedoshim is one of the most beautiful and meaningful chapters in all of religious literature. Chapter 19 of the Book of Leviticus has been termed the Holiness Code, for it outlines the responsibility of a Jew to live a life infused with sanctity and holiness. This chapter also includes a rendition of the Ten Commandments in another form. Its detail of laws, standards, modes of behavior, and faith for the individual and the community does much to explain the role of Judaism and Jewish life in this world.

The *parashah* commences with the object lesson of all of Judaism: "You shall be holy, for I, the Lord your God, am holy" (Leviticus 19:2). From this phrase, our tradition extracted the necessity of practicing *Imitatio Dei*, emulating God. How is that possible? The Talmud in *Sotah* 14a states: "Just as God clothed the naked [Adam and Eve], you should clothe the naked. Just as God visited the sick [Abraham], you should visit the sick. Just as God comforts those who mourn [Isaac], you should comfort those who mourn. Just as God buried the dead [Moses], so you should bury the dead." One of the modes of emulating God is to perform righteous activities in this world, to be involved in *gemilut ḥasadim*, deeds of lovingkindness. Holiness dictates appropriate responses to human needs.

Rudolf Otto, in his book, *The Idea of the Holy*, defines holiness as the experience of a Divine reality that evokes fear, awe, and submission. Only later, as concepts of divinity are purified and elevated, are ethical elements introduced into the idea of holiness. In this chapter, the Torah contends that holiness and ethical behavior are intertwined from the very origin of our tradition, and one of the ways to serve God is to be sensitive to the needs of His creations. This is exemplified in this reading's description of giving gifts to the poor: "When you reap the harvest of your land, you shall not reap all the way to the edges of your field, or gather the gleanings of your harvest. You shall not pick your vineyard bare, or gather the fallen fruit of your vineyard; you shall leave them for the poor and the stranger: I the Lord am your God" (Leviticus 19:9–10).

It is not by accident that these verses conclude with the phrase: "I the Lord am your God." Sixteen times in this one chapter, we are reminded of the purpose of these laws and standards: "I am the Lord." In this case, to be holy is defined as being concerned with the poor in our society. The Jewish farmer had the responsibility of caring for the less fortunate in his community. And he had to do so in a special manner.

The intention of these remarkable laws is not merely to provide for the needs of the poor but also to preserve their dignity. The Torah is not legislating a mere handout; on the contrary, the poor man is entitled to enter the field and collect what is his due without suffering the embarrassment of confronting the donor. Every Israelite learned that he was privileged to work the land and to gain from its gifts. At the same time, he learned through these laws that those less fortunate had special rights, including receiving sustenance from the landowner's harvest.

Preserving the dignity of a human being is a *sine qua non* of the concept of holiness. I believe that this is the reason why this chapter contains the famous statement identified as the golden rule: "Love your neighbor as yourself" (Leviticus 19:18). Again we learn that relationships with human beings are tied to a response to the Divine. Martin Buber understands this phrase to mean that you should remember that your neighbor deserves the same rights of respect, honor, and dignity that you want for yourself. Your neighbor, like you, is created in the image of God. Holiness, as expressed through correct conduct, is how we emulate God in this world. It is found in the small kindnesses that uplift the downtrodden, assist the poor, help the distressed, and enhance the Divine Spirit.

A Yiddish tale tells of a soul that traveled to heaven to observe the procedures of the Heavenly Court. The soul watched as a learned rabbi wished to enter. "Day and night I studied the holy Torah," the rabbi stated, expecting to find a place in heaven. "Wait here," said the ministering angel, "we will investigate your motives to see whether your study was for its own sake or for gain." Next, a *tzaddik*, a holy man, came forward. "I fasted much and chanted Psalms each day," he explained to the angel. Again the response came, "Wait here until we have completed our investigation to learn whether your motives were pure." Then a tavern keeper introduced himself. "I kept an open door and fed without charge every poor man who came into my inn," he remarked. Immediately the gates of heaven opened themselves for him to enter.

Holiness for the Jew is not found in asceticism, in running away from society. Instead, it is found in being part of the community and in upholding standards and guidelines whereby human beings can live with dignity, respect, and love for one another. If we but follow the guidelines of Leviticus chapter 19, the Holiness Code, we will live our lives emulating God and establishing societies based on justice, ethics, and morality.

EMOR
Looking Out for Others

During one of Lithuania's freezing winters over a century ago, Rabbi Israel Salanter, founder of the Mussar movement, became aware that his *yeshiva* had no money to buy fuel and that the students had to study in the numbing cold. Early one morning, Reb Yisroel, as he was called, went to the home of a wealthy, but not very philanthropic, householder. Still in his dressing gown, the man invited the rabbi in, but the rabbi chose to stay in the doorway. Seemingly unaware that the householder was shivering from the cold, the rabbi began a lengthy Talmudic discourse. The host's teeth were chattering and before long his lips had turned blue. Thinking he was about to faint, the man finally interrupted the rabbi and persuaded him to come in. As they warmed themselves before the stove, Reb Yisroel continued, "I am sure that you are wondering about my strange conduct. The students are freezing and we need money for fuel. If I had asked you to help while you were warm and comfortable, you would not have understood what it means to study in an unheated room in sub-zero weather. Now that you feel what they feel, I am sure you will help me." And indeed, the wealthy man provided the fuel for the *yeshiva* as long as he lived.

Parashat Emor contains a long passage concerning the festival cycle. Each of the major festivals, as well as Shabbat, is mentioned and its rituals briefly described. In the midst of this section, there seems to be an interpolation, a verse that simply does not belong: "And when you reap the harvest of your land, you shall not reap all the way to the edges of your field, or gather the gleanings of your harvest; you shall leave them for the poor and the stranger: I the Lord am your God" (Leviticus 23:22).

What has this verse to do with the festival cycle? Rashi, quoting the *Sifra*, puts the query into perspective: "Why did Scripture place this law here between Passover and Shavuot on the one hand and Rosh Hashanah and Yom Kippur on the other? To teach you that the person who leaves the corners of the field and the gleaning of his harvest for the poor is counted as if he built the Holy Temple and offered the sacrifices therein."

This is truly an amazing statement. And yet, this is the classic Jewish approach. In *Avot D'Rabbi Natan* 11a, the following story is told:

> Rabban Yoḥanan ben Zakkai once was walking with his disciple Rabbi Joshua near Jerusalem after the destruction of the Temple. Rabbi Joshua looked at the Temple ruins and said: "Alas for us! The place which atoned for the sins of the people Israel through the ritual of animal sacrifice lies in ruins!" Then Rabban Yoḥanan ben Zakkai spoke to him these words of comfort: "Be not grieved, my son. There is another way of gaining atonement even though the Temple is destroyed. We must now gain atonement through deeds of lovingkindness." For it is written, "For I desire goodness, not sacrifice" (Hosea 6:6).

Thus, the Torah and its later commentators insist upon our obligations to the needy members of our society. This law's placement in the passage concerning the festivals may suggest that its message was even more profound. A person might think, "Why do I have to worry about the details about helping the poor? I keep the holidays, bring my sacrifices, and perform the rituals—that is the true meaning of being a religious individual." The Torah tells us that it is one's duty to help the needy in the community, especially at times of rejoicing and observance of a festival. Thus, for example, on Sukkot we perform *ushpizin* and invite guests into our *sukkah*; on Purim we give *matanot le-evyonim*, gifts to the poor; and on Passover we distribute *maot ḥittim*, food to the needy.

Another lesson is present in this verse as well. The Torah tells us "when you reap [*u'vekutzrekhem* (plural)] the harvest of your land [*artzikhem* (plural)], you shall not reap [*lo tikhale* (singular)] all the way to the edges of your field [*sadkha* (singular)]" (Leviticus 23:22). Why does the sentence commence with the plural and then switch to the singular?

It instructs us that when people do their harvesting, no one should think that since everyone else is leaving a corner of the field for the poor, the needy will be adequately provided for and one may reap to the edge. By changing the language to the singular, the Torah emphasizes that each and every individual must remember his obligation to the unfortunate and the disadvantaged.

Once in the city of Chelm, the people looked forward with great anticipation to the marriage of the rabbi's only son. In order to guarantee a truly joyous wedding, the mayor instructed the carpenter to construct a barrel the size of a small water tower in the middle of the town square. The top could only be reached by a ladder, and the mayor decreed that each villager had two weeks to bring a bucket full of the best wine from his or her cellar and empty it into the tall barrel. On the eve of the wedding, the barrel would be tapped and all would drink the sweet wine.

Every day for two weeks a steady stream of villagers walked to the town square with pails in hand. Each one climbed the ladder to the top and poured wine into the massive barrel. The evening of the wedding finally arrived, and the mayor decided the time had come to tap the barrel and enjoy the luscious red wine.

As the mayor approached the barrel, the villagers crowded around him. He climbed the ladder, pounded the tap, placed his hand on the spigot, and said, "*mazel tov*!" Suddenly the entire village fell silent. When the mayor turned the spigot, out flowed nothing but water. Looking into each other's eyes, the villagers knew exactly what had happened. Throughout the previous two weeks, each villager supposed that he or she could get away with adding water to the barrel instead of wine and assumed the others would provide the wine. After all, what difference would one pail of water make in all of that wine? After standing silently in the square for what seemed like hours, the villagers returned to their own homes filled with shame and despair. Each person recognized his or her failure; each person made a false assumption.

The responsibility to help the needy is placed upon each of us, and we are not to pass off our obligation to others. Let us recall the words of the *midrash* on Psalms 17:14: "Consider the power of *tzedakah*, for by virtue of the coin a man gives to an impoverished person he merits and receives the Presence of God."

The Book of Leviticus is a code and framework for holiness in the home, in the sanctuary, and in the community. The Torah reminds us of our duties to all members of our community, even in the context of the festival cycle. It is our task to live up to the challenge to infuse the Presence of God in all aspects of our lives.

EMOR
The Dignity of Work

In one of Aesop's fables, a farmer who was about to die desired to impart to his sons a secret of great importance. He called them around his bedside and said, "My sons, I am shortly about to die. I would have you know, therefore, that in my vineyard there lies a hidden treasure. Dig and you will find it." As soon as their father was dead, the sons took spade and fork and searched for the treasure. They found none; however, the vines, after so thorough a digging, produced a crop such as had never before been seen.

Parashat Emor concludes with the recitation of the Festival cycle. Many verses detail the period of the counting the *omer*. From the second night of Passover, we count forty-nine days with the fiftieth day being the holiday of Shavuot.

In some ways, Shavuot serves as both a mirror image and an opposite pole to the festival of Passover. On Passover, even the smallest crumb of bread is forbidden; on Shavuot the commandment is to bring two loaves of bread. This idea of opposites manifests itself in the fact that the *omer* offering on the second day of Passover is brought from barley, the most common of grains and considered not much better than animal food. On Shavuot, on the other hand, wheat, the finest grain, was offered in the Temple. Wheat symbolizes the very essence of human food, and the consumption of bread defines a formal meal that begins with the ritual washing of hands, *Birkat Ha-motzi*, the blessing over the bread, and concludes with *Birkat Ha-mazon*, the Grace after Meals.

The journey from Passover to Shavuot represents the Exodus of our people from Egypt and their arrival at Mount Sinai. It is the story of liberated slaves who taste their first fruits of freedom and, at Mount Sinai, receive the Torah and become truly free. The agricultural journey that begins on Passover and ends on Shavuot marks the journey from barley to wheat, from matzah to bread.

When Adam and Eve are driven from the Garden of Eden, God sets forth the punishment: "Because you did as your wife said and ate of the tree, about which I commanded you, 'You shall not eat of it,' cursed be the ground because of you; by toil you shall eat of it all the days of your life: thorns and thistles shall it sprout for you. But your food shall be the grasses of the field; by the sweat of your brow shall you get bread to eat" (Genesis 3:17–19).

In *Pesaḥim* 118a, the above verses appear in a restructured dialogue between God and Adam. Rabbi Joshua ben Levi teaches that when God tells Adam "thorns and thistles shall it sprout for you," Adam weeps tears. Adam protests before God, "My donkey and I will eat from the same trough." God responds, "By the sweat of your brow shall you get bread to eat," and Adam is comforted.

At first this may seem quite odd. Don't we usually think of working by the sweat of the brow as a punishment for the sin in the Garden? This reading turns the punishment into a reprieve for Adam's troubled soul. Bread represents the essence of the meal and the crown of human achievement. The reason why Adam grows calm is that he will have his bread, albeit through the sweat of his brow. God promises Adam that he will possess human dignity if he wills it. He need not be consigned to the same animal existence as his donkey.

In our society, we have become accustomed to instantaneous commands and immediate gratification. If our computer takes too long to boot up, we simply upgrade it or buy a new one. To find an answer to a question, we only need to search Google or Wikipedia. Why waste time on something that takes the sweat of our brow?

Yet, we know that work is applied effort. Work, in its fundamental sense, is not what we do for a living but what we do with our living. William Bennett, in *The Book of Virtues*, writes, "All can be done well or poorly. All can be done cheerfully and with pride, or grudgingly and with distaste. And which way we do them is really up to us. It is a matter of choice. That is perhaps the greatest insight that the ancient Roman Stoics championed for humanity. There are no menial jobs, only menial attitudes. And our attitudes are up to us."

Why were Americans so enamored with Cal Ripken Jr.'s streak of playing in 2,632 consecutive games? It may be true that he was one of the greatest shortstops to play the game of baseball, but that was not the only reason. Was it because he went about his job quietly, efficiently, and without great fanfare for so many years? There are millions of Americans who do just that. Was it because he wasn't injured over the course of his career? For that he was most assuredly blessed. I think what endeared him to all was that Cal Ripken found nothing remarkable about just doing his job day after day, and doing the best he could. Now, most assuredly, most of us don't have a $30-million contract that rewards our work, but to see someone who enjoyed his work and went about it in a professional, humane, and responsible manner filled all of us with great pride.

Thomas Jefferson said, "I'm a great believer in luck and I find, the harder I work, the more luck I have." The farmer in Aesop's fable would agree. And for good reason, Cal Ripkin Jr. has served as an appropriate model. If we follow our *parashah*, we learn that it takes hard work to produce a good wheat crop and that nothing comes easily.

Working toward a goal with persistence, patience, and the sweat of our brow adds to the luster of human dignity and enhances human life. We sanctify God in our world through our work when we set appropriate goals and attempt to accomplish them.

BE-HAR
The Gifts of Nature

I once heard the following tale:

>On Friday afternoon, as was his custom when on the atoll of Abemama, the Last Rebbe of Bialystok went to a tidal pool with his good friend, the island's high priest. The high priest sensed that something was bothering his friend and asked what it might be.
>
>The rebbe said he wished he could have one clear, unmistakable sign of the existence of the Blessed Holy One to whom he had dedicated his life. The high priest arose and said: "It is best that you be alone."
>
>The rebbe floated in the pool, letting the warm ocean water relax his muscles. He noticed the half moon, already high in the sky well before sunset. He saw the monumental shapes of tropical clouds and watched an egret soar. He stood up and looked at the waves crashing against the outer reef as the tide flowed in. Yet the rebbe saw no sign.
>
>As the rebbe approached him, the high priest asked, "What did you see?" The rebbe answered, "I saw no sign."
>
>The high priest persisted: "I asked what you saw, not what you did not see." And the rebbe told him of the moon and the clouds and the egret and the waves and the tide. The high priest continued: "Aren't these all signs from your Holy One?" The rebbe responded, "I see them every day."
>
>The high priest replied, "If today you saw any of these for the first time, you would have considered it to be a sign, a miracle. How much more so that your Holy One lets you see them every day?"

Each day that we arise in the morning is a renewal of creation. We often become inured to the fact that miracles daily attend us. Yet, each morning in the first blessing before the *Sh'ma* we recite: "in your goodness, day after day You renew Creation." Each day is not merely a new day; it is a re-creation of the world.

In *parashat Be-har*, the Children of Israel are reminded that they are mere tenants on the face of this earth: "But the land must not be sold beyond reclaim, for the land is Mine; you are but strangers resident with Me. Throughout the land that you hold, you must provide for the redemption of the land" (Leviticus 25:23–24). The land on which they sit is a gift; they must care for it. Thus, the laws of the Sabbatical Year (*Shemittah*) and the Jubilee Year (*Yovel*) are mentioned as part of the calendar so that the Israelites shall realize that the land is God's. Once every seven years the *mitzvah* of *Shemittah* presents a reminder that we merely tend the earth but, ultimately, the land is not ours. As individuals, we are able to borrow land, utensils, and material things, but we must ultimately return them to the cycles of nature. During the *Shemittah* year the land is to lay fallow, and its produce is available to all.

The notion that humans are temporary tenants on God's earth undergirds much of Jewish environmental law. As Creator of heaven and earth, God is the true owner of natural resources. Human beings are considered *shomrim* (protectors or guardians) of the earth that God has placed in our charge. As the well-known *midrash* in *Ecclesiastes Rabbah* 9 states, "God said to Adam in the Garden of Eden: 'See My works how fine and excellent they are. For your sake I created them all. See to it that you do not spoil and destroy My world; for if you do, there will be no one else to set it right after you.'"

In the first chapter of the Book of Genesis, Adam is told: "Fill the earth and master it; and rule the fish of the sea, the birds of the sky, and all the living things that creep on earth" (Genesis 1:28). Yet, Adam must promise that, though he may be master of the world, he must respect it. In this way, the preservation of the planet is an important part of Biblical, Rabbinic, and modern Jewish thought. In fact, in the second chapter, Adam is placed in the Garden of Eden for this purpose: "To till it and tend it" (Genesis 2:15). Adam's needs were taken care of, but he also had duties to perform—to nurture and conserve the perfection of the Garden through the labor of his hands.

The proliferation of major industry, the danger of overpopulation, the use of nuclear energy, building activities on a scale unimagined in the past, the risk of global warming, and the greenhouse effect all contribute to our anxiety about the ecological state of the world. Though we have progressed greatly in society, we must realize that there has been an environmental cost. The Sabbatical and Jubilee Years remind us that we are to be stewards of the land. We are reminded that we are tenants on this earth, and, if we destroy its gifts, we leave behind a major catastrophe for the generations that follow us.

The Last Rebbe of Bialystok was looking for signs and miracles from the Holy One that would have given him greater faith. His friend the high priest, taught him well. The gifts we see each day remind us of the presence of the Creator in our lives. It is our responsibility to be God's partners in ensuring that we faithfully tend to our gifts.

BE-ḤUKKOTAI
Serious Torah Study

In his bestselling book, *Blink*, Malcolm Gladwell writes, "We live in a world that assumes that the quality of a decision is directly related to the time and effort that went into making it ... We believe that we are always better off gathering as much information as possible and spending as much time as possible in deliberation." However, he comments, "there are moments, particularly in times of stress, when haste does not make waste, when our snap judgments and first impressions can offer a much better means of making sense of the world."

Gladwell's findings suggest that "decisions made very quickly can be every bit as good as decisions made cautiously and deliberately." This very interesting theory attempts to convince us that snap judgments and first impressions can be educated and controlled. Using stories of individuals who are trained as experts in antiquities, tennis, psychology, and other disciplines, Gladwell argues that great decision makers aren't those who process the most information or spend the most time deliberating, but those who perfect the art of "thin-slicing," filtering the very few factors that matter from an overwhelming number of variables.

If Gladwell is correct, then maybe this is one of the reasons that Judaism has a tough time making it in the modern age. It is very difficult to get a singular and transformative first impression of Judaism. Instead, we teach that to be involved in our heritage takes years of learning, practice, and observance. From the earliest moment of our lives until our last breath, we grow day by day. Judaism teaches us that only with constant study and involvement can we become more learned Jews and better people.

This lesson is taught in the first verse of *parashat Be-*ḥukkotai. God addresses the Children of Israel and says, "If you follow My laws and faithfully observe My commandments" (Leviticus 26:3), I will provide blessings of the land, fertility of the soil, and safety, security, and peace in society.

Rashi, following the halakhic *midrash Sifra*, asks the following question concerning this verse: "I might think that this (refers to) the fulfillment of the commandments; (but) when it states, 'If you follow My laws and faithfully observe My commandments,' then the fulfillment of the commandments is (already) stated. How, then, shall I explain 'if you follow My laws?' That you shall toil in (the study of) Torah."

Rashi suggests that Torah study is an activity that requires commitment and effort. Serious Jewish study is often done *be-ḥavruta*, in pairs, with one member of the couple pushing the other for greater diligence in studying the text. Voices are raised, disputations are discussed, and arguments ensue, all of them in order to fully understand the text and ascertain its true meaning. Whether it is a tractate of the Talmud, a passage from Maimonides, or the *parashah* of the week, the passion for Torah study is palpable. In this setting, one can appreciate the Talmudic remark that the Torah cannot be acquired unless one expends enormous amounts of effort. As the Talmud states: "He who repeated his chapter a hundred times is not to be compared with him who repeated it one hundred and one times" (*Ḥagigah* 9b).

Most of us did not grow up in that kind of culture. Even if we were students of a serious religious school or a day school, Torah study was not always our passion. It is always a challenge, especially in the circles in which we live, to convey a true passion for *talmud Torah*. When Torah study is passionate, one feels the presence of Hillel and Shammai, Rabbi Akiva and Rabbi Tarfon, Maimonides and Rabbi Joseph Karo when delving into the text. Serious Torah study becomes an ongoing dialogue with previous generations of Jewish scholars. One feels the presence of the ancient study halls of the Land of Israel and Babylonia, the Torah sessions of Rashi and Ramban, and the halls of learning of Lithuania and Jerusalem.

Joel Grishaver writes:

> The heart of Torah learning is a kind of special dialogue. The text is read slowly, word by word. As we read, questions emerge. We struggle to solve these questions. Along the way, other voices, other Jews who have looked at these words before, join the discussion with their commentaries. They point out problems; they share their personal solutions. The conversation continues ... Between students, between teachers and students, the perceptions differ, the inferred meanings conflict, and the quest continues. In the end, the learner is left staring in his/her own text; the voices and insights of many others are heard, but for each learner the passage has yielded a personal understanding. Jewish text study is a wondrous combination of learning from others and finding out about yourself.

In many ways, this is the opposite of Gladwell's theory in *Blink*. Judaism is not about first impressions; it is a lifelong journey. As the Talmud states in *Eruvin* 54a–b: "Why were the words of Torah compared to the fig tree? As with the fig tree the more one searches it the more one finds in it, so it is with the words of the Torah; the more one studies them, the more relish he finds in them."

I am convinced that this is a true challenge of modern Jewish life. We must make the study of our tradition a passion of young people and adults. Torah study must be ongoing and serious. It should be an integral part of each person's day, as Saadia Gaon states: "We are only a people by the merit of receiving the Torah."

Jewish education is not merely for religious school students; it is a lifelong process. Today we must strengthen Jewish pre-school education and religious school education. Funds must be available for day schools and for Jewish summer camps. We need to have the resources available for our young people to participate in study programs in Israel. Continuing adult education must be a priority on the community's agenda. Learning and teaching must be seen as a noble vocation and avocation in Jewish life. If we take this lesson seriously, the future of Judaism will be blessed.

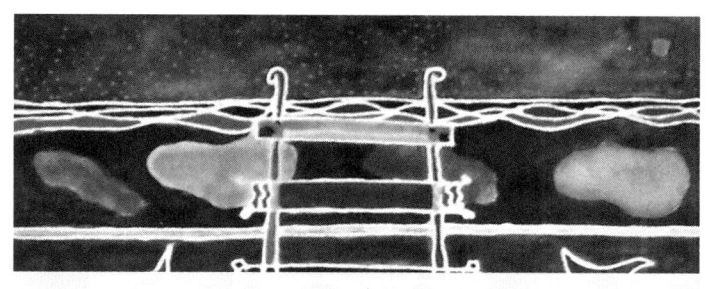

NUMBERS
במדבר
BE-MIDBAR

BE-MIDBAR
Jewish Unity

The opening chapters of the Book of Numbers set the stage for the Israelite journey in the desert. The first section of *parashat Be-midbar* deals with the census, and the second section details the arrangement of the camp of the Israelites.

The Israelite camp is arranged in a square with the Tent of Meeting as the central focus. Arranged in this fashion, it is clear that the Tabernacle, and especially the Ark of the Covenant, was to be protected physically by the Israelites. Conversely, found in the very middle of the camp, this sacred place was symbolically designed to act as a protective shield for the Israelite tribes.

The groupings of the tribes surrounding the Tabernacle are not arranged in chronological order of their birth; rather, other principles of organization are used. On the east and the south are the tribes of the children of Leah. Judah and Reuben are the leaders. On the west are the descendants of Rachel. Ephraim is the most important one in this arrangement. On the north, Dan is given prominence over the other sons of Bilhah and Zilpah (with Gad having been moved to take Levi's place).

Why this particular order and organization? Historians have shown the historical prominence of the tribes of Judah, Reuben, Ephraim, and Dan. This seems to be portrayed in the arrangement. But a closer look at the symbols of the tribes and what they represent may also be in order.

The Torah informs us that the tribes were situated in a certain fashion: "The Israelites shall camp each with his standard, under the banners of their ancestral house" (Numbers 2:2). A flag or standard is nothing more than a piece of cloth tied to a pole. The cloth by itself is almost worth nothing as is the pole on which it hangs. But put them together and the symbol is powerful. The flag of your country, your regiment, even the banner of your youth group or organization, assumes prominence far beyond its constituent parts.

As Jews, when we see the Israeli flag, we know that it represents much more than a piece of cloth tied to a pole. It represents the dream, now realized, of an independent Jewish state with its own government, anthem, symbols, and language. As a very powerful symbol, it fills us with a sense of pride.

Rabbi Zalman Sorotzkin, in his book *Oznaim Latorah*, suggests that we look at the symbols on the flags of the four most prominent tribes. Judah's symbol was a lion; Reuben's—a man; Ephraim's—an ox; and Dan's—an eagle. These four motifs represent the four celestial creatures with four faces perceived by Ezekiel in his vision of God's chariot in the first chapter of his book.

Numbers Rabbah 2:10 states: "Now in the same manner as the Holy One, blessed be He, created the four cardinal directions of the world, in like manner did He set about his throne the four creatures and above them the Throne of Glory. Corresponding to these was the order of the standards which He communicated to Moses."

What does this *midrash* suggest? Perhaps it is telling us that in the gathering of the Children of Israel, the characteristics of God's holiness are found. God's mystical Presence is found in their midst when the Israelites encamp around the Tabernacle. They give honor, protection, and respect to the Ark of the Covenant and God's word contained therein, and God, in turn, is found in their collective identity as a people. A single flag by itself is not sufficient. All must be present simultaneously to represent the chariot and God's Holy Presence.

When Israel joins together, there is peace among the tribes, not rivalry for prominence, for God is symbolically found in their midst: "So they camped by their standards, and so they marched" (Numbers 2:34). They must not only encamp together; they must travel together as well.

The concept of Jewish unity is a significant motif, not merely for Jewish survival but for comprehending the very essence of the Jewish spirit. "We are all brothers and sisters," states *Midrash Tanḥuma Naso* 1. We are dependent upon one another. We feel responsible for another Jew wherever he or she may reside. When we unite together in spirit, we are a holy people. We gain from other Jews an essence of *kedushah*, holiness. Rabbi Abraham Isaac Kook, former Chief Rabbi of Palestine, believed that every Jew was holy, and together, each Jew enhanced the sanctity of others. He wrote, "it is a grave error to be insensitive to the distinctive unity of the Jewish spirit, to imagine that the Divine stuff which uniquely characterizes Israel is comparable to the spiritual content of all the other national civilizations. This error is the source of the attempt to sever the national from the religious element of Judaism. Such a division would falsify both our nationalism and our religion, for every element of thought, emotion, and idealism that is present in the Jewish people belongs to an indivisible entity, and all together make up its specific character."

All of us stood together at the foot of Mount Sinai. All of us form an integral part of this people. Jewish unity cannot merely be a slogan. We must strive to achieve this unity, as it enhances the very foundation of our spiritual essence. With the Tabernacle in the middle of the camp, with the Israelite tribes all united surrounding it, the Israelites could not be defeated, either physically or spiritually.

Our Sephardic brothers and sisters insert a meaningful prayer into their version of *Birkat Ha-mazon*, the Grace after Meals: "May the all-merciful One grant peace among us." No greater wish could I bestow upon our people. May we unite in purpose, spirit, and vision, for when we do, no force on the face of this earth can defeat us.

BE-MIDBAR
The *Minyan*

In *parashat Be-midbar*, Moses is commanded to take a census of the Israelite people for the purpose of military conscription. Like other censuses throughout Biblical literature, the head count of the troops was always taken before a campaign and at its conclusion. In this case, the Israelites were to be counted each according to his father's household, according to their tribal affiliation.

Commentators suggest that the manner in which this census was taken was exactly in accord with that of previous countings of the Children of Israel: "Take a census of the whole Israelite community by the clans of its ancestral houses, listing the names, every male, head by head" (Numbers 1:2). The clan and its ancestral home were numbered, not the individuals.

There are other times when we count Jews and are careful how we count them. For example, a *minyan*, ten Jewish adults, is necessary for communal prayer. (In some communities, only men are counted; in others, men and women are counted). Unless that number is present, certain prayers are not recited, specifically the *Bar'khu*, the *Kaddish*, and the *Kedushah*.

Rabbi Louis Jacobs suggests that Jewish teachers give various explanations for praying in a *minyan* having to do with favoring communal over private prayer. Menahem Meiri stresses the psychological advantage: "Whenever a person is able to offer his prayers in the synagogue he should do so since there proper concentration of the heart can be achieved." The Rabbis voiced the principle that communal prayer has special value and "whenever ten pray in the synagogue the *Shekhinah* is present" (*Berakhot* 6a). In the *Kuzari*, Judah Ha-Levi, in the words of the Jewish sage, suggests that an individual, praying on his own, may pray for others to be harmed, but a community will never pray for harm to come to one of its members. Furthermore, an individual may make mistakes when mouthing the words of the prayers, whereas when people pray together, they make up for one another's shortcomings.

The Zohar offers a mystical reason: When an individual prays, his prayers do not ascend to God until there has first been a heavenly investigation to determine whether he is worthy for his prayers to be accepted. On the other hand, the Zohar states, communal prayers ascend immediately to the Heavenly Throne without any prior investigation.

A *minyan* needs to be present in a Jewish community so that communal prayer can be recited. In fact, *Sanhedrin* 17b states that, in order for a scholar to reside in a community, ten individuals need to be present, ensuring there is always a *minyan*.

I have been privileged to pray in a *minyan* in many places around the world. Whether it has been in Jerusalem, New York, Buenos Aires, Paris, Toronto, Budapest, London, Los Angeles, or Kiev, I have always been welcomed as a member of the prayer group. In some cases, I had the obligation of reciting the Mourner's *Kaddish* and was pleased that others were present so that I could offer the words of memorial and the sanctification of God's name during my time of personal mourning. At other times, I was a participant in the communal prayer service so that others could memorialize a loved one. And sometimes, the *minyan* was present not because one needed to recite *Kaddish* but simply so that we could recite the entire prayer service.

There are specific instances that stand out in my mind where a *minyan* became almost a mystical experience. One night in Moscow in June 1983, when it was not easy to be a Jew behind the Iron Curtain, Rabbi Mordecai Simon and I were present to make a *minyan* in a small synagogue in an outlying area of Moscow. We hadn't intended to be there at that time as we were extremely careful to visit Refusenik families in a secretive fashion. Yet, after one of our visits late on a Friday afternoon, we passed by a synagogue that needed two more individuals to complete the *minyan*. We were privileged to be part of it.

In Seoul, South Korea, I delivered a lecture as president of the international Rabbinical Assembly at a conference on Judaism. On a Friday night on an American Army Base in Seoul, my wife and I were present as a *minyan* was formed for communal prayer. It consisted of Americans who were on the base and a few individuals who were in Seoul on business or lived in the city. Coming from a variety of different backgrounds, we joined together to usher in the Sabbath in communal prayer. I will always remember those particular occasions.

How do we count individuals for the *minyan*? There are various ways. We don't enumerate each person individually because we are a collective. Instead there is a custom of counting not one, not two, not three, until we get to the number ten. We also have the custom of using a Biblical verse containing ten words as we enumerate those who make up the prayer community. When the requisite number is reached, a community is judged present.

Jews count others with the goal of forming community. It is significant to note that in Exodus 30:12–15, the census is taken by having each individual give a half-shekel, as it is only when one half joins another half that a whole is created. We would not be whole without another whose half we need to complete our whole.

Rabbi Jacobs suggests that, in this manner, Jews are able to form a *Kehilla Kedosha*, a Holy Congregation, caring about the well-being of one another and creating a space for God's Holy Presence in their midst.

NASO
Trusting Relationships

A story is told of two boys camping in the woods who saw a big, hungry grizzly bear ready to charge. They were both terrified. One of the boys sat down and quickly took his running shoes out of his knapsack and began to put them on. His friend said to him, "Are you crazy? It doesn't matter what shoes you wear, you can never outrun a grizzly bear." The other camper responded, "That's true, but all I have to do is outrun you."

So often, in the area of human relations, we live in this fashion. There is constant competition, lack of concern for our fellow human beings, and, even in the relationships that are the most important to us, an insufficient amount of trust. We end up being much more concerned about our own welfare than about attempting to nurture the bonds of friendship and love that join one person to another.

In *parashat Naso*, we read one of the most troubling laws of the Torah, the law of the *Sotah*, the suspected rebellious woman: "If any man's wife has gone astray and broken faith with him in that a man has had carnal relations with her unbeknown to her husband" (Numbers 5:12–13), and the husband has a fit of jealousy and suspects his wife of adultery, he should bring her to the priest and have her stand before the Lord.

The text then describes the only example in the Torah of trial by ordeal, a practice that existed well nigh into the Middle Ages in Europe. Through this ordeal, the woman's guilt or innocence would be proven. By the time of the Mishnah and Talmud, the Rabbis so restricted the possible occurrence of this situation that it was deemed impossible for it to occur. In fact, after the destruction of the Second Temple, Rabban Yoḥanan ben Zakkai abolished it altogether (*M. Sotah* 9:9).

It is a sad situation when two people in a marital relationship are brought to this stage, where the husband suspects the wife of infidelity, and the only way to prove innocence or guilt is for the woman to undergo this terrible ordeal. One wonders what happened to their union of love and respect for each other.

The law of the *Sotah* implies that fidelity is an essential element in marriage, jealousy is a legitimate sentiment, and trust is the foundation of the marital covenant. As in all situations involving private or public trust, the partners must not only be faithful but also appear to be worthy of confidence.

By the time the ordeal takes place, the marriage has already been in serious trouble. The ceremony affords the woman the opportunity of vindicating herself. If she is not guilty, the Midrash (*Sifrei Numbers* 19) informs us she will be recompensed for her ordeal: "God will ultimately compensate her for her disgrace. If she was barren, she is remembered with the gift of a child; if she bore with pain, she will bear with ease; if she had ugly children, she will give birth to fair ones."

More than anything else, the element of trust has been lost in the marital relationship. In every human undertaking, trust must be a basic building block. Building trust is not easy; destroying it is quite simple.

Many of us have participated in an exercise called a "trust walk" in which you literally put your life in the hands of another. Closing your eyes, you give another person your hand and allow him to lead you about. At first, you are reticent and fearful, lest this person cause you to fall. After a few moments, you begin to relax as you put your trust in your leader.

I have always been amazed at the ability of children to implicitly trust their elders. Have you ever seen a child jump from a stage or the top of a high structure? He has no fear. For some reason, he knows that someone will be there to catch him. But as he grows into adulthood, he loses that sense of trust in others. How many of us, as adults, would be willing to perform the same stunts we did as children and feel confident enough to trust another person to catch us?

The concept of trust implies expectation. We feel confident that others won't act in ways that will hurt us or undermine something we care about. Life based on a network of mutual trust is fundamentally different from life based on mutual distrust and suspicion. If one has a hard time trusting others, one should focus on becoming trustworthy. If you trust yourself, you will trust others.

Meaningful human relationships are based upon feelings of mutual trust. Whether the relationship is between husband and wife, parent and child, teacher and student, or friend and friend, both individuals must be worthy of trust and willing to place their lives in the hands of another. This is not easy. We are afraid, lest we get hurt. We are reticent, lest we are rejected. We are cautious, lest our feelings are not reciprocated. But without being able to trust one another, we are alone, isolated, and cut off from meaningful relationships. Every individual needs at least one person in whom he or she can place unlimited trust and know that his or her confidence is reciprocated.

To me, the tragedy of the *Sotah* is not the ordeal itself. It is the fact that a human relationship has degenerated to the point where the ordeal is deemed necessary. The element of trust in the union has been destroyed. It is not surprising to me that, since the days of Rabban Yohanan ben Zakkai, divorce became customary in cases of proven faithlessness. Trust in another human being is the cornerstone of the marital covenant. Without it, there is no way the relationship can succeed.

May we be fortunate to merit the trust of another human being and allow ourselves the possibility of building meaningful relationships by extending that trust to others.

NASO
Lessons from the Priestly Blessings

What are the most oft-repeated Biblical verses recited today? They are found in *parashat Naso* and are known as the Priestly Blessings, *Birkat Kohanim*: "The Lord bless and protect you! The Lord deal kindly and graciously with you! The Lord bestow His favor upon you and grant you peace!" (Numbers 6:24–26).

These beautiful verses are not only recited by the *ḥazzan* as the *Amidah* is repeated; they have become the traditional mode for the blessing of children on *erev* Shabbat, are offered at the *bedeken* before a wedding, are often recited under the *ḥuppah*, and are frequently quoted in benedictions.

In ancient times, only the *kohen* recited blessings on behalf of the community of Israel. The people would gather, and the *kohanim* would implore God to extend blessings upon the people. The Torah tells us that Aaron, the *kohen gadol*, was told, "Thus shall you bless the people of Israel" (Numbers 6:23). From this simple phrase, the Rabbis of the Talmud deduced several important principles concerning the posture and procedure of the *kohen* while conveying the blessing.

In *Numbers Rabbah* 11:4, we are told that the *kohen* must bless the people "while standing," and with "uplifted hands and outstretched arms." If you examine the archeological reliefs that have been unearthed throughout the ancient Near East, you will find that when the ancients wished to portray the idea of prayer, they pictured an individual with uplifted hands. The Israelite *kohen* was to follow this stance as he prayed on behalf of the community.

The *midrash* also tells us that the *kohanim* had to stand "face to face" with the Israelites when they offered the benedictions, "as a person talks to his friend," and it was, therefore, permissible to stand with their backs directed toward the east and the Holy of Holies.

In true dialogue, as described by Martin Buber, people must face each other, not only to hear the words of their counterpart, but also to understand the message of their eyes and the responses of their facial muscles. Communication skills involve active listening, intently paying attention to the other person. Unfortunately, the art of personal communication is becoming a lost art. With social media, face-to-face conversations with others are becoming less and less frequent.

Today, we face machines almost as much as we face people. You can do your banking by means of an automatic teller. You can do your shopping online. Computers, with all their advantages, create a society in which we don't need communication skills; we simply have to learn the functions of the computer to solve all our problems.

In my freshman year in college, we were required to take introductory humanities courses. Since so many people registered, courses were simulcast in different lecture halls or videotaped and shown to the students. All personal contact was absent and, I must admit, very little learning took place.

The *kohanim* were told to stand "face to face" with the people so that personal contact could ensue. For any meaningful relationship to succeed, this is a must.

Another stipulation concerns the Priestly Blessing. It must be spoken "in the holy tongue," in Hebrew. The Hebrew language is the soul of our people. It is the idiom of the Bible, the *siddur*, and the major texts of our tradition. With the rebirth of the State of Israel and the pioneering work of Eliezer ben Yehuda, Hebrew has become a living language and is not simply relegated to sacred texts and library bookshelves.

It is essential today, I think, for each Jew to possess the basic foundations of the Hebrew language. It is one of the binding ties that link Jews throughout the world. I recall my visit to the Soviet Union in 1983. On my first day in Moscow, I met Ari Volvosky who had traveled from Gorky especially for this encounter. There we were, two Jews from different parts of the globe. His English was not that good, my Russian even poorer. When he asked me whether I could speak Hebrew and I replied in the affirmative, all the barriers between us broke down. For the next three hours, in an apartment, on the street, on the bus, we spoke Hebrew; two Jews were brought together by "the holy tongue." It is for that reason that we concentrate on Hebrew in Jewish education. It is the key to unlocking our traditional texts and creating bonds with other Jews.

In 1845, Zechariah Frankel left the Reform Rabbinical Conference in Frankfurt because the reformers wanted to do away with the Hebrew language in synagogue services. He and others who followed him established the Positive-Historical School of Judaism, which was the forerunner of what we today call Conservative Judaism. The pamphlet *Emet Ve-Emunah: Statement of Principles of Conservative Judaism* states: "We pray in Hebrew to preserve all the original nuances of meaning. Hebrew has always been the primary language of Jewish worship *leshon ha-kodesh* (the holy tongue). As a result, through Hebrew prayer, we link ourselves to Jews praying in all times and places."

The Priestly Blessing is a meaningful and beautiful prayer, and we can learn valuable lessons from the Rabbinic commentaries concerning the actual procedures for its recitation. We must remember that our world is populated by human beings, not by computer chips. It is our task to encounter our fellow human beings "face to face" and establish meaningful moments of human communication. We are also taught that, as Jews, we must concentrate some of our efforts on mastering "the holy tongue," the language of our past and also of our future.

It is worthwhile to take to heart the beautiful content of the blessings as well as the procedures that surround their recitation as a lesson for our generation.

BE-HA'ALOTEKHA
Roses and Thorns

There once lived a monk who took upon himself vows of fasting and penance. He was allowed to speak two words every five years. After the first five years passed in the monastery, his words were "terrible food." Another five years passed and again he was permitted to talk. "Hard bed," he uttered. Another five years went by. His words, this time, were "miss television." When the next five years were due to end, he went to the office of the head of the monastery and said, "going home." "No wonder," replied his superior, "all you do is complain."

If you follow *parashat Be-ha'alotekha*, you might have the same impression of the Children of Israel. All they do is complain to Moses of their plight; never are they satisfied. They complain about the food, the water, Moses' leadership, God's commandments, and the dangers of the Promised Land. You name it—they had critical comments about it. The generation that had experienced God's presence at Sinai, had been saved at the Sea of Reeds, and had seen the miracle of manna was never satisfied. We read: "The people took to complaining (*mitonenim*) bitterly before the Lord. The Lord heard and was incensed: a fire of the Lord broke out against them, ravaging the outskirts of the camp" (Numbers 11:1). The Torah does not recount for us the grievous sin in great detail. What had the Israelites done that would have provoked such anger? The commentators were puzzled as to the exact nature of the sin.

Nachmanides interprets the sin as one of complaint and dissatisfaction. Not only were the Israelites not thankful for the manifold gifts that they had received, but they vented their anger and frustration upon God and Moses. Moses, after all, was an easy target, and so they cast the blame upon their leader who had taken them out of Egypt. They projected their own frustrations and inadequacies upon another, and, instead of bearing their troubles in a spirit of faith, they blamed Moses and God for their troubles and tribulations.

Rabbi Samson Raphael Hirsch, in his Torah commentary, adds a most interesting insight. The Hebrew word *mitonen* has as its root *onen*, "one who is in mourning." He translates the phrase in this fashion: "But the people were as if in mourning over themselves." According to Hirsch, the people considered themselves as if they were already dead, and they mourned themselves. They felt isolated, besieged by problems, and they gave up all hope of redemption. It was as if they felt themselves buried alive in the midst of their journey. The fire that was recorded as devouring them might, therefore, be interpreted as an all-consuming inner fire that destroyed these individuals.

What then was their sin, and what was their grievous mistake? The Children of Israel expected life to be a bed of roses. They presumed that only good things would come their way, and when faced with challenges, they crumbled. They had to learn that life is a constant series of peaks and valleys. This is a familiar theme in the Israelite desert experience with its high point of revelation and low valleys of despair and hopelessness. While the Israelites had to face the difficulties of not having enough food to eat in the desert, they also experienced the saving miracles of manna and water flowing from the rock.

Life is a set of constant challenges for all of us. While it is easy to celebrate and enjoy the good times, it is a challenge to live through and overcome the difficult moments. One of the most wide-spread illnesses of modern society is depression. This all-consuming illness initially presents itself as sadness and dissatisfaction, but can lead to a dangerous step: an utter lack of hope, a ritual of self-mourning. It is difficult to climb out of that valley for one feels almost buried alive under the morass of life's difficulties and burdens. The Children of Israel expected life to be perfect, and when it was not, they lost all hope and consumed themselves as if they were afflicted with this terrible illness.

The challenge of life is to see oneself over the rough spots and to realize that all of us experience those difficult times. Joanne Greenberg's novel, *I Never Promised You A Rose Garden*, tells the story of Deborah, a mentally ill woman who had to be placed in a mental hospital. The book describes her agonizing story of recovery. Placing her faith in those who helped her, Deborah was able to travel on the torturous road to wellness. At one point, as she almost moved to her next plateau, she experienced a serious regression and angrily screamed at her doctors and nurses who told her that she would be well. Her doctor responded, "I never promised you a rose garden. I never promised you perfect justice … and I never promised you peace or happiness. My help is so that you can be free to fight for all of these things. The only reality I offer is challenge, and being well is being free to accept it or not at whatever level you are capable. I never promise lies, and the rose-garden world of perfection is a lie … and a bore, too!"

The Children of Israel expected life to be a rose garden, and they were not capable or willing to assume life's challenges and overcome its hardships. They gave up all hope and destroyed themselves. It is sad that the generation that had seen the great glory of God could not rise above the hardships in the desert. Hopefully, we can do better.

BE-HA'ALOTEKHA
No Whining

In the mid-1980s, there was a common joke concerning a new *oleh* to Israel who emigrated from what was then the Soviet Union. After years of hardship, both physical and spiritual, this individual came to the State of Israel and made it his home. A number of months later, he was approached by a television commentator who wanted to learn about this new chapter in his life.

The commentator asked him the following question: "How was your life in the country from which you came?" The new immigrant responded: "I could not complain." The reporter continued: "And how were your living quarters there?" He answered: "I couldn't complain." The reporter asked another question: "How was your standard of living?" "I couldn't complain," he responded. The reporter was baffled and looked straight into the eyes of this Jew and said: "If everything was so swell, why then did you come here?" "Oh," replied the new *oleh*, "Here, thank God, I can complain."

Members of a free society are allowed to complain about almost everything. When one lives in a totalitarian regime, complaints are not expressed in public. Any kind of complaint may bring physical punishment or worse. We complain a great deal about the freedom we have, the gifts that are ours, and the manner in which we live our lives. Sometimes those complaints are valid, but many times they simply show us to be disgruntled individuals who can't bear disappointments and frustrations.

Parashat Be-ha'alotekha details the desert journey of the Israelites. They had been rescued from the terrible bondage of Egypt, saved miraculously at the Sea of Reeds, and stood in awe at Mount Sinai. Now, they were on a road to the Land of Canaan. Yet: "The people took to complaining bitterly before the Lord" (Numbers 11:1). In Hebrew, the word translated as "complaining bitterly" is *ke-mitonenim*. The word has a *kaf* prefix, which is normally translated as "like" or "as." A more exact translation might be: "And the people were like murmurers speaking evil in the ears of the Lord." What could they possibly be complaining about?

The sixth-century commentator Rabbenu Baḥya suggests that the Israelites had an incorrect frame of mind. They were hurt and distressed as they traveled in the desert. They received magnificent gifts, and, yet, they were never grateful. They spent their time worrying about the future. No matter what they had seen and experienced, they would never be satisfied.

We all know that complaining is part of human nature. When we are dissatisfied or frustrated, our complaining becomes worse, and many times we reveal our anger and disappointment in an inappropriate manner. In his book, *The Ten Commandments of Character*, Rabbi Joseph Telushkin states: "If you ask people what they most want from others, they will usually answer 'good character.' … The knowledge that those with whom we interact are kind and honorable is the surest guarantee that our loved ones and we will be treated well. But if you ask people what they want most for themselves, they will answer, 'To be happy and successful.'"

"In short," Telushkin suggests, "the reason we want good character from others, and happiness and success for ourselves, is that in both cases we want what is best for us." Telushkin continues, "Being grateful is not only an important aspect of good character … but it is also a prerequisite for leading a happy life … At the very moment a grateful person is cultivating gratitude, she is also cultivating a sense of being loved … An ungrateful person displays not only a stingy disposition, but also shows how unworthy of love she feels. Ungrateful people can't imagine anybody doing something for them merely out of goodwill and kindness." According to Telushkin, being grateful is a prerequisite for happiness.

In her book, *Wouldn't Take Nothing for My Journey Now*, the award-winning American poet Maya Angelou wrote the following story:

> When my grandmother was raising me in Stamps, Arkansas, she had a particular routine when people who were known to be whiners entered her store. Whenever she saw a known complainer coming, she would call me

from whatever I was doing and say conspiratorially, "Sister, come inside. Come." Of course I would obey.

My grandmother would ask the customer, "How are you doing today, Brother Thomas?" And the person would reply, "Not so good." There would be a distinct whine in the voice. "Not so good today, Sister Henderson. You see, it's this summer. It's this summer heat. I just hate it. Oh, I hate it so much. It just frazzles me up and frazzles me down. I just hate the heat. It's almost killing me." Then my grandmother would stand stoically, her arms folded, and mumble, "Uh-huh, uh-huh." And she would cut her eyes at me to make certain that I had heard the lamentation.

At another time a whiner would mewl, "I hate plowing. That packed-down dirt ain't got no reasoning, and mules ain't got good sense. ... Sure ain't. It's killing me. I can't ever seem to get done. My feet and my hands stay sore, and I get dirt in my eyes and up my nose. I just can't stand it." And my grandmother, again stoically with her arms folded, would say, "Uh-huh, uh-huh," and then look at me and nod.

As soon as the complainer was out of the store, my grandmother would call me to stand in front of her. And then she would say the same thing she had said at least a thousand times, it seemed to me. "Sister, did you hear what Brother So-and-So or Sister Much to Do complained about? You heard that?" And I would nod. Mamma would continue, "Sister, there are people who went to sleep all over the world last night, poor and rich and white and black, but they will never wake again. Sister, those who expected to rise did not, their beds became their cooling boards, and their blankets became their winding sheets. And those dead folks would give anything, anything at all for just five minutes of this weather or ten minutes of that plowing that person was grumbling about. So you watch yourself about complaining, Sister. What you're supposed to do when you don't like a thing is change it. If you can't change it, change the way you think about it. Don't complain."

The Israelites could have used the lesson that Maya Angelou's grandmother taught her. No matter what the Israelites saw around them, they complained, they were never satisfied, they were disgruntled, they were never contented with their lot, and, therefore, they were never happy.

Let us be contented with our lot. By simply giving up complaining and whining, we will become happy and satisfied human beings. As *Pirkei Avot* 4:1 teaches us, "Who is rich? One who is happy with his portion."

SHELAḤ-LEKHA
Being Honest to Oneself and Others

A newspaperman once asked Sam Rayburn, the former speaker of the House: "Mr. Speaker, you see at least one hundred people per day. You tell each one 'yes' or 'no.' You never seem to take notes on what you have told them, but I have never heard of your forgetting anything you have promised them. What is your secret?" Rayburn replied, "If you tell the truth the first time, you don't have to remember."

For most of us, telling the truth can be a rather interesting phenomenon. We are never quite sure how much of the truth to tell, to whom we should speak, and under what circumstances we are permitted to keep some of the truth from coming out into the open. Truth, more often than not, falls into the realm of perception.

If nothing else, *parashat Shelaḥ-Lekha* teaches us that truth can easily be found in the eye of the beholder. The *parashah* describes how Moses dispatched twelve scouts to survey the land of Canaan. They return with identical reports concerning the beauty of the land: "We came to the land you sent us to; it does indeed flow with milk and honey" (Numbers 13:27). All the scouts agree on the objective data. But the interpretation of the data brings disagreement. The majority, ten of the scouts, report that they would not be successful in their attempt to conquer the inhabitants. But Caleb and Joshua disagree: "Let us by all means go up, and we shall gain possession of it, for we shall surely overcome it" (Numbers 13:30). All see the same facts and, yet, come to different conclusions. If the majority report is correct, then Caleb and Joshua are mistaken; if the latter are right, then the former are wrong.

So often, the truth is hard to find, difficult to discover, and almost impossible to evaluate. Rabbi Louis Jacobs points out that when we find praises of truth in the Biblical texts, these often refer to three kinds of truthfulness: truthfulness to God, to one's fellow, and to oneself.

How, we might ask, can we not be truthful to God? After all, can we hide anything from the Creator of the universe? Is it possible for us to cover up factual data from God's all-knowing powers? Maimonides suggested an interesting observation about the relationship between religion and inner truth. A scriptural injunction states that a good animal set aside for sacrifice must not be exchanged for one of inferior quality. Conversely, an inferior one cannot be exchanged for one of superior quality (Leviticus 27:9–10). The Rambam suggests that being truthful to God means that we must give the best we can offer.

A story is told of a wealthy man on board a ship that was besieged by a violent storm. The man began to pray to God: "Oh Lord, if I survive this voyage, then I shall give all my wealth to charity." The storm soon abated. The man then had second thoughts. "Perhaps," he said to himself, "I shall only give away one-half of what I own." Immediately the storm began anew. He looked up to the heavens and declared, "O Lord, can't you tell I was only fooling?" Being truthful to God means establishing high ideals and living by them.

The second aspect of truthfulness is integrity in one's dealings with others. The Torah is very strict in its legislation, informing us of the need to be truthful and just in all our relationships and our business dealings: "You must have completely honest weights and completely honest measures" (Deuteronomy 25:15). Ethical behavior is the rule in all our business and commercial endeavors as well as in our relationships with others.

The words we utter must be truthful, and we should be loyal to our word. A story is told about a man who married a woman because he was promised a dowry of $25,000 by her father. After the wedding, the father-in-law took his new son-in-law aside and gave him the check. "Son, now that you are part of the family, I want you to know that we keep no secrets from one another. We always tell the truth. The check I just gave you, it's no good. It isn't worth the paper it is written on."

Being truthful to one's fellow dictates honesty and absolute integrity in all matters: in words, in thoughts, and in actions.

The third aspect of truthfulness is being true to oneself. Too often, we are prone to rationalize our failings and find excuses for not being able to achieve personal goals of success.

A Peanuts cartoon strip shows Peppermint Patty calling Charlie Brown on the telephone. "Guess what, Chuck," she said. "Today was the first day of school, and I got sent to the principal's office. It was your fault, Chuck." "My fault?" he responded. "How could it be my fault? Why do you always say everything is my fault?" "You're my friend, aren't you, Chuck? You should have been a better influence on me."

Being truthful to oneself suggests the need to admit personal failures and mistakes. Scapegoating may bring a temporary sense of relief, but it won't do anything for ultimate success. The Kotzker Rebbe believed that the commandment "Thou shalt not steal" should be interpreted as "Thou shalt not steal from thyself." And we remember the words of William Shakespeare who wrote in *Hamlet*, "This above all, to thine own self be true."

The Talmud in *Shabbat* 55a states: "The seal of the Holy One, blessed be He, is truth." In all matters, we must be truthful: to God, to our fellow human beings, and to ourselves.

Perhaps this was the grave sin of the scouts. Their data was correct, but they colored the truth in such a way that it was impossible for them to be objective. They were not truthful to God. They didn't give Him the best they had, and they were prepared to settle for much less. They were not truthful to their fellow Israelites. And they were not truthful to themselves. They convinced themselves that they were bound to fail and were unable to assume personal responsibility for their actions.

May we learn appropriate lessons from the consequences of their misdeeds.

SHELAḤ-LEKHA
The Sounds of Silence

Albert Einstein once gave his formula for success in life. "If A is success in life," he said, "then the formula is A=X+Y+Z. X is work; Y is play." "What is Z?" he was asked. "Z," he said, "is keeping your mouth shut." Sometimes, we could all afford to learn that formula for success.

Silence is an important commodity in our world, yet it is not often found. We live in a very noisy environment. Sometimes, we are forced to listen for the sounds of silence because noise is so much a part of our lives.

Parashat Shelaḥ-Lekha considers a special kind of silence. The story tells us that Moses sends out twelve scouts to view the Land of Canaan and bring back a report. Ten of the scouts relay an optimistic report that describes the beauty of the land; yet, they express pessimism about the Israelites' ability to successfully overcome the great obstacles that stand in their way. Two of the scouts, Caleb and Joshua, understand those obstacles but believe that victory is ultimately attainable.

The first text narrates the giving of the majority report. One can imagine that as the Children of Israel listened, there was great clamor, noise, and much shouting. The people began to get restless around Moses and wondered why God had rescued them from the safety and security of Egypt. At that moment of commotion, "Caleb hushed the people before Moses and said, 'Let us by all means go up, and we shall gain possession of it, for we shall surely overcome it'" (Numbers 13:30).

Amidst the shouting, Caleb had to get the attention of the Children of Israel. The Hebrew word *va-yahas* conveys this sense onomatopoetically, using the sound of the word. In a number of scribal editions, the word is written with a large *samekh* to make sure it is pronounced properly. Both the Hebrew word and the JPS English translation, "hush," are perfect. Before Caleb could give his report, he had to hush the people and gain their attention. As Rashi states: "He caused all of them to be silent."

Only then could Caleb proceed with an optimistic report of their future ascent to the Land of Canaan.

Silence has many purposes in the world. There is the silence of acceptance or resignation. In the Book of Leviticus, we read the story of the death of the sons of Aaron. The Torah records Aaron's reaction: "And Aaron was silent" (Leviticus 10:3). Aaron was dumbfounded in the face of this great tragedy. As difficult as this event was for him, he resigned himself to it and God's judgment. Often, this kind of silence is an appropriate reaction to tragedies both personal and communal. Silence in the face of tragedy is often our only response and generally signifies sad acceptance.

At other times, silence expresses a sense of indifference. This kind of silence may signify a sense of benign neglect or a sense of indifference and implied malice. This silence can bring disaster upon its recipients. The Jewish people have been on the receiving end of this type of indifferent silence too often in the course of our history. We still are angered by the indifference of the world as six million Jews were slaughtered in the Nazi onslaught. While, clearly, the perpetrators can never be forgiven, we have learned that many bystanders could have made a difference but, for reasons we will never understand, never lifted their voices or gave orders to rescue those in danger.

The silence of indifference can be deafening. Many times, it is injurious to individuals, to communities, and to nations. When presented with the Congressional Gold Medal in 1985, Elie Wiesel remarked: "What have I learned in the last forty years? Small things. I learned the perils of language and those of silence. I learned that in extreme situations when human lives and dignity are at stake, neutrality is a sin. It helps the killers, not the victims." He continued, "I have learned the danger of indifference, the crime of indifference. For the opposite of love, I have learned, is not hate but indifference."

Silence can lead to disaster. Yet, it can also be used to portray positive human feelings and emotions. Rabbi Abahu said in the name of Rabbi Yoḥanan: "When the Holy One, blessed be He, gave the Torah, no bird twittered, no fowl flew, no ox lowed, the *ophanim* did not fly, the *seraphim* did not utter the *Kedushah*, the sea did not roar, the creatures did not speak; the universe was silent and mute. And a voice came forth: 'I am the Lord your God.'" (*Exodus Rabbah* 29:9).

The Psalmist tells us, "To You silence is praise" (Psalms 65:2). Arriving at the highest understanding of the Divine, a person is reduced to stillness before the power of the Creator. Abraham Joshua Heschel taught: "In a sense, our liturgy is a higher form of silence. It is pervaded by an awed sense of the grandeur of God which resists description and surpasses all expression." This is the silence for which we crave, the silence of praise for God heralding a time of renewal and hope.

There are moments in our lives when silence is laudatory and when we must listen rather than talk. Shimon, the son of Rabban Gamliel, teaches in *Pirkei Avot* 1:17: "Throughout my life, I was raised among the scholars, and I discovered that there is nothing more becoming a person than silence." This silence can lead to a potential for reconciliation, rebirth, and renewal of spirit and faith. May we engage in this type of positive silence rather than in the silence of indifference.

KORAḤ
Defining Wickedness

Rasha ma hu omer? "What does the wicked one say?" This phrase is familiar to all of us from the Passover *Haggadah*. As we enumerate the narrative of the four sons and their possible roles in the retelling of the Exodus story, we recount the deficiencies of the wicked son.

But how does one define such an individual? Who is considered wicked, and under what conditions is he so described? *Parashat Koraḥ* tells the story of the rebellion against Moses' leadership. To the Rabbis of the Midrash, Koraḥ represented all that was evil in the community and all that could be wrong in human character. The Midrash amplifies the description of Koraḥ's life and activities and suggests that his mode of behavior aptly outlines the prototype of one who is viewed as *rasha*, "wicked."

Midrash Tanḥuma Koraḥ 8 states: "Our Rabbis taught: Four types of people are called wicked." The passage then proceeds to enumerate each category: "one who puts out his hand against his fellow to strike him, even though he has not actually struck him." The threat alone is enough to label this individual as a wicked person. We usually see the man of violence as a wicked person. Here, the Rabbis teach us that those who even threaten violence are in the same category whether or not they carry out their threat.

Is the parent or dominant spouse who continually threatens his or her weaker counterpart included in this category? Is the bully who threatens the weaker kids in the schoolyard such an example? What about one who threatens a community with possible violence? To create fear in the heart or mind of another is seen as a form of wickedness by the Rabbis. This kind of behavior cannot be countenanced.

A second category describing the *rasha*, according to the Midrash, is "one who borrows and does not repay." I am sure that banks, credit unions, and loan institutions would be sensitive to this particular definition. Clearly, the text does not refer to those who have unexpected financial reversals. But, then, we must ask, what do the Rabbis mean by this description?

This person is considered evil because he betrays the trust that another puts in him as he loans him money. The betrayal of trust is a significant misdeed. Trust is a most important human commodity. It is a basic building block of every human undertaking. You can trust others only if they can trust you, and that trust must be mutual. The Rabbis of the Midrash suggest that the *rasha* is one who cannot be trusted; he is one who betrays the trust of others.

The third category is an interesting one: "One who shows insolence and who is not ashamed in the presence of one greater than himself." Every family and every society must have a clear sense of authority. If that authority breaks down, chaos and anarchy may ensue. Jewish tradition has understood the lesson well. In *Pirkei Avot* 3:2, Rabbi Ḥananiah, the Deputy High Priest, taught: "Pray for the welfare of the Government, for if people did not fear it, they would swallow each other alive." Respect is critical for the ordered evolution and development of a society.

Respect for authority is also necessary in human relations. We are taught not only to honor our parents, but to respect our elders: "You shall rise before the aged and show deference to the old" (Leviticus 19:32). Even those who have forgotten most of what they learned about Jewish tradition in childhood have often incorporated this basic lesson into their daily lives. For example, on reaching the age of eighty-five, George Burns observed that he had reached a very comfortable stage of life. "I was always taught to respect my elders," he said, "I've now reached the age when I don't have anybody to respect."

According to the text, one who has no respect for his elders, for symbols of authority in the family, community, and society is to be considered a *rasha*, and his attitude will eventually lead to disaster.

The final category suggests that "one who is given to contentiousness" is to be considered a *rasha*. Discussion, even disagreement, is an important part of human experience. Continual discord, however, leads to conflict, disharmony, and may lead to enmity and hatred. While there is a way to express differing opinions and dissenting points of view, one can go too far and become unpopular. One who always disagrees for the sake of argument is viewed with a great deal of skepticism.

Pirkei Avot 5:19 instructs us that the controversy caused by Koraḥ and his associates was not for the sake of heaven or a noble purpose. Instead, the initiators of the rebellion were only interested in creating discord and in achieving greater honor for themselves. Therefore, these people are to be branded as wicked individuals.

The Midrash thus outlines four categories of wickedness. We learn not only from the positive attributes of Biblical characters but also from their failings. By extension, Koraḥ and his comrades represented all that was evil in society. They lacked respect for authority and trust in their fellow man. They based their leadership on discord and threats of punishment for those who did not agree with them. Their victory would have meant the breakdown of society, the destruction of community. It is our task to ensure the opposite by creating families and societies in which people base their common values on the high ideals of trust, respect, and the willingness to build together communities of friendship, love, and concern for one another.

KORAḤ
The Almond Tree

Parashat Koraḥ tells the story of the rebellions against the leadership of Moses, his brother Aaron the High Priest, and God. One would think that the miracle of the ground opening up and swallowing Koraḥ and his 250 followers, along with the plague with which the Israelites were afflicted, would have been enough for God to prove the point that only God will decide who will lead the Israelite people in the desert. However, there is more to the story.

God tells Moses to assemble twelve staffs, each representing one of the twelve tribes. He is to leave these in the Tent of Meeting: "The staff of the man whom I choose shall sprout" (Numbers 17:20). When the people returned to the Tent the next day, they found that one of the rods had blossomed: "The staff of Aaron of the house of Levi had sprouted: it had brought forth sprouts, produced blossoms, and borne almonds" (Numbers 17:23).

This must have been quite a scene to prove God's point. Rashi asks, "Why did almonds appear on Aaron's rod?" We, trained in a logical mode of thought, might respond with the proverbial Jewish answer, "Why not almonds?" But the commentators on the Biblical text, who were very deliberate about every detail written in the Torah, were not satisfied.

The almond as a metaphorical image occurs a number of times in Biblical literature. In the first chapter of Jeremiah, the prophet receives a call from God. Jeremiah is told that he has been chosen to bring the word of God to Jerusalem. Jeremiah sees a vision. "What do you see, Jeremiah?" God asks. "I see a branch of an almond tree" (Jeremiah 1:11). Jeremiah is then told of the doom that will befall Judea.

Why the almond? The almond tree blooms in Israel in January or February while the other fruit trees are still bare. It actually blossoms before it is covered with leaves. Thus, according to the commentators, the almond is used to signify the speedy fulfillment of the prophecy. Similarly, in this *parashah*, the almond quickly blossoms on Aaron's rod to convey God's support of his leadership.

The almond tree is also mentioned in the Book of Ecclesiastes (*Kohelet*). In a difficult passage, the cynical author of *Kohelet* instructs the people concerning the short cycle of human life: "When one is afraid of heights and there is terror in the road.— For the almond tree may blossom, the grasshopper be burdened, and the caper bush may bud again; but man sets out for his eternal abode, with mourners all around in the street" (Ecclesiastes 12:5).

Although the almond tree blossoms early, the fruit only ripens late in the summer. It is pink at its base when it blooms in January, but it becomes white at the tip within a month. Thus, the almond tree represents the white hair of the elderly, the aging process. *Kohelet* describes the loss of physical powers as one advances in age. In our text, the almond tree represents the sagacity and wisdom of lived experience represented by the leadership of Aaron.

This image of the almond tree can teach us much about life and its accompanying lessons. While the almond fruit takes only a month to go from pink to white, its blossoms start early. Like the exuberance of youth, ready to proceed forward with full speed ahead, it jumps into the world with great excitement. But over time, it matures and its color turns. Like the process of human life, the tree is transformed in various stages.

All of us are on a life's journey. We age each day. Our hair turns a little whiter, we may lose some of the exuberance and vitality of youth, yet, hopefully we recognize that the process is one of growth and realization.

Sherwin Nuland, in *How We Die: Reflections on Life's Final Chapter,* writes that knowing we will die "makes more precious each hour of those we have been given; it demands that life must be useful and rewarding." Each of us must contribute to an evolving process. While Nuland attempts to demythologize the process of dying for his readers, he also teaches much about living: "The greatest dignity to be found in death," he writes, "is the dignity of the life that preceded it ... Hope resides in the meaning of what our lives have been."

The almond tree produces two kinds of fruit. Some trees produce sweet nuts; others have bitter ones. Sweet nuts are considered a delicacy; bitter ones are not edible and are only used for oil. Even the fruit of the tree symbolizes the journey of life.

No person's life is without peaks and valleys. We may be on top of the world one day only to find that we cannot ride the crest of the wave all the time. Life's challenges and successes are part of the journey of life. Each of us may taste those sweet almonds and, unfortunately, may also endure the bitter taste of the other type of almonds during our lifetime.

From its early blossoms to the white tips of its fruit, the almond tree establishes the pattern of the journey of life. Bitter or sweet is the fruit. Life is not only lived in the actual tasting of the fruit, but in the flavor that remains in our mouths. Can we overcome the bitter moments and relish the sweet ones? Are we able to put it all in perspective as we proceed from the exuberance of youth to, we pray, the white hair of advanced years?

"Why the almonds?" Perhaps because they teach us much about life itself. Aaron's leadership was seen by God as blessed and praiseworthy. But the rebellious Israelites saw Aaron as a recipient of undeserved favoritism. Everything depends on one's vantage point and attitude. As we move through the journey of life, may we learn to savor the sweet fruits and endure the bitter ones, putting the entire range of experience in proper perspective.

ḤUKKAT
To Whom Could Moses Turn?

In *parashat Ḥukkat*, we read the enigmatic story of the sin of Moses. God tells Moses to speak to the rock so that water will flow from it and the people may drink. Moses, taking God's staff in front of the assembled people, raises his hand, strikes the rock twice with his staff, and water flows forth from the rock. God then says to Moses and Aaron: "Because you did not trust Me enough to affirm My sanctity in the sight of the Israelite people, therefore you shall not lead this congregation into the land that I have given them" (Numbers 20:12).

This is the entire episode. Aaron had already tried God's patience in the Golden Calf episode, but God does not explain Moses' grievous sin any further. For that reason, commentators throughout the centuries have struggled with this passage. What, indeed, was the terrible sin that Moses committed that denied him his most cherished goal? What was the heinous crime that merited so severe a punishment?

Many interpretations have been suggested. Rashi, following the opinion of many of the Rabbis, states that it was because Moses hit the rock rather than speaking to it. In this way, Rashi suggests, Moses showed his lack of faith and trust in God. But I am convinced that the reason is much deeper than that. Two of the most interesting comments on this passage come from sages of the Middle Ages. Maimonides hints that the fault was found in Moses' personality itself. He describes the sin of Moses as being that of anger. It was anger and frustration that forced Moses to lose control of his reasoned restraint. As the people assemble before him, Moses shouts, "Listen, you rebels" (Numbers 20:10). The intense anger within him spewed forth as he cursed the people and hit the rock.

The Ramban, Nachmanides, described the sin of Moses as fear. Immediately before this passage, the Israelites murmur against Moses and Aaron, forcing them to flee the anger of the people.

The sins of fear and anger are the reason that Moses was not permitted to lead his people into the Promised Land. What a sad picture of this great man!

We must ponder the question of whether it is really surprising that Moses possessed these deep-seated feelings of anger and fear. His task was not an easy one. He was forced to lead a people from slavery into freedom. Even after the great Exodus, the Israelites were dissatisfied with his leadership and constantly complained and murmured against him. Many times, Moses was forced to serve as an intermediary between God and the Israelites so that they might not be destroyed, yet, he was never appreciated, never even thanked. These feelings of frustration, anger, and anxiety boiled within him because he had no one with whom he could share his innermost feelings and darkest secrets. There was simply no one to trust as a true friend and confidant.

According to the Biblical record, Moses had very little family life to speak of. In the Book of Exodus, we are told that he married Zipporah and that she gave birth to two sons, Gershom and Eliezer. But never again are they mentioned. What was his relationship with his wife? Could he share his troubles, fears, and anxieties with her? Was she present for him? Did he have an unhappy home life? Zipporah is not mentioned in the narrative of the desert experience, leading us to ask questions about their relationship.

Did Moses have friends, people with whom he could honestly share his private concerns? It does not look that way. Even Aaron and Miriam, his brother and sister, with whom he shared some of the tasks of leadership, conspire at one point to hurt him. They gossip openly about his private life and mention the Cushite woman he had married (Numbers 12:1), but we know nothing about her. His siblings attempt to shame Moses in public for their own personal glory.

So, there was Moses alone at the top with no friends, no close family, no one whom he could trust. He was never part of a caring and sharing community. He was successful, but his body was rife with inner fears and doubts gnawing away at him. Is it any wonder that Moses finally explodes? He is simply sick and tired of carrying his burdens, unable to cope with the pressures of life and leadership. He can no longer keep the lid on his anger and is simply incapable of leading his people. A new leader must be found who can approach the tasks ahead, not with anger, but with a spirit of reconciliation.

Doubts, fears, and anxieties are part of all of us. There is no one alive who does not feel these emotions some time in life. They are a component of every human relationship: husband/wife, parent/child, teacher/student, and friend/neighbor.

We must build those types of relationships and communities in which we feel secure enough to share with others our fears and anxieties, our joys and sorrows. Every person carries burdens. We must learn to listen to our mates, our children, and our friends, and to be attentive to their concerns. We must organize those types of communities in which we can be appreciated and accepted for who we are. We must provide conditions in which people can experience trusting relationships that allow for personal growth. Only by sharing those concerns can we learn to care about others in our families and in our communities.

Moses exploded because he was not a member of that type of community. All we can do is feel sorry for him. How different his life might have been if he had the support of others with whom he could have shared his fears, anxieties, and worries.

May we create communities based on caring and mutual support where we can feel loved and accepted.

BALAK
Simply *Tzniut*

In *parashat Balak*, one of the most famous phrases in Biblical literature is voiced by Balaam, a non-Jew. He attempts to curse the Israelites as directed by Balak, the king of Moab. However, Balaam is unable to do so, and each time he sees the Israelite nation, he offers words of praise in their honor. One of his blessings has become one of the most beloved phrases in Jewish literature.

As he stands on a cliff and looks down upon the Israelite encampment, Balaam states: "How fair are your tents, O Jacob, your dwellings, O Israel" (Numbers 24:5). This phrase has become part of our liturgy. Upon entering the synagogue for daily prayer, we offer these words from the Bible in Numbers which express how Balaam's praise of the Israelite encampment represents synagogues and houses of study. As we enter the synagogue, we recognize how fortunate we are to enter a place of Jewish worship where we can gather for prayer and community.

The Rabbis suggest an interesting spin on this verse, "As Balaam looked up and saw Israel encamped tribe by tribe" (Numbers 24:2). Rashi, quoting the Talmud (*Baba Batra* 60a), explains that Balaam noticed something unusual in the Israelite encampment: "He saw that the doors of their tents did not exactly face one another so that one could not peer into the other's tent."

Balaam recognized that the Israelites were concerned about each other's privacy. They made sure that the opening of each tent did not face the opening of another. They were not concerned about what was going on in the homes of their neighbors; their focus was on what was occurring in their own homes. Thus, their encampment demonstrated a sense of modesty and privacy. The manner in which they lived showed that they were concerned not merely for their own welfare but for the welfare of their neighbors as well.

This presents a valuable lesson for architects. Individuals who live in tall apartment buildings that face other buildings know that they have to be careful to close their curtains lest someone see directly into their homes. Balaam's words can serve as a reminder that buildings should be constructed to allow private access and respect for neighbors' modesty.

But Balaam's comment can be taken even further. The Jewish concept of *tzniut*, modesty or privacy, is present not merely in the way buildings are constructed, but in dress, language, and behavior. We are supposed to dress appropriately, understanding that the way we present ourselves tells a great deal about us. American society has little concern for modesty in dress. Instead, our public advertising seems to suggest that modesty is old-fashioned and should be relegated to the past. Only deeply religious societies that seem to be out of touch with the modern world are expected to live up to that ideal.

There is also a great deal of immodesty with regard to language. As children, we are taught of the importance of choosing our words appropriately and speaking properly to others. But when we consider the modern media in America, it is apparent that this lesson needs to be learned in adult society as well. Immodest and inappropriate language has become normalized. Newspapers, magazines, television, radio, and the Internet have produced a society in which gossip has become a normal course of life. Everyone seems to be interested in the lurid details of the lives of public individuals, and very little is left out of the public arena. In Jewish law, this is considered inappropriate as everyone deserves a sense of privacy. As the Talmud states: "Why is gossip like a three-pronged tongue? Because it lulls three people at once: the person who says it, the person who listens to it, and the person about whom it is said" (*Arakhin* 15b).

A young minister complained to one of his older colleagues that his sermons did not seem to accomplish much. He had been preaching to his congregation for a number of years, and the conduct of his congregants did not change. His senior colleague replied, "If during the time of your preaching you have prevented your congregation from indulging in gossip and slanderous remarks, you have already accomplished a great deal."

We have a tendency to be immodest in our language, and when we talk about another individual, we may be defaming his or her reputation in a manner that is irreversible. Respect for others is a key Jewish value.

Tzniut is not merely a mode of conduct reserved for the ultra-religious; it is incumbent upon us all in dress, language, and behavior. It is imperative that we uphold these standards and teach the next generation the importance of speaking properly, respecting others, and appreciating the privacy of our neighbors.

Balaam, in examining the Israelite camp, was so inspired by their sense of respect that he uttered the words that have become part of our daily worship. May we also be able to say: "How fair are your tents, O Jacob, your dwellings, O Israel," and demonstrate respect and modesty in our homes, our synagogues, and in the course of our daily lives.

PINḤAS
Teaching by Example

In *parashat Ḥukkat* we read about Moses' transgression, and in *parashat Pinḥas* we learn about the consequences. God had told Moses to speak to the rock and bring forth water, but Moses did not do as he was commanded. Instead, he hit the rock twice. At that point, God told him that since he did not listen to God's word, he would be punished and would not enter the Promised Land.

It must have entered Moses' mind that perhaps God would forgive him. After all, look how many chances God had given the Children of Israel. They had sinned over and over again. After the episodes of the Golden Calf, the scouts, and Koraḥ, God gave many of the people a second or third chance. Surely, their sins were more grievous than that of Moses. But in *parashat Pinḥas*, Moses is told to ascend Mount Abarim where God reiterates the judgment. Moses will not be given a second chance. God expects more from a leader than from the common Israelite.

According to the Midrash, after the daughters of Zelopheḥad were granted their father's inheritance, Moses petitioned God: "The time is opportune for me to demand my own needs. If daughters inherit, it is surely right that my sons should inherit my glory." God then told Moses that was not to be. Joshua would be the one to inherit the mantle of leadership "seeing that he has served you with all his might, he is worthy to serve Israel" (*Numbers Rabbah* 21:14). Even this secondary wish of Moses was not to be granted. His sons played no role in the journey to the Promised Land. What could Moses do? He could reject God's wishes or accede to His request. Moses, being the good servant, listens to God and asks Him to give the people a worthy leader, a person of strength, courage, and spirit. Joshua is to be that person.

How would Moses prepare Joshua for this moment? Had he trained him properly for this role? The Torah does not inform us of Joshua's training. However, it does infer that since Joshua accompanied Moses in the desert and observed his daily activities, he learned the responsibilities of leadership from his master. It was Joshua who went up Mount Sinai together with Moses. It was Joshua who came down the mountain with Moses and was the first to hear that something was awry in the encampment. It was Joshua who fought the Amalekites at the behest of and under the direction of Moses. And it was Joshua who was jealous of Moses' leadership when Eldad and Medad continued to prophesy after the spirit of God had left the seventy elders.

We know very little about the words that were exchanged between the two concerning leadership and responsibility. Yet, Moses must have been a good teacher, for Joshua was an exemplary student and made a great leader of the Israelite nation. Moses' concept of teaching was to set an example for others. He taught by deed, not by word. This type of leadership sets a pattern for a student who is willing to learn from a master. Moses was such a teacher, and Joshua, a prized student.

Teachers—and all adults are teachers—have the responsibility to be appropriate models to young people. A study by the United States Bureau of Education suggests that to be a successful teacher, a thorough knowledge of the subject matter is necessary but insufficient. An excellent teacher is characterized by either an intuitive or a trained understanding of human beings and an interest in their welfare. The subject matter is merely a tool for a more all-encompassing goal. Teaching may be defined as caring and leadership by example.

I. L. Peretz's well-known short story, "If Not Higher," teaches the lesson well. Peretz writes of a rebbe who never recited the penitential prayers with his followers. One day, a critic of the rebbe decried the apostasy of this great teacher. His followers demurred and were certain of the rebbe's good deeds. Then, early one morning, the critic followed the rebbe and watched him dress like a peasant, go out into the words, and chop wood for an old woman who needed it for heating and cooking. The critic soon became a great follower of the rebbe. Without hearing one word of the rebbe's speeches or lessons, he learned of the rebbe's righteousness and compassion by observing his deeds.

Moses understood well that leaders teach by example. Statistically, no army has suffered more losses of its high-ranking officers than the Israel Defense Forces. The model of the IDF is based on the notion of *aḥarai*, "after me." Commanders lead their soldiers into battle; they demonstrate bravery, courage, and commitment by setting an example for their troops.

If we truly want to train others, especially those of the younger generation, we must learn to teach by example, to pattern our lives so that others can look to us and gain from observing our everyday activities. By demonstrating kindness and caring, we teach more than all the words we may utter. A number of years ago, the American Cancer Society had a wonderful motto: "Children learn from people they respect; what do they learn from you?"

Moses was the kind of teacher who taught by deed and not by word. Joshua followed his mentor, observed him, and was capable of taking on that role after the death of Moses. May we raise a generation that can learn by our example and then take our place to carry on our work.

PINḤAS
The Wonder of Creation

What is the world's greatest miracle? To my mind, it is the creation of the human being. According to the Mishnah in *Sanhedrin* 4:5, an individual who is to give testimony in a capital case is reminded of the severity of punishment that could be carried out based on his testimony. Thus, he is warned to be cognizant of the ramifications of his words: "Therefore, was a single being created to teach you that if anyone destroys a single soul (of Israel), Scripture charges him as though he had destroyed a whole world, and whosoever rescues a single soul (of Israel), Scripture credits him as if he had saved a whole world … To teach you the greatness of the Holy One, blessed be He, for a man stamps many coins with one die and they are all alike one with the other, but the King of Kings, the Holy One, blessed be He, has stamped all mankind with the die of the first man and yet not one of them is like his fellow. Therefore everyone is duty-bound to say, 'For my sake was the universe created.'"

While we have learned a great deal about the human body, the fact that we understand a little more about the composition of DNA and how the body works does not in any way decrease our sense of wonder at the creation of human life and the distinct nature of each person.

Each morning, in private prayers before we begin the *Shaḥarit* service or after relieving ourselves, we recite: "Praised are you, Lord our God, King of the universe who with wisdom fashioned the human body, creating openings, arteries, glands and organs, marvelous in structure, intricate in design. Should but one of them, by being blocked or opened, fail to function, it would be impossible to exist. Praised are You, Lord, healer of all flesh who sustains our bodies in wondrous ways."

Too often, it is only when our bodies are in travail that we recognize the importance of these words. Jewish tradition teaches that creation is renewed each day, and that we, the crown of creation, are part of that endeavor.

In *parashat Pinḥas,* Moses is told to ascend the Mountain of Abarim and behold the land that God has given to the Children of Israel. Though he will not be privileged to enter the land because "in the wilderness of Zin, when the community was contentious, you disobeyed My command to uphold My sanctity in their sight by means of the water" (Numbers 27:14), Moses does not offer a plea to God. Rather, he asks that a leader be appointed to follow in his stead: "Moses spoke unto the Lord saying, 'Let the Lord, Source of the breath of all flesh, appoint someone over the community who shall go out before them and come in before them, and who shall take them out and bring them in'" (Numbers 15–17).

In *Midrash Tanḥuma Pinḥas* 10, the Rabbis comment on this particular verse and offer an interesting comment:

> If a man sees great multitudes of people he should say, "Blessed are you, O Lord our God, King of the universe, who knows their innermost secrets." For, as their faces are not like each other's, so are their temperaments not like each other's; every individual has a temperament of his own. In this strain it says, "He makes a weight for the spirit" (Job 28:25), implying that God does so for the spirit of each individual human being. There is proof that it is so from the request that Moses made of the Holy One, blessed be He, in the hour of his death. He said to him: "Sovereign of the universe, the mind of every individual is revealed and known unto you. The minds of your children are not like one another. Now that I am taking leave of them, appoint over them, I pray you, a leader who shall bear with each one of them as temperament requires; as may be inferred from the fact that it says 'Let the Lord, the God of the spirits (*Elohei Haruḥot*) of all flesh appoint'; it is not saying 'the spirit' but 'the spirits.'"

The *midrash* seems to be saying that, although there is a commonality among human beings, each of us is different. No two individuals have ever or will ever be created exactly alike. Each of us is endowed with a spirit that is separate and unique. Since Joshua was to be appointed to lead the people, Moses hoped that this new leader could recognize the individuality of each human being. The unique and precious soul of each individual must be treasured individually.

This is the true greatness of God. Though each human being, according to the Biblical text, is created in God's image, each of us is unique. Thus, we must learn to treat each person as an individual and precious soul. As the Mishnah in *Sanhedrin* states, the human being was created individually to recognize that each soul represents a complete universe. To diminish that soul is to diminish creation, and to enhance that soul is to enhance creation.

This is the ultimate religious lesson that informs all of scientific endeavor. We do not negate the findings of science; rather we applaud how science attempts to explain our world. At the same time, science does not negate the sense of wonder we feel for the magnificence of God's creation that is renewed each and every day.

MATTOT
Causeless Love

In *parashat Mattot*, the Children of Israel prepare to cross the Jordan River and conquer the Land of Canaan. However, the tribes of Reuven, Gad, and half of Menashe approach Moses and ask that they remain on the other side of the Jordan River. "It would be a favor to us … if this land were given to your servants as a holding; do not move us across the Jordan" (Numbers 32:5).

Moses is extremely upset by the request. He believes that these tribes demonstrate selfish disregard for Israel's unity, and he compares them with the scouts in chapters 13 and 14 of Numbers who undermined the unity of Israel and triggered Divine wrath and punishment. Moses asks, "Are your brothers to go to war while you stay here? Why will you turn the minds of the Israelites from crossing into the land that the Lord has given them?" (Numbers 32:6–7). Eventually, they work out a compromise in which those of fighting age will join the Israelites as they cross the Jordan to conquer the Land of Canaan, while their children and wives remain behind and wait for their return.

The unity of the Jewish people is an extremely important concept, and those who undermine it usually lead us to disastrous consequences. This *parashah* is always read around the time we commemorate Tisha B'Av, the saddest day on the Jewish calendar. We are taught that when the month of Av begins, we are to lessen our joy as we prepare to commemorate with fasting and mournful dirge the destruction of the Temples and other calamitous events that befell the Jewish people on this date (*M. Ta'anit* 4:6).

Rabbinic literature contains many stories about the legends of destruction. Why was it that the Temple, the House of God, and Jerusalem, the Holy City, were destroyed? *Gittin* 55b–56a in the Talmud states:

In the city of Jerusalem, there lived a man who had a friend named Kamtza. This same man had an enemy named Bar Kamtza. One day this man made a large feast, a feast that was attended by all the people in the city. Among the guests there were important people. The man wanted his friend Kamtza to attend the feast, so he sent the beadle to invite him.

But the beadle made a mistake and invited Bar Kamtza, the enemy of the man, to the feast. Bar Kamtza was quite surprised when he heard that his enemy had invited him. He thought, "Maybe the man wants to make peace with me," and so Bar Kamtza came to the feast. When the host saw him he got angry and shouted, "Why are you in this house? I don't want you in this house. Leave!"

But Bar Kamtza did not want to leave, and pleaded, "Please don't chase me from your house. I'll pay you the price of the meal, just please don't force me to leave." The host, however, shouted angrily, "Leave my house!" All the other guests heard the argument but remained silent. Bar Kamtza looked around the room and yelled, "I'll bet you all want me to leave the house. You're enjoying seeing me suffer. I won't forget it!" And he then stormed out of the house.

Bar Kamtza then went to the Roman emperor and said, "Your Highness, the Jews are revolting against you." The emperor asked, "How can I be sure you are telling me the truth?" Bar Kamtza answered, "Send a sacrifice to the Temple. If they accept it, then they are not revolting, but if they refuse it, then they are indeed revolting." The emperor followed this suggestion and sent a sacrifice to the Temple. On the way, however, Bar Kamtza blemished the animal. When the *kohanim* saw the blemish, they refused to sacrifice the animal. The emperor, therefore, believing that the Jews were revolting, sent his army against Jerusalem.

The Rabbis felt that destroying Jewish unity undermined the Jewish people and led to the destruction of the Temple. In *Yoma* 9b, the Rabbis state: "Why was the First Temple destroyed? Because three evils were practiced in it: idolatry, immorality, and bloodshed ... But why was the Second Temple destroyed, when during the time it stood, people occupied themselves with Torah, with observance of precepts, and with the practice of charity? Because during the time it stood, hatred without rightful cause (*sinat ḥinam*) prevailed. This is to teach you that hatred without rightful cause is deemed as grave as all the three sins of idolatry, immorality, and bloodshed together."

History shows that *sinat ḥinam* destroyed Jerusalem and caused the exile of our people from the land. We need to be aware of this and serve the needs of our people by showing respect for every Jew. At times, it seems that we have not learned the lesson well, as we spread causeless hatred within our own people. We need to be mindful of the Rabbinic understanding of what caused the destruction of the Second Temple and ensure that we learn its lesson well. Jewish unity was essential for our people in ancient times and is essential today as well. The former Chief Rabbi of Palestine, Rabbi Abraham Isaac Kook, taught that what we need today is *ahavat ḥinam,* "causeless love." This will ensure the survival of our people.

Moses understood this lesson and attempted to teach it to the tribes of Reuven, Gad, and half of Menashe. They learned the lesson and followed through on their promises. The lessons of Tisha B'Av remind us that we must continue in the path of caring for the welfare of our people, working for their safety and security, and sharing our causeless love with all of them.

MASE'EI
The Responsibility of Leadership

In *parashat Mase'ei*, the Israelites are told to prepare six cities of refuge, three on each side of the Jordan River. In Biblical times, it was an accepted fact that if one person killed another, it was the responsibility of the deceased's nearest of kin to avenge the death of his family member. The *goel hadam*, the blood avenger, took matters into his own hands to mete out strict punishment upon the murderer.

Should a killing occur, the killer could flee to one of these cities to protect himself from the vengeance of the blood avenger. If, in a proper court of justice, the killing was deemed premeditated, then the killer would be punished. However, if the killing was deemed accidental, the individual would be safe from the justice of the blood avenger as long as he remained within the confines of the city. But that did not mean it was a vacation resort. Instead, the Mishnah in *Makko*t 2:1 refers to it as *galut* (exile). The person is not allowed to leave the city on penalty of death, for the blood avenger could then take matters into his own hands. "And there he shall remain until the death of the High Priest who was anointed with the sacred oil" (Numbers 35:25).

What is it about the death of the High Priest that allows the individual to go free? The Torah itself does not supply us with an answer, and we turn to commentaries to help us understand the circumstances.

Among the most interesting explanations offered is that of Rashi who suggests that it was not the death of the High Priest that was significant, but his life. Following the Talmud in *Makkot* 11b, Rashi suggests that the High Priest bears some responsibility for his own death and for the eventuality of the killer fleeing to the city of refuge: "The High Priest should have prayed that this horrible event should not have occurred during his tenure." In other words, it was the High Priest's task to set the moral tone for the community and, thus, he bore some responsibility for what occurred on his watch.

Rashi understands the importance of the burdens of leadership and the immense responsibilities that accompany it. A leader is responsible for the welfare of his community whether he is in contact with every single citizen or not. Leaders must be held accountable for the actions of the community—this is what democracy is about. In democratic countries, as people proceed to elections, an incumbent is held responsible for his or her record. In totalitarian regimes, or in hereditary monarchies, the right to decide on a ruling authority is not given to the ordinary citizen. Instead, decisions are made for the people.

I would like to suggest that the principle of democracy could be taken even further. It is the responsibility of each person to care about others. Ultimately, we are all held accountable for the actions of society as a whole. Abraham Joshua Heschel taught that the opposite of good is not evil; the opposite of good is indifference.

This principle was operational during the Nuremberg trials. The Nazi war criminals were held responsible for their actions. It was not enough for them to say that they were just following orders. The entire society and each individual are to blame for the transgressions of the leaders of their regime.

If we understand this principle properly, then we recognize our own responsibility not to remain indifferent to those who need our assistance. The prophetic tradition instilled in the people of its time an understanding that ritual practice alone is not enough. It is the community's duty to clothe the naked, care for the disadvantaged, and shelter the homeless. If we live in a society in which we are indifferent to the needs of others, then we are personally to blame.

We are reminded of this truth over and over again in our ritual practices and life cycle events. As we sit down to the Passover Seder, we recite an invitation to anyone who is hungry to join us at our Seder. Before we have the privilege of eating our Passover meal, we have to ensure that others are cared for. When we recite the names of the ten plagues, we spill drops out of our full glasses of wine symbolizing the fact that we cannot rejoice over the downfall of our enemies. And at the moment of supreme joy for a bride and groom, we break a glass at the end of the wedding ceremony as a reminder that we cannot fully rejoice until all people live in harmony, peace, and fulfillment.

The High Priest, who in those days was an individual with immense influence, had the responsibility to set the proper tone for all members of society. If he did not, Rashi states, then the resulting punishment would ensue. The High Priest needed to ensure that murder did not occur in his society, that there was no reason for the institution of the avenger, and that all people should live in harmony. If he was unable to do this, he was not deserving of the responsibility of leadership and could not complete his tenure as High Priest, and the murderer would go free.

We must learn to care for all human beings and respond to the needs of all members of society. This teaching is at the heart of Jewish ethics and should serve as a guide for our communities and our leaders.

DEUTERONOMY
דברים
DEVARIM

DEVARIM
The Meaning of Tisha B'Av

Parashat Devarim is always read on the Shabbat preceding Tisha B'Av. The 9th of Av on the Jewish calendar is considered the black day of our tradition as we commemorate the destruction of the Temples in Jerusalem as well as other calamities that befell the Jewish people.

Since the rebirth of the State of Israel, many have questioned whether we should continue to observe Tisha B'Av. After all, we again have a Jewish commonwealth, we have returned to Jerusalem, and the dreams of the restoration of our land are coming to fruition. Does it make sense to continue the observance of a day that reminds us of the destruction and desolation of Jerusalem and, in particular, the Temple Mount? Is Tisha B'Av still relevant today for the modern Jew?

One of the great leaders of Modern Orthodoxy, Rabbi Joseph B. Soloveitchik, suggested that there are three reasons for the continued observance of this day of mourning.

His first reason is that Jews have a unique collective memory and awareness of time. We do not see ancient historical events as past occurrences. Instead, we relive them as contemporary experiences. What is Shabbat but a re-creation of God's seventh day of rest? What is Passover but a review of the events concerning the Exodus from Egypt? What is Sukkot but reliving our ancestors' experience in the desert as they traveled toward Canaan? Our Torah is not an ancient manuscript relegated to a library shelf; we reenact revelation each week as we read its lessons.

Isaac Bashevis Singer said that Jews suffer from many diseases, but amnesia is not one of them. Our memories affect our responses to contemporary events and situations. Without our memories, we would suffer from amnesia and lose track of who we are.

As individuals, we relive past events throughout the course of our lifetimes. As a people, we do very much the same. We recall both the good times and the bad times in our history and attempt not only to remember them but to learn from them as well. Soloveitchik suggests that Tisha B'Av is necessary because we need to relive the anguish that befell our people during those terrible days. As part of our collective memory, Tisha B'Av should motivate us to ensure that the destruction of Jerusalem never occurs again.

The second reason to continue the commemoration of Tisha B'Av is that the day represents more than simple mourning or even a recollection of mourning. What did Jews do during the Second Temple period? Was the 9th of Av observed during this period or not? According to a number of sources, it was. However, it must have posed a very strange paradox. How could the High Priest conduct the daily Temple service and then weep over the Temple's loss? Soloveitchik suggests that in its time, Tisha B'Av was not a day of mourning but a day of prayer. On Tisha B'Av, Jews prayed that such a calamity should not occur again.

Prayer is a significant part of our tradition. In our Shabbat morning liturgy, we recite the prayer for the State of Israel and the prayer for those who serve in the Israel Defense Forces. Those few moments unite us with the people in the State of Israel. Prayer is meant to lead to action, and, while it is hoped that the efficacy of prayer can stand on its own, we know that the act of reminding ourselves of the welfare of our brothers and sisters in Israel motivates us to work on their behalf.

The third reason mentioned by Soloveitchik concerns the Book of *Eikhah* (Lamentations) that we recite on Tisha B'Av. This text connects to a verse in our *parashah* which begins with the word *eikhah* and is translated: "How can I bear unaided the trouble of you" (Deuteronomy 1:12). The Book of *Eikhah* also begins with the word *eikhah* and the first verse is translated: "Alas! Lonely sits the city once great with people!" (Lamentations 1:1). The word *eikhah* is used to express the poet's incredulity regarding the tragedy that he is witnessing.

This leads to the question that Jews have asked throughout the ages. How is it that we have endured so much suffering, generation after generation? Why were the great centers of Jewish learning in France and

Germany destroyed by the Crusaders? How could the Inquisition have occurred, expelling Jews from Spain on this date in 1492? Why did our people endure the pogroms of 1648–49 under the leadership of the ruthless Bogdan Chmielnicki? On Tisha B'Av, we recall all of these events.

Tisha B'Av gives us cause to stop and ponder these questions. We have no answers to these calamities, to the Shoah, or to other terrible events in Jewish history. However, the day does force us to ask difficult questions and invites us to wonder at the remarkable survival of our people over the centuries.

Tisha B'Av reminds us that while the questions remain, we continue to be a proud and resourceful people. The Talmud assures us that "all who mourn the destruction of Jerusalem will merit seeing it in its joy" (*Ta'anit* 30b). In fact, our Sages tell us that even as we ponder these questions, we are to remember that the Messiah is to be born on Tisha B'Av (Jerusalem Talmud *Berakhot* 2:4), and this will ultimately lead to the redemption of our people.

I believe that Tisha B'Av is still relevant for our day, and it is important that we commemorate the tragedies of the past. Yet, even as we do so, we must commit ourselves to the ongoing restoration of our people in the Land of Israel, the reconstruction of the Holy City of Jerusalem, and the welfare of all of our brothers and sisters who live there.

May Tisha B'Av be transformed from a day of mourning to a day of rejoicing when the redemption of our people will occur and peace and security will come to Israel and to our brothers and sisters throughout the world.

DEVARIM
Constructive Criticism

The title of the fifth book of the Bible, the Book of Deuteronomy, is derived from the Greek term "Second Law" and follows the Rabbinic name for the book, *Mishneh Torah*. The Book of Deuteronomy is basically a review of the history of the Children of Israel as they journey from Egypt to the edge of the Jordan River where they hear the laws spoken by Moses before he is taken from this world by a kiss from God.

Moses wishes to spend his last few days with the people instructing them in the ways of God by suggesting that they follow the commandments. One might expect that Moses would offer words of encouragement and gently urge the people to do his bidding. Instead, he is very critical of the Israelites, recalling their misdeeds and telling them that if they do not obey God, they will be punished.

The Midrash (*Deuteronomy Rabbah* 1:4) immediately recognizes this fact: "It would have been more fitting for the criticisms and the warnings to have come from the mouth of Balaam and the blessings to come from Moses." Balaam, the prophet, was asked by Balak to curse the Israelites. Each time he saw the Israelites in their encampment, instead of cursing them, he blessed them. One would have thought that Moses, the great leader of the Israelite people, the one sent by God to redeem them from the Land of Egypt and to be the interlocutor for them at Mount Sinai, would have offered words of blessing before he left them on the edge of the Land of Canaan. Likewise, one would have expected that Balaam would have criticized and cursed the Israelite people as Balak had requested of him.

However, the Midrash responds to this puzzle as follows: If Balaam had criticized the people, the Israelites would have said, "We don't have to take these words seriously; after all, an enemy of ours is uttering them." And if Moses had blessed the people of Israel, the nations of the world would have stated, "How could you expect anything different from their leader and their admirer?"

The Midrash understands human psychology very well. When people criticize us, we want to know the source and context of the remark. If the criticism is voiced by an enemy, an adversary, or a competitor, we tend to discount it. However, if we are criticized by someone we respect and trust, we tend to take it more seriously.

Some of the greatest lessons that we learn in life are based on criticism that we hear from our loved ones, our friends, and respected teachers. The Torah states: "Reprove your kinsman" (Leviticus 19:17). We are instructed to reprove and offer positive criticism to people we care about. However, the Sages forbid carrying reproach to the point of causing embarrassment to another person. The obligation to reprove is limited to cases in which one has reason to believe the reproof will bring about a change in behavior. At the same time, the Torah hints that we should accept the criticism that is offered and take it seriously.

Very often we become defensive when others, especially those closest to us, offer criticism that they believe to be in our best interest. Frequently, it takes a great deal of courage for them to say it, and it often hurts them to share these criticisms with us.

This is best exemplified in the relationship between a parent and a child. In the normal course of events, a parent is called upon to discipline the child. Invariably, the child often feels that the parent is picking on him and that the criticism is unjust. The parent, on the other hand, believes that she has the best interests of the child at heart. Discipline is not easy for the parent, nor is it easily accepted by the child. Hopefully, because of the parent's love and role as advisor and counselor, the discipline will be appropriate and, over a period of time, the child will realize this as well. This can be a learning experience for the child if he or she recognizes that the parent is looking out for his or her best interests. At the same time, this confers responsibility upon the parent to act fairly and appropriately in all matters.

The fact that Balaam blessed the people allowed his words to be taken seriously. His words carried even greater weight as he was not an admirer of the Israelite people and would not normally offer these words of praise. If we receive words of admiration from a worthy adversary, a challenger, or a competitor, we feel that these words are offered with a great deal of respect. If compliments come from a person who may not necessarily be in our corner, we accept them with a great deal of gratitude. On the other hand, if Moses was offering reproof to the Children of Israel, his words would more than likely be taken very seriously by his listeners.

The Midrash teaches us that we should offer positive criticism to our friends and convey respect and admiration to our adversaries. This is what the Torah teaches when it reminds us that each of us is created in the image of God, that we should reprove our neighbor, and at the same time, love our neighbors as ourselves (Leviticus 19:17–18). It is not an easy task to live up to all of these responsibilities. Yet, doing so makes our lives more worthwhile and the world a better place in which to live.

VA-ETHANNAN
Re-experiencing Jewish History

The generation that left Egypt was radically changed by the experience of Sinai and should have been expected to follow the words of the covenant. Though we know there were serious lapses in the Israelites' behavior, they had lived through a number of significant experiences that were part of the fabric of their lives. But what about their descendants? How are the later generations supposed to relate to the covenant?

Moses expresses concern about this sense of continuity. He warns the people: "But take utmost care and watch yourselves scrupulously, so that you do not forget the things that you saw with your own eyes and so that they do not fade from your mind as long as you live. And make them known to your children and your children's children" (Deuteronomy 4:9).

Moses is addressing the second generation after the Exodus. They may not have witnessed the Exodus, the miracle at the Sea of Reeds, or the revelation at Sinai, but they had heard about these events directly from their parents. They could internalize the experiences and appreciate what their parents had been through. But what about future generations?

Moses is concerned with what will happen once the Israelites are established in their own land. He knows that they will be victorious in the Land of Canaan, but with stability, it will become difficult for the people to understand the difference between slavery and freedom, the sanctity of the covenant, and the special relationship that they are to have with the God of Israel. As they become further removed generationally from the actual events of the Biblical record, how will they internalize the experiences and the lessons of the preceding generations?

This challenge continues to be one of the major issues of Jewish life. As Jews have established a sense of security in the United States, we need to understand the nature of our communal and religious bonds.

Many young Jews growing up in this country do not have the personal experiences of witnessing vital Jewish communities whose level of knowledge, observance, and attachment to Judaism formed the warp and woof of the fabric of daily life. We have established countless committees to discuss issues of Jewish identity and continuity. Our religious organizations and our secular agencies have studied what brings Jews closer to the center of Jewish life, allowing them to create meaningful Jewish affiliations. Yet, we have learned from statistics and surveys that many American Jews no longer find Jewish life a necessary aspect of their daily existence.

Jewish memories alone will not guarantee a vibrant Jewish community. Moses tells those assembled before him that they must make their individual commitments to the covenant and recognize their responsibilities to educate future generations: "The Lord our God made a covenant with us at Ḥoreb. It was not with our fathers that the Lord made this covenant, but with us, the living, every one of us who is here today" (Deuteronomy 5:2–3).

In contemporary Jewish life, we must be sensitive to the fact that the youngest generation will not personally have experienced the two major events of modern Jewish history. For most Jews today, the Holocaust is history. They may hear stories from members of their families or other survivors; they may watch movies or television programs; they may even visit museums, but the event remains surrealistic and, in some cases, impossible to comprehend. It is imperative that we translate the events of the Holocaust for the young people of today. Our goal is not to frighten them with concerns of anti-Semitism or to create, as Salo Wittmayer Baron inveighed against in 1928, a "lachrymose theory" of Jewish history, but instead to make them realize that Jewish life was changed forever by the events in Europe during World War II. Thus, it is critical that survivors tell their stories and be involved in the education of future generations of leaders. It is important that our young people visit Holocaust museums and study the events of that period. And it can be a life-changing event for them to go on educational tours of destroyed Jewish communities to witness the places where the Holocaust actually occurred.

This same generation also does not know a world without the State of Israel. For 2,000 years, our people were bereft of a homeland. Those born today take it for granted that the State of Israel exists and cannot begin to imagine the unbelievable sacrifices that were necessary in order for the State to survive over the years. In order for them to appreciate this magnificent miracle of our day, it is imperative that our young people and their families travel to the State of Israel to see, experience, and learn of its great challenges and its magnificent promise. Statistics show that Israel educational and experiential programs immeasurably enhance the Jewish identity of our young people. It is sad that roughly only a third of American Jews have even visited the State of Israel. No wonder they cannot understand the attachment of our people to our ancient land and the need for all of us to support Israel and its people.

Moses understood that the generation that would become comfortable in the Land of Canaan might forget its past, since it had not personally witnessed or experienced the saving acts of God and the revelation at Sinai. If the parents who had been privy to these miracles could be led astray, how much more so could their children? Thus, as they begin their preparations to enter into the Land of Canaan, Moses warns them about the future. It remains the duty of every generation to teach those who follow the importance of standing once more at Sinai, accepting the covenant with God, and strengthening our commitment to our people's history and its future.

VA-ETHANNAN
Loving Your Fellow, Loving God

A ḥasid once asked a *tzaddik*, "Why is it customary to say *le-ḥayim* before reciting the benediction over wine? Is it not disrespectful to bless mortals before blessing the Immortal One?" The *tzaddik* responded, "The word *ve-ahavta*, you shall love, occurs three times in the Torah. It first occurs in the famous phrase, 'Love your neighbor as yourself' (Leviticus 19:18). The second time it occurs in the phrase, 'You shall love him [the stranger] as yourself' (Leviticus 19:34). It finally appears in *parashat Va-ethannan* (Deuteronomy 6:5): 'You shall love the Lord your God with all your heart and with all your soul and with all your might.'" The *tzaddik* continued, "Why is it that God is mentioned last? Because if you do not love people, you cannot love God."

This is a marvelous lesson for our world. You cannot love God without loving other human beings. You cannot show respect for the Divine Presence in this world unless and until you show respect for God's creations, for those created in God's image. The two of them are tied together and cannot be separated.

We often quote the phrase, "Love your neighbor as yourself." However, we rarely conclude the verse as it appears in chapter 19 in the Book of Leviticus, "I am the Lord." If you love your neighbor, another human being, and treat him or her with the utmost respect, admiration, and affection, then, and only then, do you demonstrate that God can be recognized as "I am the Lord." It is again important to look at the sequence: first the love of a fellow human being, then "I am the Lord."

This lesson is deeply relevant for our times. Though we have made great strides in medicine, science, technology, the humanities, and overall quality of life, we still need to incorporate this lesson into our lives. We still have not learned how to treat others, to respect the rights of all, to reduce the suffering of humanity. There are people in this world who still experience the effects of racism, prejudice, enmity, and hatred, and they need someone to show them respect. There are individuals who go to bed hungry, without shelter or adequate clothing, and there are those who are subject to both verbal and physical abuse. We have the means to ameliorate the situation for many of these individuals, and sometimes all it takes is determination.

The Shabbat after Tisha B'Av is known as *Shabbat Naḥamu*, the Sabbath of Consolation. It begins a period known as the Seven Weeks of Consolation, which begins with *parashat Va-etḥannan* and ends with the celebration of Rosh Hashanah. The *haftarah* on the Shabbat of *Va-etḥannan* is from the 40th chapter of the Book of Isaiah: "Comfort, oh comfort My people." The prophet recognizes that there will be a time when Israel will rise from destruction, and peace and redemption will occur.

Our ancient sages were puzzled about the process that leads to that redemption. Who will bring about those days of redemption for Israel? There were two schools of thought. One suggested that we should leave it all to God. God alone will signify that day, and we have very little say in the matter. Others suggested that human beings had a significant role to play in the process and related the following folktale, "The Field of Brotherly Love":

> When it came time to build the Temple in Jerusalem, King Solomon did not know where it was to be placed. One night he heard a voice, "Arise and go up to Mount Moriah in Jerusalem." He did but found nothing special there except a field. He learned that the field had been left to two brothers and each lived in a house built at opposite ends of the field. The first brother was married and a father of four children. The second brother lived alone. Together they tilled and tended the field and shared the harvest.
>
> While King Solomon watched, the two brothers tossed in their beds. The first brother said to himself, "How fortunate I am. I have a wife and children who will take care of me when I grow old. But my brother has no one." The second brother also could not sleep and said to himself, "I have only myself to feed. My brother has six mouths to feed with the food that he has. He needs more than I do."

So each brother got out of bed and went to the granary where he took some sheaves of wheat and left them in the granary of his brother. When they awoke they were surprised to see that their amount of wheat had not changed. This continued every night for almost a week until the brothers met in the middle of the field and fell into each other's arms.

Solomon knew why this field had been chosen. It was a field of brotherly love, and it would house the Temple of God. The love of human beings dictated the place where the Temple would stand.

We are to love God with all our hearts, with all our souls, and with all our might (Deuteronomy 6:5). It is the same with regard to our fellow human beings. Let us recognize the importance of this message as we reach out to one another to create fields of brotherly and sisterly love so that the Kingdom of God shall reside here on earth.

EKEV
Saying Yes

One of the last sections of *parashat Ekev* should be very familiar to us. Chapter 11, verses 13–21, encompasses the second paragraph of the *Sh'ma*, which we recite both morning and evening as part of our daily services: "If, then, you obey the commandments that I enjoin upon you this day, loving the Lord your God and serving Him with all your heart and soul, I will grant the rain for your land in season, the early rain and the late" (Deuteronomy 11:13–14). The section goes on to state that good things will come if we observe God's laws and to remind us to express our willingness to accept these laws through educating our children and by placing these words in the *mezuzot* of our doorposts and in our *tefillin*.

The paragraph suggests that we have free choice, an idea that is found throughout the Book of Deuteronomy. We have the ability to choose to follow God's ways, and we also have the ability to refuse to do so. Throughout the desert experience, the Children of Israel were given that opportunity. In his final discourses to the people, Moses impresses upon them the need to adhere to God's commandments and warns them of the outcome of their actions if they disobey these instructions.

This reading marks an instructive period in the Jewish calendar. Beginning with the Shabbat after Tisha B'Av and proceeding until the Shabbat before Rosh Hashanah, we recite seven *haftarot* known as *Shivata de-Neḥemata*, or the Seven Weeks of Consolation. All the prophetic readings during this period speak of the consolation, solace, and comfort offered to the Children of Israel during their time of difficulties and travails. It is interesting to note that on each of these seven weeks, we read a selection from the second half of the Book of Isaiah, as the prophet comforts the people after their exile from Jerusalem and the destruction of the First Temple.

This selection of readings puzzled the ancient scholars. The Midrash in *Yalkut Isaiah* asked the question: "Why are all of the *haftarot* of the Seven Weeks of Consolation taken from Isaiah the prophet? After all, are there not other prophets—what about Jeremiah, Ezekiel, Amos, or Micah?"

The Midrash explains as follows: Isaiah, they suggest, was different from all of the other prophets. Of all of those prophets summoned by God to assume a role of leadership and to serve as God's messengers, only Isaiah answered without hesitation: "Here I am, send me." Many of the other prophets, including Moses, Jeremiah, and Jonah, attempted to find excuses or chose to flee rather than assenting to God's requests.

Isaiah was one of the original Jewish "yes men" in the best sense of the term. He did not know the meaning of the word "no." He was immediately ready and willing to accept his personal responsibility in Jewish life and jump right into his task. Therefore, Isaiah was the prophet who was selected to comfort the people for the seven weeks after Tisha B'Av.

There are many Jews today who bear the title "Jews by Choice." This is a new term often used for a person who converts to Judaism. There is no accurate statistical count today of how many Jews in America are "Jews by Choice," but their numbers are definitely in the six figures. We welcome their participation in our faith and our people.

However, if we take a broader picture of the American Jewish community, we can all be called "Jews by Choice." While many of us are born Jewish, we must be willing to choose Judaism in our lives. It is so easy to assimilate into American culture and to be like everyone else. Today in America, one can live a life with a Jewish name and ancestry and not be concerned about being singled out for discrimination or bias. Being actively Jewish is truly a choice today. One must deliberately decide to be involved in Jewish life, to express religious belief, to promote Jewish identity, and to recognize one's role in the destiny of the Jewish people. This is a positive response to being born Jewish. It is a true declaration of being a "Jew by Choice."

The task of the Jew of today is to become a "yes man" in Isaiah's context, to willingly accept the responsibility of actively contributing to Jewish life and the Jewish community. Judaism requires us to reply "yes" to God's demands. It requires us to live in accordance with the ritual dictates of our faith. It requires us to uphold moral and ethical standards. It requires us to set high standards for our community and to abide by them. And it requires us to be concerned about those in our extended Jewish family and reach out to all others in need and attempt to better their situations.

Henry Slonimsky, a Jewish scholar, remarked that being Jewish is "bad for the nerves but good for the soul." Being a Jew today means not knowing the word "no"—only the word "yes" as a response to serving God and our fellow human beings.

Dag Hammarskjöld, the former United Nations secretary general, in his book *Markings*, wrote, "at some moment I did answer *Yes* to *Someone*—or *Something*—and from that hour I was certain that existence is meaningful and that, therefore, my life, in self-surrender, had a goal." Being a "Jew by Choice" means saying "yes" and allowing that "yes" to change our lives, as we give our minds, our bodies, and our souls to Jewish life and experience.

Let us follow the example of the prophet Isaiah whose words we read from Tisha B'Av to Rosh Hashanah, sharing a message of affirmation, consolation, and comfort. At the same time, let us abide by the teachings of the second paragraph of the *Sh'ma*, found in *parashat Ekev*, following God's teaching and impressing upon the generations that follow us to do the same.

EKEV
Yirat Shamayim

Some say that it is hard to be a Jew, and most of us would probably agree. Some feel that it is hard to be a Jew because it often seems that the world is still not in favor of our continued existence. Others feel it is hard to be a Jew because so much is expected of us.

According to Rabbinic tradition, non-Jews have seven commandments. Based on instruction given to Noaḥ in the Torah as he and his family emerged from the ark, these are known as the Seven Commandments of the Children of Noaḥ. As enumerated in *Sanhedrin* 56b, these commandments are: "social laws; to refrain from blasphemy, idolatry, adultery, bloodshed, robbery, and eating flesh from a living animal."

We, on the other hand, have 613 commandments (*mitzvot*) to follow. These laws establish a framework for lives of justice and morality, even as we follow in minute detail ritual enactments concerning the way we eat, the manner in which we dress, and even how we have sexual relations.

It is hard to be a Jew because the demands on us are even greater than one might think. The prophet Micah enumerates the responsibilities for all humanity: "He has told you, O man, what is good, and what the Lord requires of you: only to do justice and to love goodness, and to walk modestly with your God" (Micah 6:8). According to Micah, this is the standard by which all societies and individuals are judged.

Yet, the Jewish people, as discussed in *parashat Ekev*, have additional obligations to follow. Moses states: "And now, O Israel, what does the Lord your God demand of you? Only this: to revere the Lord your God, to walk only in His paths, to love Him, and to serve the Lord your God with all your heart and soul, keeping the Lord's commandments and laws, which I enjoin upon you today, for your good" (Deuteronomy 10:12–13).

The key concept here is that the Israelite people are to revere, or, literally, to fear God. As Rabbi Harold Kushner points out in the *Etz Hayim ḥumash*, "Reverence and obedience are perhaps the only virtues we cannot learn by imitating God, because God has no one to revere or obey." Thus, we are on our own. We must learn reverence for God through our own instincts.

What is this concept of "the fear of God?" Rabbi Louis Jacobs, in *A Jewish Theology*, states: "the Fear of God in the Bible frequently refers to an extraordinary degree of piety and moral worth." He quotes the Book of Psalms: "The fear of the Lord is the beginning of wisdom" (Psalms 111:10). This is where it all begins. If we fear God, then everything else follows.

Rabbi Byron Sherwin, in an essay on the fear of God in the book, *Contemporary Jewish Religious Thought*, states: "In Judaism the religious person is not characterized primarily as a believer who assents to a given creed, as in other religions. Rather, the religious person is depicted as one who has *yirat shamayim* or *yirat ha-Shem*, fear and awe of God."

This is the reason that the anonymous author of the medieval ethical treatise *Orḥot Tzadikkim* states: "The Torah is of no use to an individual but for *yirat shamayim*, for it is the very peg upon which everything hangs" (paragraph 590). The concept impels us to appreciate our place in the universe and to live by the moral and ethical dictates of our tradition, ennobling human life on the face of this earth. As Rabbi Jacobs observes, a religion devoid of *yirat shamayim* tends to become reduced to comfortable sentimentality.

This is our daily responsibility. Ḥasidic rabbi Baruch Ha-Levi Epstein suggests that in order to accomplish all of the *mitzvot*, one needs other tools that are ultimately part of God's world. *Yirat shamayim*, however, is totally dependent upon human endeavor. He points out that, in order to fulfill the *mitzvah* of *tzitzit*, one must have a four-cornered garment; to observe the *mitzvah* of *mezuzah*, one must have a doorpost in a house; to keep the laws of *kashrut*, one must have food. However, *yirat shamayim* must be experienced at all times and in all places under all occurrences and is totally in the hands of each and every individual. As the Talmud in

Berakhot 33b states, basing itself on the Biblical verse: "Everything is in the hands of heaven, except *yirat shamayim*, the fear of heaven."

Yirat shamayim is a concept we need to bring back into Jewish life. It is laudable to establish a society of ethics, morality, and justice, but it is even more desirable to understand that the fear and awe of God lead us in that direction, and ritual and ethical conduct, morality, and justice simply follow apace.

A student once visited Reb Yosef Ber of Brisk. The rabbi asked him how he was doing. "Thank God," he responded, "everything is going well. My business has brought me great wealth." A few moments later, the rabbi asked him the same question. "How are things going?" The student answered him exactly the same way. A third time the rabbi asked, and this time the student began to give him details of his business dealings. Finally, Reb Yosef Ber stopped him and said, "We have learned that everything is in the hands of heaven, and, thus, whether you do well or not in business dealings is really a gift from God. However, one thing is transferred into the hands of human beings and that is *yirat shamayim*. When I asked how you were doing in life, I was not concerned with the gifts that God has presented to you. I was more concerned with how you were dealing with your *yirat shamayim*."

Yes, it is hard to be a Jew, but it is also a great privilege. We need to follow not merely the words of Micah but also the dictates of Moses. May our *yirat shamayim* positively affect our daily activities.

RE'EH
The Prophetic View

Girolamo Cardano, a sixteenth-century Italian mathematician and astrologer, was renowned in Europe for the accuracy of his prognostications. He was a steadfast believer in his so-called science, and he constructed a horoscope predicting the hour of his own death. When the day dawned, however, he was in good health and safe from harm. Rather than having his prediction falsified, Cardano killed himself.

I think this is rather drastic. People offer visions of the future all the time. Read the newspaper columns written by political pundits; they think they know everything. When things don't turn out exactly as they had predicted, they always find an adequate excuse.

In *parashat Re'eh*, the Children of Israel are warned: "If there appears among you a prophet or a dream-diviner and he gives you a sign or a portent, saying, 'Let us follow and worship another god'—whom you have not experienced—even if the sign or portent that he named to you comes true, do not heed the words of that prophet or that dream-diviner" (Deuteronomy 13:2–4). Even if they can foretell the future, even if they produce some supposedly supernatural signs, if they are attempting to lead you astray from the God of Israel, do not follow them.

The prophet is one who speaks out for God. He may receive his message in a variety of ways—in dreams, visions, or by direct address. However, Moses is the only one who communicates directly with the Divine. While the prophet may foretell the future, he does much more than that. The message he conveys is one of great import brought to the Children of Israel from their God.

In Biblical tradition, there are many prophets. The early ones in Israelite history are miracle workers. Elijah and Elisha performed signs and wonders, miraculous events that spoke of their devotion to the God of Israel and loyalty and fidelity to the law.

The classical prophets, on the other hand, such as Isaiah, Jeremiah, Ezekiel, as well as those known as the twelve minor prophets, are not miracle workers in the same sense of the term. In their case, the message is all-important. They tell the Israelites of both the northern and southern kingdoms predictions that they do not necessarily want to hear. God demands of them ethics, justice, and moral behavior as well as ritual observance. God will hold the Israelites responsible for keeping their part of the covenant, and if they do not follow in God's path, they will be punished. However, God will never abandon them; He will eventually redeem them.

In his book, *The Prophets: Who They Were, What They Are*, Norman Podhoretz attempts to review the messages of the major prophets of the Bible and examine whether they have relevance for our day. He contends that conservative and liberal Christians, modern Reform Jews, and the secular left have distorted the message of the Biblical prophets. While the prophets were concerned about broad humanism and universalism, Podhoretz asserts "they did *not* elevate morality over ritual; they did *not* constitute a party of the 'spirit' in opposition to a rigidly legalistic priestly 'establishment'; and they did *not* feel or give expression to a 'tension' ... between 'universalism' and 'particularism.'" Thus, the prophets defended monotheism, the exclusive worship of the one invisible God who created everything, and opposed pagan religion. Paganism's central fault was the worship of false and non-existent gods and goddesses in the form of idols. When idolatry faded, so did the prophets.

In the last part of his book, Podhoretz outlines what he sees as the relevance of the prophet's message for today's America. To Podhoretz, paganism worships the self, and American culture has become guilty of the same sin. When interviewed about the book, he remarked that the besetting sin in American culture is narcissism and that the prophets have much to say about such self-worship.

Podhoretz's views will not be popular with everyone. He moves from being a student of Biblical literature to a commentator on the American way of life. One may or may not agree with his theories about what ails

American society and his recommended solutions. However, if nothing else, he raises questions concerning the role of the true prophet.

In our day and age, who can be deemed a prophet? The true prophet is in conflict with his times. When things are going well materially, he notes what is wrong morally. According to most traditional commentators, if the message is painful for the prophet to utter and painful for the people to hear, then it is likely an authentic message from God. In the Book of Jeremiah, the so-called prophet Ḥananiah tells the people optimistic lies rather than the hard truths that they need to hear. Jeremiah, on the other hand, the true prophet, castigates the people for their behavior, their treatment of others, and their lack of observance of God's laws.

Who is to call us to task these days? Who will be our models? Who will understand that, even if one may be unpopular, one must stand up for what is right, just, and equitable? While we may not concur with Podhoretz's entire thesis, it is clear that we need a prophetic voice that will impel us to establish a society based on the highest ideals of our faith.

It is not an easy task to be a prophet or one who listens to his message. The challenges that were presented by the true prophets of old are still very much with us today. How we respond to them will ultimately tell the story of our culture, our society, and our way of life.

RE'EH
The Loving Parent

I always inform couples with whom I do pre-marriage counseling that parenting is both the greatest blessing and the most awesome challenge. To have a new life in your home presents a tremendous opportunity not only to shape that young person but also to shape his or her future. Not only during their formative years, but throughout the course of their lives, parents have the responsibility to treat children with respect and not to see them merely as "*nachas* machines."

In *parashat Re'eh* God is seen as a concerned parent. Moses, in describing the relationship between God and the Children of Israel, states: "You are children of the Lord your God" (Deuteronomy 14:1). This statement led to a debate in *Kiddushin* 36a. Rabbi Yehudah states: "When you (the Jewish people) behave like children should, you are considered the Children of God. When you do not, you lose that designation." Rabbi Meir disagrees: "In both cases you are called the Children of God."

The debate between Rabbi Yehudah and Rabbi Meir is over the question of the ability of the Jewish people to survive. The destruction of the Second Temple, the loss of sovereignty over the land, and the exile were accompanied by profound national depression. Rabbi Yehudah is echoing the judgmental side of God's attributes. When Israel violates filial responsibility, it forfeits the special relationship it possesses with the God of Israel. Rabbi Meir insists, as do the prophets of the exile, that this filial relationship is never vanquished. Despite the nation's foolishness, its lack of faith, its moral corruption, and even its seeming rejection of the covenant itself, the Jews are always God's children and will eventually be redeemed.

It is not uncommon to view God as a parent. On Rosh Hashanah and Yom Kippur, we describe God as *Avinu Malkeinu*, "Our Father, Our King." We would like to believe that God is a supportive parent, caring about His children, and lovingly tending to their needs. In Yiddish, in loving fashion, God is referred to as *Tatenyu*, our loving parent, expressing our desire to feel close to God's loving care and nurturing providence.

Parenting is not easy, for a parent always has high expectations for his or her child. We set lofty standards, expecting appropriate conduct and moral behavior. What happens when the child does not live up to that responsibility and those high standards? What happens when the child disobeys and fails to take heed of the parent's advice and counsel?

Rabbi Yehudah seems to possess extremely high standards. He believes that if the child does not live up to the expectations of the parent, then the child may lose parental love. Perhaps this threat will lead the child to fulfill necessary responsibilities. Rabbi Meir is more understanding. He appreciates that children make mistakes, and that even under difficult circumstances, parents must always be there for them.

Rabbi Meir, however, is not ready to relieve Israel of its spiritual and moral responsibilities. Regardless of how firm and unbreakable the covenant may be in the eyes of Rabbi Meir, the threatened punishments will nevertheless be severe enough to hold them to proper commitments. In other words, a parent has to be ready to deliver a scolding rebuke to a child and to punish appropriately, if necessary. A parent is not a friend who lets things go and who simply wants to be loved by the child. A parent has the obligation to ensure that the child understands that standards are set for him to which he must adhere.

It is, of course, the parent's responsibility to live by the same high standards and moral dictates. It is the obligation of the parent to be an appropriate role model so that the child will see that parents do not simply "talk the talk but also walk the walk." Parenting is a most awesome responsibility and challenge.

Rabbi Akiva felt that this verse in Deuteronomy had a great lesson attached to it. In *Pirkei Avot* 3:18 he states: "Israel is beloved, for they are called God's children. They are exceedingly beloved for it was made known to them that they are God's children, as it is written, 'You are children of the Lord your God'" (Deuteronomy 14:1). According to

Rabbi Akiva, it is a great privilege to be a child of God and to know that God is our parent.

The lesson applies to the relationship between parents and children. It is not enough to love our children; we need to demonstrate our love as well. Sometimes, that love has to be tough and judgmental in order to teach appropriate lessons. When things are going well, it is easier to show that love; it is more difficult when tense moments occur. Not only must we always show that love, but our children need to know we love them no matter what. They need to hear it, they need to feel it, and they need to know it.

The parent/child relationship, whether between God and humanity or between one generation and the next, is not an easy one. There are always trials and tribulations, moments of great joy and times of distress and frustration. However, I can't agree with Rabbi Yehudah that we can only be fair-weather parents or that God is as well. Instead, we must always be loving parents and advocates for our children, and we must pray that God follows the same pattern. If parenting is a challenge for us, I can only presume that God, as the Eternal Parent, finds it difficult as well. Hopefully, we can make it easier for God by embracing the covenant, establishing a better world here on earth, and, at the same time, being proper parental models for our children and grandchildren.

SHOFETIM
The Sin of Indifference

On April 12, 1999, as part of the Millennium Lecture Series hosted by President Bill Clinton and First Lady Hillary Rodham Clinton in the East Room of the White House, Holocaust survivor and Nobel Laureate Elie Wiesel delivered a very moving speech on "The Perils of Indifference."

Wiesel framed the following question: "We are on the threshold of a new century, a new millennium. What will the legacy of this vanishing century be? How will it be remembered in the new millennium? Surely it will be judged, and judged severely, in both moral and metaphysical terms." He went on to enumerate the great tragedies of the last century and then concluded: "So much violence, so much indifference."

Wiesel then spent the rest of his speech on the significance of indifference. For him, indifference is more dangerous than anger and hatred. "Anger," he stated, "at times can be creative. Even hatred at times may elicit a response. But indifference is not a response. It is not a beginning, it is an end, and it is always a friend of the enemy. It is not only a sin, it is a punishment, and this is one of the most important lessons of this outgoing century's wide-ranging experiment in good and evil."

If Elie Wiesel has spent his life voicing opposition to indifference, Raul Hilberg, the noted Holocaust historian, defined the field of Holocaust studies through looking at the perpetrators, the victims, and the bystanders. In his book, *Perpetrators Victims Bystanders*, Hilberg defines the bystanders as those who neither participated in the machinery of genocide nor were its victims. Their principal reaction was indifference. For most, there was "a dull awareness" of the catastrophe and little more.

While we mourn the victims of the Holocaust and condemn the actions of the perpetrators, how do we react toward the bystanders? Are they just as guilty? Could they claim they didn't know what was going on? Are they to be seen as victims themselves of the Nazi onslaught? Or did their indifference lead to the mass murder of millions of people because they wouldn't stand up for appropriate morality?

In *parashat Shofetim*, we read a description of the *eglah arufah*, the ceremony of the broken-necked heifer. The passage tells us that if a corpse is found lying in the open, and the identity of the slayer is unknown, then it is the responsibility of the elders and magistrates to go out and measure the distance from the corpse to the nearby towns. The elders of the town nearest to the corpse then take a heifer, bring it down to an ever-flowing wadi, and break its neck. The elders then wash their hands over the heifer and make this declaration: "Our hands did not shed this blood, nor did our eyes see it done" (Deuteronomy 21:7). At that point, they ask God, "do not let guilt for the blood of the innocent remain among Your people Israel" (Deuteronomy 21:8).

This statement of the elders as they declare their innocence is most interesting. Why should we assume that the elders need to atone for some misdeed? Are we concerned that they murdered or caused the murder of this slain individual? Why must they ask atonement for themselves and the for people of their city?

The Mishnah in *Sotah* 9:6 asked the same question, and here the elders respond: "It is not so that he came into our hands and we sent him away without food, nor did we see him journeying and leave him with none to accompany him." In other words, we surely didn't kill him, and we are not even accessories to the murder. If he had been in our city, and he needed some help, we would have been of assistance. If he was on his journey and needed someone to accompany him, we would have been there.

The Torah instructs us not to be bystanders. It teaches us not to profess indifference. If there is any way for us to make a difference in the world, then we must act immediately. If there is a life to be saved, a person to be fed, a sojourner to be housed, a solitary individual needing hospitality, we must be there. While the elders were not suspected of actual murder, they could not even profess indifference to the plight of another human being.

What is our record today, and have we learned anything from the past? Are we indifferent to the plight of the poor and the needy? Are we insensitive to those who need our assistance and aid? Do we appreciate the lessons of the last century that bystanders can cause almost as much evil as perpetrators? Or do we simply go about our own individual lives, concerned merely for our own well-being without spreading our compassion to others?

Wiesel states: "Indifference is never an option. It is not the beginning of a process; it is the end of a process. The opposite of love is not hate; it's indifference. The opposite of art is not ugliness; it's indifference. The opposite of education is not ignorance; it's indifference. The opposite of faith is not heresy; it's indifference. The opposite of life is not death; it's indifference."

It is important to learn from history and from the teachings of *parashat Shofetim*. Do not be indifferent. Do not be bystanders. Instead, live life with a caring heart, a sensitive soul, and the capacity to assist others when necessary. The elders of the town had to ask for forgiveness, lest in some way they may have caused the death of one human being. May we learn the lesson well and never be accused of indifference to the plight of another.

SHOFETIM
To Be Someone

The following obituary notice was placed in a church bulletin:

> Our church was saddened to learn this week of the death of one of our most valued members, SOMEONE ELSE. SOMEONE's passing creates a vacancy that will be difficult to fill. ELSE has been with us for many years, and for every one of those years, SOMEONE did far more than a normal person's share of the work. Whenever there was a job to do, a class to teach, or a meeting to attend, one name was on everyone's list, 'Let SOMEONE ELSE do it.' Whenever leadership was mentioned, this wonderful person was looked to for inspiration as well as results: 'SOMEONE ELSE can work with that group.' It was common knowledge that SOMEONE ELSE was among the most liberal givers in our church. Whenever there was a financial need, everyone just assumed SOMEONE ELSE would make up the difference.
>
> SOMEONE ELSE was a wonderful person, sometimes appearing superhuman. Were the truth known, everybody expected too much of SOMEONE ELSE. Now SOMEONE ELSE is gone. We wonder what we are going to do. SOMEONE ELSE left a wonderful example to follow, but who is going to follow it? Who is going to do the things SOMEONE ELSE did?

While this obituary was, of course, not factual, it points out how we are always ready to pawn off our responsibilities on someone else. We can always find excuses to be lenient on ourselves and to expect another person to pick up the necessary responsibilities and obligations. Too often, we don't see those obligations falling upon our shoulders; instead, we expect someone else to fulfill them.

Parashat Shofetim is concerned with establishing the Israelite society as a place of justice and equity for all. Judges and magistrates are to be appointed who will follow appropriate judicial demeanor and not be blinded by bribes and persons of high status. At all times, they are to follow through on the principles of equality and fairness for all.

The judges were to be people of impeccable character who could be relied upon to uphold the highest values of the Israelite community. Maimonides, in his *Mishneh Torah* (Laws of the *Sanhedrin* 2:7), stipulates that these people had to be learned in the law, trustworthy, fair, and above suspicion of wrongdoing. Before they could make judicial decisions and administer justice, they had to be worthy of sitting in judgment of others.

Mishnah *Sanhedrin* 2:1 states: "The High Priest may judge and be judged, testify and be testified against." Since the High Priest is an individual who occupies the highest ritual office, one should expect that he would be of the highest moral character.

In other words, first one must take care of one's responsibilities before one can expect others to do so. Thus, a High Priest may sit in judgment only because he can also be judged. He is not above the law; he is subject to it. And, thus, he should understand his responsibility to the law, both as a member of Israelite society and as one who is privileged to sit on the judiciary panel. One cannot eschew responsibility; one must assume responsibility for one's own conduct. Someone else cannot be expected to pick up the obligation if you can do it yourself. The magistrates and the officials who sit in the Israelite courts must be individuals of the highest noble character. They must be subject to the laws of society before they can execute those laws upon others.

Rabbi Jacob Joseph of Polonne, in *Toledot Yaakov Yosef*, published in 1780, suggests that we should see this not merely with respect to administering justice or in terms of leadership in a community but on a personal level as well. He states: "Do not be lenient with your faults while judging the same faults in others; do not overlook sin in yourself while demanding perfection of others." Before you judge another person, judge yourself. Before you demand of others, demand of yourself. Before expecting someone else to assume obligations, assume them yourself.

Rabbi Israel Salanter taught that we have two eyes for a reason. With one eye, we look at our neighbors, fastening our gaze on their goodness, excellence, and most desirable qualities, while refraining from criticism, slander, and gossip. With the other, we turn inward to see our own weaknesses, imperfections, and shortcomings so we can correct them. This is not an easy task, but it is a necessary one if we are to become better human beings.

In 1980, Rabbi Haskel Lookstein gave a fiery Rosh Hashanah sermon to his congregation. He told them that they needed to be better people, that they should conduct their business in a truthful manner, that they should live with honesty and integrity, and that they must improve themselves in the coming year. After the sermon, many congregants said to him: "Boy, oh boy, Rabbi, you really gave it to THEM!!"

It is not enough to suggest that others need to improve their conduct; we must do so as well. In fact, we must do so first. When leadership is called for, we cannot rely on SOMEONE ELSE. As Hillel taught in *Pirkei Avot* 2:6: "Where there are no worthy persons, strive to be a worthy person." When we examine our lives and those of others, we should be lenient on them and harsh on ourselves.

May we establish communities of honesty, equality, and integrity. May we be proud of ourselves and our conduct.

KI TETSE
The Beauty of Small Deeds

Parashat *Ki Tetse* outlines many different laws in all realms of Jewish endeavor. Some of the laws relate to ritual matters, but most stipulate the values and ethical imperatives that are needed to constitute a holy society in which there is reverence for human life and respect for God.

One of the most interesting laws is called the law of the bird's nest: "If, along the road, you chance upon a bird's nest, in any tree or on the ground, with fledglings or eggs and the mother sitting over the fledglings or on the eggs, do not take the mother together with her young. Let the mother go, and take only the young" (Deuteronomy 22:6–7).

On the surface, this law simply instructs us that we must be compassionate and kind. We are entitled to take the young birds or the eggs but should not subject the mother bird to witnessing our actions. We must not demonstrate cruelty to animals. We must learn to be sensitive to all forms of life. The concept of *tzar ba'alei ḥayim*, cruelty to animals, is deemed a violation of Jewish law, and we might think that this law simply follows that prescription.

However, this law is somewhat unusual. Rarely does the Torah mention a specific reward for the performance of a *mitzvah*. In this case it does: "in order that you may fare well and have a long life" (Deuteronomy 22:7). What made this law different from so many others in the Torah that recompense needed to be mentioned?

This reward is mentioned only one other time in the Torah, in association with one of the more famous commandments: "Honor your father and your mother, that you may long endure on the land that the Lord your God is assigning to you" (Exodus 20:12). The Rabbis of the Midrash (*Deuteronomy Rabbah* 6:2) realized that one could only understand our text when it is compared with the commandment of honoring parents. "God did not reveal the reward for the precepts except in two cases: the most difficult and the least."

Honoring of parents is one of the most difficult of all Biblical commandments to properly fulfill. Being a child presents us with situations fraught with difficulty. While parents bring us into the world, nurture us, educate us, and care for us in our early years, there must come a time of individuation, of separation, of rebellion against parental authority. Throughout life's stages, the relationship may experience stress. As well, the parent-child relationship changes over time, as children grow up, parents age, and a role reversal is sometimes inevitable. From the youngest of ages and even after death—with the recitation of the Mourner's *Kaddish* for eleven months for a parent—Jewish tradition recognizes the special nature of the parent-child relationship. It may, therefore, not be altogether too surprising that this commandment stands out from others in the Torah.

But what about the law of the bird's nest? It is, after all, one of the simplest of all Biblical commandments to fulfill. How often during our lifetimes will this particular possibility present itself to us? How often are we tempted to take the eggs from a nest as we pass by a tree and see the mother bird hovering over its young? Perhaps that is exactly the reason it is so important. "If you chance upon a bird's nest," instinctively you must realize the right thing to do.

Great and momentous deeds are important. The honoring of parents, for example, is seen by all societies to be a cornerstone of family life. From the earliest of ages, we are taught to honor our parents, and Jewish tradition provides many texts that describe how that honor is to be enacted. We are, therefore, not surprised that it is enumerated as one of the Ten Commandments. However, the law of the bird's nest teaches us that the small things also matter.

The great artist Michelangelo had a friend who visited him when he was in the last phase of work on a statue. Soon after, the friend visited again and noticed that the sculptor was still working on the same project. His friend said to him, "Nothing much has changed. You must have been idle since I last came." "By no means," replied the sculptor, "I have retouched this part and polished that; I have softened this feature and brought out this muscle; I have given more expression to this lip and more energy to that limb." "Well," said his friend, "but these are all trifles." "It may be so," replied Michelangelo, "but I believe that trifles make greatness and greatness is no trifle."

Greatness is not necessarily found in grandiose actions but rather in the simple things, in the trifles of life. Greatness is found in a warm smile, a comforting touch, a kind word, or a hospitable welcome. Greatness is found in clothing the naked, visiting the sick, and comforting the mourner. These are the very cornerstones of life. They take little personal sacrifice, and, yet, they define greatness by demonstrating our love for fellow human beings and for God.

While there is no doubt that honoring parents is a crucial *mitzvah*, the Rabbis of the Midrash recognized that the Torah was teaching us a great lesson by making the reward the same for these two commandments. It is not only the large deeds that matter; the simpler and less substantial actions are also meaningful. The law of the bird's nest teaches us that no deed is insignificant. May our small deeds become great ones as they change our world for the better.

KI TETSE
Remembering and Forgetting

We are a people of memory. No less than 169 times in the Bible does the verb *zakhor,* "remember," appear. We are to remember our history, our special relationship with God, our responsibility to our neighbor, and the narrative of recalling that our deeds make a difference in this world.

In Yosef Ḥayim Yerushalmi's powerful book, *Zakhor,* he explicates the term *zakhor* as follows: "the verb is complemented by its obverse—forgetting. As Israel is enjoined to remember, so it is adjured not to forget." For example, we are told in *parashat Ki Tetse*: "Remember what Amalek did to you on your journey, after you left Egypt ... Do not forget!" (Deuteronomy 25:17, 19).

In discussing the importance of memory in Jewish tradition, Yerushalmi writes: "Only in Israel and nowhere else is the injunction to remember felt as a religious imperative to an entire people." Throughout the Bible, and especially in the Book of Deuteronomy, the Israelite people are told to remember what occurred to them, to understand the implications of that memory, and to act upon it. As Yerushalmi writes: "Both imperatives [to remember and not to forget] have resounded with enduring effect among the Jews since Biblical times. Indeed, in trying to understand the survival of a people that has spent most of its life in global dispersion, I would submit that the history of its memory, largely neglected and yet to be written, may prove of some consequence." As Jews, we are enjoined to remember on a constant basis who we are, what has happened to us, and what is expected of us.

Think, for example, of the Passover Seder. The entire experience is predicated upon the fact that we are to remember what happened to us in the Land of Egypt. We are to recall God's saving grace of bringing us out from slavery and bondage to enjoy liberation and freedom. We enact that liberation in the story we tell, the foods we eat, and the actions we perform. The Seder allows us to see ourselves personally coming out of Egypt and invites the experience to resound in our modern lives.

On a communal level, remembering is normative and carries with it an obligation. Recalling ancient times is not simply nostalgia; by resurrecting the past, we bring it into the present. The Exodus from Egypt is not a one-time historical event. It is an everyday activity. Recalling the evil nature of Amalek is not a one-time occurrence in history. It is a constant reminder of the importance of creating goodness in the world. Remembering the Sabbath day to keep it holy is not merely an intellectual event; it is an enduring practice that impresses upon us the sanctity of the day and our responsibility to care for the world.

This collective memory shapes the obligation of the individual Israelite. He is to remember that he was a stranger in Egypt, and, therefore, he is responsible for befriending the strangers in his community. He is to recall that, as part of his ongoing responsibility, he has to care for the less fortunate in his society. He has the responsibility to care for the land because he is a mere tenant on it, placed there by God. And he is to remember being present at Sinai so that he can relive the covenantal nature of his relationship with the God of Israel.

As important as remembering is, there are times when forgetfulness is also helpful, at least if it is done consciously. On Rosh Hashanah, which is also called *Yom Ha-Zikaron* or the Day of Remembrance, we state: "You remember every deed, and nothing in creation can be hidden from You." But if God remembers everything, what chance do we have of doing *teshuvah*, repentance? We make mistakes on a continual basis. How can we come before God and expect atonement for our errors in judgment, word, and deed? We hope that God will decide to forget our misdeeds and transgressions and, with grace, forgive our trespasses. Sometimes conscious forgetting is a good thing.

Clara Barton, the founder of the U.S. Red Cross, was alleged never to have held grudges. She was once reminded by a friend of a wrong done to her some years earlier: "Don't you remember?" asked her friend. "No," replied Clara, "I distinctly remember forgetting that."

Sometimes, it is better to forget than to remember. Sometimes, we actually have to work at it in order to allow another person a second chance, to effect reconciliation and forgiveness, to create a relationship where one may have been destroyed.

Memory may lead to action, but bad memories often lead to inaction. Sometimes, it is important to remember to forget and to move forward on both a personal and a spiritual basis. It is not easy, but many times forgetting is crucial to the process of making life meaningful. If God can somehow forget our misdeeds, transgressions, and sins, then we can most assuredly do so with others in our lives.

Our Sages recount that when God finished creating the world, He suddenly realized that He had omitted an indispensable ingredient without which life could not endure. God had forgotten to include the power to forget. And so God blessed the world with that special gift and was content that the world was now ready for human habitation.

May we use the power to remember and the power to forget appropriately in our relations with others. May we remember and not forget our roles as members of a sacred nation in covenant with our God. And may God forget our misdeeds and transgressions and always remember us for good.

KI TAVO
The Blessing of True Happiness

Passing through Rome in 1961, the legendary golfer Sam Snead stopped for an audience with Pope John XXIII. He had not been playing well for some time and confessed to one of the Papal officials: "I brought along my putter on the chance that the Pope might bless it." The Monsignor nodded sympathetically. "I know, Mr. Snead," he said. "My putting is absolutely hopeless, too." Snead looked at him in amazement. "If you *live* here and can't putt," he exclaimed, "what chance is there for me?" We all want to be blessed, whether in our golf game or our business ventures. We want to be blessed with the good things in life.

Parashat Ki Tavo contains the blessings and the curses. According to Biblical theology, the conduct of the people of Israel in the Land will bring either reward or punishment. While the curses are a long litany of doom and disaster, the blessings are short and direct: "Blessed shall you be in the city and blessed shall you be in the country" (Deuteronomy 28:3). "The Lord will give you abounding prosperity in the issue of your womb, the offspring of your cattle, and the produce of your soil" (Deuteronomy 28:11). This, one would think, would bring true happiness to those so blessed. They would have all they could desire. The problem is that many people confuse being happy with being blessed.

Rabbi Jeremy Collick writes, "The happiest people I have met in my life did not always *have* the best of everything; they just seem to *make* the best of everything. That's why I believe that happiness is a state of mind—our mind." I know of many people who seem to be blessed, seem to have it all, but, many times, these people are miserable rather than happy. And this story is not unique. A man had an income of well over a million dollars a year, and yet he was miserable. He was asked why he always looked so morose. "Money is a test," he said, "and I have failed the test."

Solomon ibn Gabirol, the eleventh-century Jewish poet, wrote: "The wise will realize that the search for happiness is one of the main sources of unhappiness in the world." We may be entitled to "life, liberty, and the pursuit of happiness" according to the Declaration of Independence, but this last phrase has caused more unhappiness and discontent in our society than we truly understand. For what is happiness, and how and why should it be pursued?

Pirkei Avot 4:1 states: "Who is rich? One who is happy with his portion." Contentment becomes the key to happiness. This does not necessarily inhibit personal initiative. We should reach higher if we can acquire something honestly through creativity and sacrifice. But we must be realistic. Some things are not ours to attain.

A story is told of two dogs that were having a conversation. A large dog had been chasing his tail, and a small dog was incredulous. "Why are you always chasing your tail?" he asked. "I chase my tail," the large dog responded, "because I know that if I catch my tail I shall be happy. For whenever I am happy, my tail wags." The little dog answered, "I also know that happiness is in my tail. But whenever I chase my tail, it keeps running away from me. I have discovered that if I go about my business, then happiness, like my tail, will come after me."

Pursuing happiness is like a dog chasing its tail. It is a futile enterprise, for happiness is a by-product of achievement, of working hard to reach one's goals. A story is told of a newspaper in London that offered a prize to the happiest person in the city. Three people received prizes: a craftsman who whistled as he worked at his craft, a mother who sang at night after bathing her baby, and a surgeon who completed a successful operation in which he saved the life of his patient. Each person was not pursuing happiness; each was totally absorbed in his or her activities. By going about their business, they opened the door to allow happiness to gently slip in.

The nineteenth-century Kotzker Rebbe taught: "Happiness is the midpoint between too little and too much. When what we are is what we wish, that is happiness. When envy appears, happiness will vanish."

This is indeed a lesson all of us should learn. Many of us have more than our parents could ever have wished for us. But material well-being never brings happiness in and of itself. Think of your happiest moments, and I daresay you will recall moments of tenderness, times of love and friendship, periods of quiet and serenity, moments of supreme joy with children and grandchildren, times of achievement and success, or the moment one learns something new and finds a solution to a seemingly insoluble problem. These are examples of happiness and joy, and they bear no direct relationship to material luxuries.

Happy are those who have found their soulmate in life, those who have been healed from disease or injury, or those who were saved from accident or natural disaster. And there is no one happier than one who knows that he has helped his fellow human being. How good it feels to share your energy, your resources, or your time with another person!

There is, I think, a difference between being blessed and being happy. Being blessed acknowledges that the gifts we receive are not totally dependent upon us. As Jews, we recognize they come from God, and we must be grateful for them. Perhaps that is the reason why Moses instructs the Israelites to recognize the blessings that will come their way (Deuteronomy 26:1–10).

May we always be blessed and in those blessings find true happiness.

KI TAVO
Tikkun Olam—A True Story

As Moses prepares to take leave of the Children of Israel, he reminds them that they possess the freedom of choice. It is up to them whether they produce blessings or curses, whether they choose life or death.

I once heard Shlomo Riskin, the Chief Rabbi of Efrat, tell a story about how he finally understood the challenge of fulfilling the Jewish people's mission of *tikkun olam*, the perfection of the world. One of his *yeshivot* was under heavy attack during the Intifada. Each Thursday, Rabbi Riskin would give a Torah lecture to the IDF soldiers protecting the school. One particular Thursday, he noticed one of the soldiers was unlike any of the others; this soldier took copious notes and stood out because he was very tall and very black.

In a discussion with him after class, the young man told Rabbi Riskin that he was from Nigeria and his name was Dan. He became Jewish because of the concept of *tikkun olam*. He explained that when a delegation of post-army Israelis came to Nigeria as "peace corps" ambassadors to impart new techniques in agriculture and medicine, he was befriended by one of the Israelis who happened to be an observant Jew. This man taught him about *tikkun olam* and they stayed in touch. A year later Dan came to Israel, converted to Judaism, and served in the IDF, which he considered to be *tikkun olam*.

The concept of *tikkun olam* has become synonymous with performing acts of lovingkindness, of creating a better world. But *tikkun olam* is far from a modern concept. It is first recorded in Mishnah *Gittin* chapter 4 where it functions as a concept for creating social order. The laws mentioned there are concerned with a diverse spectrum of activities such as delivering and receiving a *get* (a divorce document), freeing of slaves, redemption of captives, and participation in fair business practices. It does not relate to social action projects and deeds of lovingkindness. The ordinances are described as having been instituted "to make the world a better place."

Over time, in kabbalistic thinking, the concept of *tikkun* was given special meaning. According to Isaac Luria, the renowned sixteenth-century kabbalist, God created the world by filling vessels with Divine Light. But as the light was poured into the vessels, they catastrophically shattered, tumbling down toward the realm of matter. Thus, our world consists of countless shards of the original vessels trapping sparks of the Divine Light. The work of *tikkun olam* is necesary to join the shattered pieces of the whole back together so that the unique sparks of light and truth may shine forth.

In our liturgy, the concept is brought to our consciousness three times a day. In the second paragraph of the *Aleinu* prayer, we recite the words "perfecting earth by Your kingship." We, the Jewish people, have a special mission to accomplish, to create of this world a heavenly abode. We can do so by trying to unite the shards that were broken through a hands-on approach to life as we participate in the world through our daily activities. Emanating from our will, Divine sparks bring God's presence into our universe and help humanity at the very same time. Rabbi Joseph Telushkin suggests that this is the very purpose of Jewish existence: "Human beings are obligated to bring mankind to a knowledge of God, whose primary demand of human beings is moral behavior."

In *parashat Ki Tavo*, Moses tells the Children of Israel: "You have affirmed this day that the Lord is your God, that you will walk in His ways, that you will observe His laws and commandments and rules, and that you will obey Him" (Deuteronomy 26:17). Our Rabbis wondered how it was possible to walk in the ways of God. After all, we are only flesh and blood. They suggest in *Sotah* 14a that we walk in God's ways by following God's attributes. In the same way that God clothes the naked (Adam and Eve), visits the sick (Abraham), comforts those who mourn (Isaac), and buries the dead (Moses), so should we. As we follow God's ways, we perform tasks of *tikkun olam*, creating a better world order, a more humane society that allows the Divine sparks to shine forth.

Rabbi Riskin continued his story by telling us that he invited this young man to join him for a Friday night dinner at his home. The man accepted the invitation for the following week, but he never made it. He was killed in the line of duty. Only the people from the *yeshiva* attended his funeral; his family in Nigeria was informed, but never responded.

Rabbi Riskin reported that about six weeks later his wife woke him up from a Shabbat afternoon nap and apologetically explained that he had guests. He found a middle-aged black couple sitting on the living room sofa. They said, "We don't understand why our son became Jewish or why he joined the IDF. We don't know why our son had to die … Everyone told us that you had a serious conversation with him before he was killed." Rabbi Riskin had difficulty explaining all of it to the parents of this young man.

About two years later, Rabbi Riskin received a call from Dan's father. They had enrolled in an ulpan in Netanya, and were converting to Judaism. They invited Rabbi Riskin to put up the *mezuzah* in their new home. At the dedication, Dan's mother said, "I know all of you are questioning why we left Nigeria and why we're living in Israel … We have decided to cast our lot with the Jewish people in the Jewish homeland. We have decided to stand alongside all of you in your fight against terror. The reason is very simple: *tikkun olam*."

We have been given freedom to choose good or evil, blessing or curse. It is our task to work for the perfection of the world by performing deeds of lovingkindness, allowing the Divine sparks to shine forth in our lives and our world.

NITSAVIM
Community and Faith

There is a legend of a woman in mourning who pleaded with a wise man to return her only son whom she had just lost. The wise man told her that he could comply with her request on one condition. She would have to bring him a mustard seed taken from a home entirely free from sorrow. The woman set out on her quest. Years elapsed, and she did not return. One day, the wise man chanced upon her, but he hardly recognized her, for now she looked so radiant. He greeted her and then asked her why she had never kept their appointment. "Oh," she said in a tone of voice that indicated she had completely forgotten about the mustard seed. "I'll tell you what happened. In search of the mustard seed, I came into homes so burdened with sorrow and trouble that I could not walk out. Who better than I could offer them the sympathy they needed? So I stayed in each home for as long as I could be of service. And," she added apologetically, "please do not be angry, but I never again thought about our appointment."

All of us experience low points in life. There is no greater sorrow than the loss of a loved one. Many also experience debilitating physical, mental, and emotional illnesses, deep disappointments, and tragic failures. When people need support and help, they often turn to community and to faith in God.

In *parashat Nitsavim*, Moses begins his farewell address to the Israelites by stating how the people are to stand. The text reads, "Your tribal heads, your elders and your officials, all the men of Israel, your children, your wives, even the stranger within your camp, from woodchopper to water drawer" (Deuteronomy 29:9–10). Israel is a community joined together in bonds of love and commitment, Moses suggests. When we recognize those standing next to us as a part of our community, our larger family, then we know that we are not alone, that there are others who are with us and who support us. At the same time, we recognize our concomitant role in ensuring each person's well-being by supporting the needs and desires of others.

A Jew lives in community. We bear responsibility for each other. "All Israel is responsible one for the other" (*Yalkut Shimoni* 247) is not merely a slogan for us; it is a way of life. Even in the Middle Ages, when Jewish experience was wretched and discriminatory, each Jewish community had a *kehilla*, a communal organization. Soup kitchens, *hakhnassat orḥim* (hospitality organizations), medical services, educational stipends, and community *tzedakah* collectives were always part of communal responsibilities. No Jew would be left behind while another Jew grew prosperous or more successful.

We pray together, celebrate life cycle events together, and at times of sorrow, cry together. The entire experience of *shiva* allows the community to respond to an individual's grief. The *kehilla* is responsible for providing food, the presence of a *minyan*, and the physical support of the mourner. No one should be left alone at his or her time of sorrow.

And the same principle should apply if one is ill. *Bikkur ḥolim* societies, organizations designed to visit the sick and infirm and support their families are part of the *kehilla* structure. Today, most of that responsibility has been delegated to the professionals of the Jewish world: the rabbi, the *ḥazzan*, and the Jewish chaplain. But the responsibility lies with the entire community. It is a great *mitzvah* to care about others and extend oneself to help. Being part of the *kehilla* is a necessity for all of us, and we can only expect in return what we ourselves are ready to give.

In addition to community support, faith in God is also necessary at moments of great travail. For seven weeks between Tisha B'Av and Rosh Hashanah, we read a series of seven *haftarot* from the second part of the Book of Isaiah. The prophet was speaking to the exiles of Babylonia who were despondent and yearning for a return to Zion. Isaiah prophesied of a time when they would return and rebuild Jerusalem.

In his book, *The Healer of Shattered Hearts*, Rabbi David Wolpe uses this title to describe God. When it seems as if God has abandoned us, we need support and seek it out. Wolpe writes, "All the elements of care, concern, love, and protection that we associate with a caring parent, the Rabbis associate with God." Wolpe continues, "In the presence of a loving parent there is a security that time and growth do not diminish. No voice is more reassuring, no love more unconditional and embracing. The tolerance and love of a parent, although sometimes strained, is finally inexhaustible. These are the wondrous attributes that the Rabbis vested in God." It is a reassuring picture of security that the Psalmist paints for us when he records: "Though I walk in the valley of the shadow of death, I fear no harm, for You are with me" (Psalms 23:4). This is the kind of support that is necessary at life's most difficult moments.

Community and faith are the two pillars upon which each individual Jew has pledged his or her life from Biblical times to today. While we look forward to and plan for happy events and celebrations, we know that along the path of life, moments of sorrow, despair, and loss are inevitable. We pray that we have the courage and faith to meet those moments and make ourselves available to support others during their time of need.

VA-YELEKH
No Regrets

Like most congregational rabbis, I receive many *b'nai mitzvah* and wedding invitations. I could probably do a study of the American Jewish value system just by analyzing all the invitations that I receive in the mail.

Often, at the bottom of the invitation or on a separate card are the words "regrets only." While the phrase may be very legitimate in its use for a response to an invitation, it conveys a whole set of different meanings when it is attached to this period of the year when we read *parashat Va-yelekh*, coinciding with the period of the High Holy Days.

For many people, this phrase, "regrets only," becomes a constant life theme. No matter what success there may be, some people always look on the bleak side of events and never appreciate the gifts they do receive.

A nineteen-year-old man was in Las Vegas for the first time in his life. He sat down at the blackjack table and played cautiously, even frugally. The bets were small; the risks were low. Before too long he had a winning streak. After each hand, he was incredulous that he kept winning. "I should have doubled-down," he said. "I should have increased my bet; I should have split my cards," he kept saying. The dealer, exasperated by the young man's incessant whining, looked at him and retorted: "Young man, you can't live your life with 'should'ves.'"

During this time of the year, we are bidden to examine our conduct. How many times have we second-guessed our choices? Do we live our lives with "regrets only" or can we legitimately say, "I did the best I could; I have no regrets; I'm not living my life with 'should'ves.'"

In this section of the Torah, we read about the last days of *Moshe Rabbeinu*. His greatest dream was not realized. He wanted to enter the Promised Land and lead his people into the Land of Canaan, the land of their ancestors. But Moses is informed, "You shall not go across yonder Jordan" (Deuteronomy 31:2). Was Moses saddened by the turn of events?

Most assuredly he was. Did he wallow in self-pity, engage in a chorus of "I should not have hit the rock; I should not have been angry with the Israelite people," or the like? He realized that he was human, that he was bound to make mistakes, and that he had to bear the consequences of his actions.

What did Moses do? He looked toward the future and did not let himself become engulfed by feelings of inadequacy and regret: "Then Moses called Joshua and said to him in the sight of all Israel: 'Be strong and resolute, for it is you who shall go with this people into the land that the Lord swore to their fathers to give them, and it is you who shall apportion it to them'" (Deuteronomy 31:7). Rather than lament the past, Moses appreciated his role in bringing the Israelites to the bank of the Jordan River and appointed Joshua to complete the task of crossing it.

Our lives are filled with successes and accomplishments, along with some regrets. It is important to focus on the accomplishments and not live with "regrets only." If we only do the latter, then we will judge our lives to be failures and never learn to appreciate what we actually have accomplished.

Yet, there are times when we need to admit that we have made mistakes. That is what the concept of *teshuvah* teaches us. Maimonides in his *Laws of Repentance* encourages us to admit those mistakes, to ask for forgiveness, and to make sure never to repeat those particular modes of behavior. "I'm sorry" is not easy to say. In fact, many times the most difficult thing for a person to do is to admit he made a mistake and be willing to accept blame for the consequences of his actions. Human nature simply does not allow it. Each year, the High Holy Day period reappears on the Jewish calendar and encourages us to admit that we are only human and, therefore, imperfect. There is always need for improvement. Regret, in this case, is positive, life-affirming, and behavior-modifying. It is an integral part of the concept of *teshuvah*. As we recognize our regret, the process of *teshuvah* should ultimately motivate us to examine the consequences of our action or inaction the next time the same opportunity is presented to us.

The Mishnah in *Ḥagigah* 1:6 describes the obligation of bringing a festival sacrifice on the pilgrimage festivals. What happens if the first day of Sukkot passes, and the person has not brought his sacrifice? The Mishnah states: "He may bring it during the entire festival week, even on the last day." However, should he miss that period, he is not bound to bring the sacrifice any longer because: "A twisted thing cannot be made straight; and what is not there cannot be numbered" (Ecclesiastes 1:15). In other words, an opportunity lost is an opportunity wasted.

Life passes us by very quickly, and there are so many missed opportunities. Before we know it, we begin living our lives with "should'ves" once more. We get few second chances in life. In the concert notes to a Mozart symphony program were the words: "The first melody is the one you have to relish, for it does not re-occur." In this particular piece of music, Mozart used the melody only once. If you missed it, you missed it; it was not to be repeated.

We need to understand that we cannot live our lives with "regrets only" or with "should'ves." Only with a proper combination of opportunities grasped, successes tallied, and mistakes acknowledged can we put our lives into proper perspective. May we learn to balance the demands of all three.

HA'AZINU
The Singular Soul

In the glorious song with which Moses addresses the congregation, he invites people to think of the Torah, the covenant with God, as if it is like rain that waters the ground and brings forth its produce: "May my discourse come down as the rain, my speech distill as the dew, like showers on young growth, like droplets on the grass" (Deuteronomy 32:2).

God's word is like rain in a dry land. It brings life and makes things grow. No matter what we do in terms of work on the land, unless the rains fall, nothing will grow. So it is, according to the text, with Israel; no matter what success it may achieve, a good portion of the credit is due to God.

The Sages, however, sensed something more in the analogy. In *Sifrei Deuteronomy* 306:2, they suggest: "Just as the rain is one thing, yet it falls on trees, enabling each to produce tasty fruit according to the kind of tree it is, the vine in its way, the olive tree in its way and the date palm in its way, so the Torah is one, yet its words yield Scripture, Mishnah, laws, and lore. Just as showers fall upon plants and make them grow, some green, some red, some black, some white, so the words of Torah produce teachers, some worthy individuals, some sages, some righteous, and some pious."

Rabbi Jonathan Sacks, the Chief Rabbi of England, in his commentary on this particular Biblical verse and *midrash*, suggests, "the Torah is compared to rain precisely to emphasize that its most important effect is to make each of us grow into what we could become. We are *not* all the same, nor does the Torah seek uniformity." In other words, we all understand the words a little bit differently; we are all unique souls. While it is true that individuals make up the whole, the whole is also made up of individuals, and each individual has his or her own special nature and uniqueness.

In Mishnah *Sanhedrin* 4:5, human creative ability is compared with God's: "To teach you the greatness of the Holy One, blessed be He, for a man stamps many coins with one die and they are all alike one with the other, but the King of Kings, the Holy One, blessed be He, has stamped all mankind with the die of the first man and yet not one of them is like his fellow." No two human beings on this earth are exactly the same. Each person is a unique individual possessing a soul precious unto itself.

The message comes forth rather clearly in the liturgy of Rosh Hashanah and Yom Kippur. As the *U-Netaneh Tokef* prayer states: "All that lives on earth will pass before You like a flock of sheep. As a shepherd examines the flock, making each sheep pass under the staff, so You will review and number and count, judging each living being, determining the fate of everything in creation, inscribing their destiny." This magnificent image brings forth the metaphor of God lovingly considering each individual human being, each unique soul, and judging each one on his or her own merit.

In the enormity of numbers, the individual tends to lose his or her own importance. After the Holocaust, we are still attempting to understand what it means to lose six million of our brothers and sisters. It is simply unfathomable. If we really want to understand the tragedy, we have to break it down, not simply by the number of people lost in each region or even each city, town, or village, but by each individual soul whose life was cut short by racial hatred and bigotry.

What is it that makes us unique? We are created in the image of God, and unlike any other living being, we can be God-like. We have been given souls that we must tend and nurture. Each day as we begin our morning services, we recite the prayer that states: "The soul which You, my God, have given me is pure. You created it, You formed it, You breathed it into me; You keep body and soul together. One day You will take my soul from me, to restore it to me in life eternal. So long as Your soul is within me I acknowledge You, Lord my God, my ancestors' God, Master of all creation, sovereign of all souls. Praised are You, Lord who restores the soul to the lifeless, exhausted body." Each person has a unique soul planted in him by God, giving each of us a distinct sense of worth and dignity.

Toward the end of tractate *Sotah*, there is a long list detailing the attributes of each individual sage: "When Rabbi Meir died, the composers of fables ceased. When Ben Azzai died, the assiduous students ceased. When Ben Zoma died, the expositors ceased. When Rabbi Akiba died, the glory of the Torah ceased. When Rabbi Ḥanina ben Dosa died, men of deed ceased. When Rabbi Jose Ketanta died, the pious men ceased. When Rabbi Yoḥanan ben Zakkai died, the luster of wisdom ceased" (*Sotah* 49a). Each sage was a unique individual and made his own contribution to our collective heritage. Their deaths created a vacuum in the community.

No individual is the same as the next, and each individual is special. This is a great lesson of Judaism. Rabbi Sacks states: "The miracle of creation is that unity in Heaven produces diversity on earth. Torah is the rain that feeds this diversity, allowing each of us to become what only we can be."

It is a constant challenge to live up to our potential, to make a difference in the lives of families and community, to treasure our unique souls, and to appreciate the diversity of the people with whom we live. When the day comes that our souls will be judged by God, one by one, let us hope and pray that we will be deemed to have met that challenge.

HA'AZINU
Mitzvot of Heaven and of Earth

"Give ear, O heavens, let me speak; Let the earth hear the words I utter!" (Deuteronomy 32:1). With these words, Moses begins his final discourse to the entire people. But this is an odd way to begin. Why must he call heaven and earth to be witnesses before he talks to his people? Most of the commentators suggest that Moses wanted eternal witnesses to remind the Children of Israel that they had taken an oath that obligated them to remain steadfast to the covenant. They could never claim that they were unaware of the obligations of that oath, as heaven and earth would be there for eternity to remind them of their promise.

Sifrei Deuteronomy 306:1 suggests another reason why Moses calls forth both heaven and earth at this particular moment: "It was taught: why did Moses call heaven and earth to bear witness over Israel? The heavens, to bear witness for the *mitzvot* of the heavens; the earth for the *mitzvot* of the earth."

Rabbi Baruch Ha-Levi Epstein, in his commentary *Torah Temimah*, published in 1902, offers two interesting comments on this particular *Sifrei* passage. He suggests that the *mitzvot* of heaven include the blessing over the new month and the setting of the times for the festivals and the related laws; the *mitzvot* of the earth include such laws of the tithes, the gleanings, the forgotten sheaf, the corner of the field, and similar laws.

Rabbi Epstein suggests that there are certain laws in our tradition that are wholly incumbent upon heaven. Our calendar, for instance, is based upon the moon and its phases. We know that Rosh Hashanah is never late or early; it always comes on time, beginning on the first day of the month of Tishrei. The English date, though, is different from year to year. Because of the discrepancy between the lunar year and the solar year, we must always make sure that Passover is celebrated in the spring. While we have a role in the sanctification of the new month, or at least we did in the times of the Temple, the calendar is based upon the activities of the heavens.

The *mitzvot* of the earth, on the other hand, are totally dependent upon us. Whether we leave our gleanings or the corners of the fields to the poor is our choice. The heavens have little role to play. It is our task to take care of those less fortunate than we. It is our duty to make sure that everyone has food, clothing, and shelter.

A Ḥasidic parable tells us that even atheism has its place. How so? The parable says, when a poor person asks you for *tzedakah*, you must be an atheist; don't tell him "God will provide" or "The Almighty will look after you" or the like. Rather, you must rely only on yourself to help him. According to this view, the words of the Psalmist ring true: "The heavens belong to the Lord, but the earth He gave over to man" (Psalms 115:16).

Rabbi Epstein also offers another interesting interpretation of this passage from the *Sifrei*. The heavens are "the *mitzvot* between people and God" and the earth "the *mitzvot* between one person and another." Most of us would distinguish between the ritual commandments that are directed toward God and the ethical commandments that are directed toward people. But are they really different?

In our tradition, they are not. One is obligated both for the commandments between people and God and the commandments between one person and another. There is no difference.

This is evidenced on Yom Kippur as we recite the long confessional, the *Al Ḥet*. The sins that are enumerated are not ritual sins, they are not commandments between us and God; rather, they are the commandments between us and our fellow human beings. For example, we recite these words: "We have sinned against You by defrauding others … We have sinned against You through foul speech." We are also taught that before atonement can be effectuated between ourselves and God, we must ask for forgiveness from our fellow human beings (*Yoma* 85b).

Ultimately, Moses may have called heaven and earth to witness his great song because Israel bears a responsibility for the covenant in all of its aspects. We are obligated in both directions, both the vertical and the horizontal axes. Both must be present.

The ritual laws without the ethical commandments are like the human skeleton without the flesh that overlays it. Our ancient prophets inveighed against focusing on ritual laws exclusively. It was the prophet Isaiah who also called heaven and earth to listen and give ear to his tirade against the people when he said: "'What need have I of all your sacrifices?' (Isaiah 1:11) says the Lord ... 'Cease to do evil; learn to do good. Devote yourselves to justice; aid the wronged. Uphold the rights of the orphan; defend the cause of the widow'" (Isaiah 1:16–17).

Ritual without ethics may be like bones without skin, but ethics without ritual is like skin without bones. Just as we have a responsibility to our fellow human beings, we bear obligations toward God. Jewish tradition informs us that observing *kashrut* and Shabbat, being involved with daily prayer, and performing the other ritual commandments bring us closer to God and to experiencing the Divine in our lives.

Moses may have called both heaven and earth to bear witness to symbolize that the Children of Israel have an ongoing responsibility for keeping the *mitzvot* of the heavens and the earth. May we be constant in our devotion to that mission.

Bibliographic Notes

Biblical translations are from the *Jewish Publication Society TANAKH* (1999). Prayer translations and excerpts from *Pirkei Avot* are from *Siddur Sim Shalom* (Rabbinical Assembly, 1985), and High Holiday prayer translations are from *Mahzor Lev Shalem* (Rabbinical Assembly, 2010). In several instances I veered from the translations for literary purposes.

Talmudic quotations are from the Babylonian Talmud except where a quotation from the Jerusalem Talmud is indicated.

Bere'shit: **A Closer Look.** The quote from Rabbi Milton Steinberg is from his sermon, "To Hold With Open Arms," in his book, *A Believing Jew* (Harcourt, 1951). Ronnie Schreiber's comments were posted on the Mail.Jewish Mailing List, Vol. 15, No. 31, on September 24, 1994; see www.ottmall.com/mj_ht_arch/v15/mj_v15i31.html. Jack Borden's comments are based on his article, "Look to the Sky" (*Orion Afield*, Vol. 3, No. 2, Spring 1999). The quote from Henry David Thoreau is from *The Journal of Henry David Thoreau* (Dover Publications, 1962).

Bere'shit: **The World Gone Wrong.** Freud wrote about the Oedipus complex in *The Interpretation of Dreams*, by Sigmund Freud, translated by A. A. Brill (Macmillan, 1913).

Noah: **Lurking Evil.** Simon Wiesenthal's story is based on his book, *The Sunflower: On the Possibilities and Limits of Forgiveness* (Opera Mundi Press, 1969).

Noah: **The Power of Words.** The story about the Angel of Fire is found in *A Complete Treasury of Stories for Public Speakers*, edited by Morris Mandel (Jonathan David Publishers, 1974).

Lekh Lekha: **Abram, Melchizedek, and the Act of Giving.** The commentary on the two kings is based on *The JPS Torah Commentary: Genesis (Bereshit), The Traditional Hebrew Text with New JPS Translation,* by Nahum M. Sarna (Jewish Publication Society, 2001).

Va-yera: **Biblical Family/Modern Problems.** The anecdote about the religious school teacher is from *Heart of Wisdom: A Thought for Each Day of the Jewish Year*, by Bernard S. Raskas (Burning Bush Press, 1973). Leslie Farber's essay, "The

Family Reunion," originally appeared in *Commentary* magazine, January 1974, and is included in his book, *Lying, Despair, Jealousy, Envy, Sex, Drugs, and the Good Life* (Basic Books, 1976).

***Hayyei Sarah*: The Last Days of Abraham and David.** The Viktor Frankl quotes are from his book, *Man's Search For Meaning* (Beacon Press, 1959, 2006). The poem by Rabbi Alvin I. Fine appears in the Reform movement's *Gates of Repentance: The New Union Prayerbook for the Days of Awe* (CCAR Press, 1996); an adaptation and Hebrew translation also appear in the Conservative movement's *Maḥzor Lev Shalem*, edited by Rabbi Edward Feld (Rabbinical Assembly, 2010).

***Toledot*: Jacob or Esau?** The translation of Genesis 27:18–19 is from the *ArtScroll Series Tanach* (Mesorah Publications, 1993). Discussion of the *Or Ha-Ḥayim* and *Sefat Emet* interpretations are based on *Genesis: The Beginning of Desire,* by Avivah Gottlieb Zornberg (Jewish Publication Society, 1995). See especially, "Jacob Becomes Esau: The Ironic Posture." Quotes from Rabbi Irving Greenberg are from "The Ethics of Jewish Power" in *Contemporary Jewish Ethics and Morality: A Reader*, edited by Elliot N. Dorff and Louis E. Newman (Oxford University Press, 1995). The essay is also available as a PDF file from www.wexnerheritage.org.

***Toledot*: The Five Senses as a Source of Blessing.** The non-Jewish theologian quoted is Wilhelm Bousset and is mentioned in *The Authorized Daily Prayer Book*, by Joseph Herman Hertz (Bloch Publishing Co., 1959).

***Va-yetse*: Eyes to See.** Rabbi Lawrence Kushner's story, "Inaudible Screams," is from his book, *God Was in This Place & I, i Did Not Know: Finding Self, Spirituality, and Ultimate Meaning* (Jewish Lights Publishing, 1991).

***Va-yetse*: The Dual Axis.** Rabbi Shlomo Carlebach's story about the hunchback street sweeper is titled "The Holy Hunchback" and is recounted in several sources including *Storytelling and Spirituality in Judaism,* by Yitzḥak Buxbaum (Jason Aronson, 1994) and *Shlomo's Stories: Selected Tales by Shlomo Carlebach with Susan Yael Mesinai* (Jason Aronson, 1994). The *Etz Hayim* commentary is from *Etz Hayim: Torah and Commentary*, edited by Rabbi David L. Lieber (Rabbinical Assembly, 2001). Rabbi Harold Schulweis' comments and quotes are from his book, *Conscience: The Duty to Obey and the Duty to Disobey* (Jewish Lights Publishing, 2008). Rabbi Ḥayim of Brisk's remarks on the function of the rabbi are from *Halakhic Man*, by Rabbi Joseph B. Soloveitchik (Jewish Publication Society, 1983). Rabbi Joseph B. Soloveitchik's comment is also from this book.

Va-Yishlah: **Jacob's Encounter.** The interview with the poor worker in Warsaw is adapted from *Heart of Wisdom*: *A Thought for Each Day of the Jewish Year*, by Bernard S. Raskas (Burning Bush Press, 1973).

Va-Yishlah: **Deborah's Legacy.** Wendy Mogel's quote is from her book, *The Blessing of a Skinned Knee*: *Using Jewish Teachings to Raise Self-Reliant Children* (Simon and Schuster, 2001). The quote about success in life is attributed to Bessie Anderson Stanley and appeared as "Definition of Success" for a contest held in *Brown Book Magazine* (first published in 1904); the quote is often incorrectly attributed to Ralph Waldo Emerson or Robert Louis Stevenson.

Va-yeshev: **Joseph's Core Values.** Rabbi Walter Wurzburger's comments and his quote about Rabbi Joseph B. Soloveitchik are from *Ethics of Responsibility*: *Pluralistic Approaches to Covenantal Ethics*, by Walter S. Wurzburger (Jewish Publication Society, 1994).

Va-yeshev: **The Challenge of Good Fortune.** Rabbi Hugo Gryn's story is titled "My Father's Spiritual Heroism: The Margarine Menorah (Germany, 1944)" and appears in *A Different Light*: *The Hanukkah Book of Celebration*, by Noam Zion and Barbara Spectre (Devora Publishing, 2000).

Mikkets: **Joseph and Other Jewish Dreamers.** Leo Oppenheim's remark is taken from his book, *The Interpretation of Dreams in the Ancient Near East, with a Translation of an Assyrian Dream Book*, Transactions of the American Philosophical Society, Vol. 46, Part 3, September 1956 (American Philosophical Society, 1956). Sigmund Freud's views on dream interpretation are discussed in *The Interpretation of Dreams*, by Sigmund Freud, translated by A. A. Brill (Macmillan, 1913). Theodor Herzl's diary entry can be found in *The Complete Diaries of Theodor Herzl*, edited by Raphael Patai, translated by Harry Zohn (Herzl Press and Thomas Yoseloff, 1960). The other Herzl quote is from *A Jewish State*: *An Attempt at a Modern Solution of the Jewish Question*, by Theodor Herzl (The Maccabaean Publishing Co., 1904). Martin Luther King, Jr. delivered his "I Have a Dream" speech on August 28, 1963, at the Lincoln Memorial in Washington, D.C. The full text and audio of his speech are available from www.americanrhetoric.com/speeches/mlkihaveadream.htm.

Mikkets: **Making a Difference.** The full title of Elie Wiesel's book is *The Jews of Silence*: *A Personal Report on Soviet Jewry* (Schocken, 2011). For more about Natan Sharansky, see *The Case for Democracy*: *The Power of Freedom to Overcome Tyranny and Terror*, by Natan Sharansky and Ron Dermer (Public Affairs, 2009). The second translation of *Pirkei Avot* 2:6 is the *ArtScroll* translation from *Pirkei Avos*

Treasury Set: *The Sages' Guide to Living*, by Moshe Lieber, edited by Nosson Scherman (Mesorah Publications, 1996).

Va-yiggash: Responsible for One Another. Rabbi Norman Lamm discusses the synthesis of Torah and *derekh eretz* in *Torah Umadda*: *The Encounter of Religious Learning and Worldly Knowledge in the Jewish Tradition*, by Norman Lamm (Jason Aronson, 1990).

Va-yiggash: Jewish Identity. The story about Charles Laughton's reciting Psalm 23 is recounted in *What God Can Do for You Now*: *For Seekers Who Want to Believe*, by Robert N. Levine (Sourcebooks, 2008).

Va-yeḥi: The Value of Tears. The quote from Rabbi Abraham Twerski is from *Positive Parenting*: *Developing Your Child's Potential*, by Abraham J. Twerski and Ursula Schwartz (Mesorah Publications, 1996). Dr. Nahum Sarna's comments are based on *The JPS Torah Commentary*: *Genesis (Bereshit), The Traditional Hebrew Text with New JPS Translation*, by Nahum M. Sarna (Jewish Publication Society, 2001).

Va-yeḥi: The Secret of the Two Yuds. The quote from John Wesley is from *Letters of John Wesley*, by John Wesley and Augustine Birrell, edited by George Eayrs (Hodder and Stoughton, 1915). The quote from Ann Landers' reader is found in *Janie's Unbelievable Journey*: *Inspirational Letters Along the Way*, by Janie Wilkins (Tate Publishing, 2011).

Shemot: Yihiye Tov—"It Will Be Good." The song, "*Yihiye Tov*" (*Things Will Get Better*) was written by Yonatan Geffen (lyrics) and David Broza (music) (1978). The quote from Sigmund Freud is from his book, *Moses and Monotheism*, translated by Katherine Jones (Hogarth Press and the Institute of Psycho-Analysis, 1939). The quote from Emmanuel Ringelblum's diary is from *Notes from the Warsaw Ghetto*, by Emmanuel Ringelblum and Jacob Sloan (Ibooks, 2006). The New Year's quote is from "365 Clean Pages," which appeared on the *New York Times* op-ed page, January 1, 1991.

Shemot: The Book of Names. The Herman Wouk quote is from his book, *Inside, Outside* (Little, Brown and Company, 1985). The poem, "Each of Us Has a Name," by Zelda (Zelda Schneurson Mishkovsky) was first published in Hebrew in 1968; it was translated from the Hebrew by Marcia Falk and appears in *The Spectacular Difference*: *Selected Poems of Zelda* (Hebrew Union College Press, 2004). An English translation also appears in *Maḥzor Lev Shalem* (Rabbinical Assembly, 2010).

***Va-era*: A People Who Dwell Apart.** The Prager and Telushkin quote is from *Why the Jews? The Reason for Antisemitism,* by Dennis Prager and Joseph Telushkin (Simon and Schuster, 2003). Gunther Plaut's concept is drawn from *The Torah: A Modern Commentary*, by W. Gunther Plaut (URJ Press, 1981).

***Bo*: Beyond Remembering.** The quote from Abraham Joshua Heschel is from his book, *The Insecurity of Freedom: Essays on Human Existence* (Farrar, Straus and Giroux, 1965). The full quote from Heinrich Heine reads: "Since the Exodus, freedom has always spoken with a Hebrew accent."

***Bo*: The Challenge of Darkness.** Remarks by Maryanne Bruce and reflections of other survivors from U.S. Airways Flight #1549 are adapted from "After Miracle on Hudson, Many Promises to Keep," by Michael Wilson, published in *The New York Times*, January 14, 2010.

***Be-shallah—Shabbat Shira*: The Ultimate Song.** The comment from Rabbi Abraham Joshua Heschel is adapted from *Moral Grandeur and Spiritual Audacity: Essays*, by Abraham Joshua Heschel, edited by Susannah Heschel (Macmillan, 1997).

***Be-shallah—Shabbat Shira*: Embodying Faith in Life.** The quote from Rabbi Abraham Joshua Heschel is from *Moral Grandeur and Spiritual Audacity: Essays*, by Abraham Joshua Heschel, edited by Susannah Heschel (Macmillan, 1997).

***Yitro*: To Listen and To Hear.** To learn more about Bernard Baruch, see *Baruch: The Public Years,* by Bernard Mannes Baruch (Holt, Rinehart and Winston, 1960). The comment by Bernard Baruch is adapted from *Raising Your Child to be a Mensch,* by Neil Kurshan (Atheneum, 1987). The conversation between Mark Twain and the businessman is adapted from *A Man of God: Essential Priorities for Every Man's Life,* by Jack Graham and Chuck Norris (Crossway, 2007).

***Yitro*: The Tenth Commandment.** The comments and quotes from Rabbi Nilton Bonder, including his quote from the Rabbi of Radvil, are from his book, *The Kabbalah of Envy: Transforming Hatred, Anger, and Other Negative Emotions* (Shambhala, 1997). The translation of Leviticus 19:18 is based on *The Soncino Chumash* from the Soncino Books of the Bible, edited by Abraham Cohen (Soncino Press, 1947). The story about Angela and Charlotte is adapted from "Always Return Your Phone Calls" (anonymous author) in *Chicken Soup for the Teenage Soul: 101 Stories of Life, Love, and Learning,* by Jack Canfield, Mark Victor Hansen, and Kimberly Kirberger (Health Communications, 1997). David Noel Freedman's comments are from his book, *The Nine Commandments: Uncovering the Hidden Pattern of Crime and*

Punishment in the Hebrew Bible (Doubleday, 2000). The commentary from Rabbi J. H. Hertz is from *The Pentateuch and Haftorahs*: *Hebrew Text, English Translation, and Commentary,* edited by Rabbi J. H. Hertz (Soncino, 1960).

Mishpatim: Home, Sanctuary, Community—The Threefold Cord. See *The Pentateuch and Haftorahs*: *Hebrew Text, English Translation, and Commentary,* edited by Rabbi J. H. Hertz (Soncino, 1960). Commentary by Dr. Nahum Sarna is from *The JPS Torah Commentary*: *Exodus (Shemot), The Traditional Hebrew Text with New JPS Translation,* by Nahum M. Sarna (Jewish Publication Society, 1991). Comments from Rabbi Samson Raphael Hirsch are from *The Hirsch Chumash*: *Complete Set,* by Rav Samson Raphael Hirsch (Feldheim Publishers, 2009). For further reading on the issues of home, house of worship, and community, see my article, "Civic Morality," by Rabbi Vernon H. Kurtz in *The Observant Life*: *The Wisdom of Conservative Judaism for Contemporary Jews,* edited by Martin S. Cohen and Michael Katz (Rabbinical Assembly, 2012).

Mishpatim: Derekh Eretz. The story about United States Ambassador Averell Harriman appeared in *The New Yorker* on May 3, 1952, and can be found in *Far-flung and Footloose*: *Pieces from The New Yorker, 1937–1978,* by Ely Jacques Kahn (Putnam Publishing Group, 1979). Rabbi Simcha Bunim's commentary is based on "Coming Down from the Mountain While Still Being There," by Laura Geller in *10 Minutes of Torah,* Union of Reform Judaism, February 8, 2010. See also *Torah Gems,* Vol. 2, compiled by Aharon Yaakov Greenberg, translated by Rabbi Dr. Shmuel Himelstein (Yavneh Publishing House, 1998). The anecdote by Yitzhak ben Zvi is from *A Treasury of Jewish Anecdotes,* by Lawrence Jeffrey Epstein (Jason Aronson, 1989).

Terumah: It Depends on Us. The quote from the witness to the first atomic explosion and the quote from William L. Laurence are adapted from *Heart of Wisdom*: *A Thought for Each Day of the Jewish Year,* by Bernard S. Raskas (Burning Bush Press, 1973).

Tetsavveh: Who Is a Leader? The Churchill quote is from *The Definitive Wit of Winston Churchill,* edited by Richard Langworth (Random House, 2009). The story about Rabbi Judah Zvi is told in *Torah Today*: *A Renewed Encounter with Scripture,* by Pinchas Peli (University of Texas Press, 1987).

Tetsavveh: Using Knowledge for Good. For a discussion of the ethical considerations in using data obtained by Nazi doctors, see Baruch C. Cohen, "The Ethics of Using Medical Data from Nazi Experiments," *Jewish Law Articles*: *Examining*

Halacha, Jewish Issues and Secular Law (2003). Cohen's article is available at www.jlaw.com/Articles/NaziMedEx.html. The quote from Rabbi J. David Bleich is from the article, "Survey of Recent Halakhic Periodical Literature: Utilization of Scientific Data Obtained Through Immoral Experimentation," by J. David Bleich, first printed in *Tradition* magazine, Vol. 26, No. 1, Fall 1991, published by the Rabbinical Council of America. The article is reprinted in *Contemporary Halakhic Problems*, Vol. 4, by J. David Bleich (KTAV Publishing House, 1995). The quote by J. Robert Oppenheimer is from *Heart of Wisdom*: *A Thought for Each Day of the Jewish Year*, by Bernard S. Raskas (Burning Bush Press, 1973).

***Ki Tissa*: Partners with God.** The Arthur Schopenhauer quote is from *Parerga and Paralipomena*: *Short Philosophical Essays*, Vol. 2, by Arthur Schopenhauer and E. F. J. Payne, edited and translated by E. F. J. Payne (Oxford University Press, 1974).

***Ki Tissa*: Two Sets of Tablets.** The story about Thomas Jefferson is adapted from "Compassion is in the Eyes" (anonymous author), in *Fresh Packet of Sower's Seeds*: *Third Planting*, by Brian Cavanaugh (Paulist Press, 1994). The quote from Ḥayim Nahman Bialik is based on his essay, "*Halakah* and *Aggadah*" which appears in *Law and Legend or Halakah and Aggadah*, translated by Julius L. Siegel (Bloch Publishing, 1923).

***Va-yakhel*: The Beauty of Shabbat.** The quote and commentary from Dr. Nahum Sarna are from *The JPS Torah Commentary*: *Exodus (Shemot), The Traditional Hebrew Text with New JPS Translation,* by Nahum M. Sarna (Jewish Publication Society, 1991). Rabbi Abraham Joshua Heschel's description of Shabbat appears in his book, *The Sabbath* (Farrar, Straus and Giroux, 1951). The comment by Roland de Vaux is from his book, *Ancient Israel*: *Its Life and Institutions* (Darton, Longman, and Todd, 1961). The Rabbinical Assembly's "A Responsum on the Sabbath," by Morris Adler, Jacob Agus, and Theodore Friedman was originally published in 1950 and can be found in *Proceedings of the Committee on Jewish Law and Standards of the Conservative Movement, 1927–1970*, edited by David Golinkin (Rabbinical Assembly, 2001). The quote from Rabbi Pinchas Peli is from his book, *Shabbat Shalom*: *A Renewed Encounter with the Sabbath* (B'nai B'rith Center for Jewish Identity, 1990). Joseph Lieberman's quotes are from his book, *The Gift of Rest*: *Rediscovering the Beauty of the Sabbath* (Howard Books, 2012).

***Pekudei*: The Ideal and the Real.** Daniel J. Levinson's theory of life transitions is adapted from his book, *The Seasons of a Man's Life* (Random House Publishing Group, 1986). For additional information about Norman Cousins, see *Anatomy of an Illness as Perceived by the Patient*: *Reflections on Healing and Regeneration*, by

Norman Cousins (Norton, 1979) and *The Healing Heart: Antidotes to Panic and Helplessness*, by Norman Cousins (Avon, 1984).

***Va-yikra*: Good Manners.** The quote from Philip Anderson is from his book, *Church Meetings That Matter* (Pilgrim Press, 1987).

***Va-yikra*: Taking Responsibility.** The quote from Bahya ben Asher is from *In Partnership With God: Contemporary Jewish Law and Ethics*, by Byron L. Sherwin (Syracuse University Press, 1990). The Alan M. Dershowitz quotes are from his book, *The Abuse Excuse: And Other Cop-Outs, Sob Stories, and Evasions of Responsibility* (Little, Brown and Company, 1994).

***Tsav*: The Path of Judaism.** Rabbi Joseph Telushkin's story of Rabbi Schwadron and his remark are from *A Code of Jewish Ethics, Volume 1: You Shall Be Holy*, by Joseph Telushkin (Harmony, 2006).

***Shemini*: Swimming Upstream.** Irving M. Bunim's commentary is from his book, *Ethics from Sinai: A Wide-Ranging Commentary on Pirkei Avos, Vol. 1* (Feldheim Publishers, 1986). The Alan Dershowitz quotes are from his book, *The Vanishing American Jew: In Search of Jewish Identity for the Next Century* (Little, Brown and Company, 1997). Principles of the Conservative movement are described in *Emet Ve-Emunah: Statement of Principles of Conservative Judaism*, by Robert Gordis and the Commission on the Philosophy of Conservative Judaism (The Jewish Theological Seminary of America, 1988).

***Shemini*: Using Time Well.** The quote from Herman Wouk is from his book, *The Caine Mutiny* (Back Bay Books, 1992).

***Tazria*: Ultimate Wonder.** The quote from Albert Einstein is from his essay, "The World As I See It." The essay appears in the book of the same title, *The World As I See It*, by Albert Einstein (Filiquarian Publishing, LLC., 2006). The Darwin quote is from *The Origin of Species*, by Charles Darwin (P.F. Collier & Son, 1909).

***Aḥarei Mot*: Adding Meaning to Life.** The Agnon story is based on "The Celebrants" from *The Bridal Canopy*, by Shmuel Yosef Agnon, translated by Israel Meir Lask (Syracuse University Press, 2000). Rabbi Sidney Greenberg's quote is from his sermon, "On Being Fully Alive" in his book, *Lessons for Living: Contemporary Reflections on the Weekly Bible Readings and on the Festivals* (Hartmore House, 1985).

***Kedoshim*: The Holiness Code.** Rudolf Otto's definition of holiness is from his book, *The Idea of the Holy: An Inquiry into the Non-Rational Factor in the Idea of the Divine and its Relation to the Rational* (Oxford University Press, 1958). The translation of Leviticus 19:18 is based on *The Soncino Chumash* from the Soncino Books of the Bible, edited by Abraham Cohen (Soncino Press, 1947). Martin Buber's comments are based on *Two Types of Faith*, by Martin Buber, translated by Norman Panter Goldhawk (Syracuse University Press, 2003).

Emor: **Looking Out for Others.** The story about Rabbi Israel Salanter is adapted from "A Story: Fundraising as Consciousness Raising" in *A Day Apart*: *Shabbat at Home*, by Noam Zion and Shawn Fields-Meyer (Haggadahs-R-Us, 2004).

Emor: **The Dignity of Work.** The quote from William Bennett is from his book, *The Book of Virtues*: *A Treasury of Great Moral Stories* (Simon and Schuster, 1993). Aesop's fable, "The Farmer and his Sons" also appears in Bennett's book.

Behar: **The Gifts of Nature.** The opening story is from *The Last Rebbe of Bialystok*, by Neil M. Levy (Creative Arts Book Company, 2003).

Be-hukkotai: **Serious Torah Study.** The Malcolm Gladwell quotes are from his book, *Blink*: *The Power of Thinking Without Thinking* (Little, Brown and Company, 2005). The Joel Grishaver quote is from his book, *Learning Torah* (UAHC Press, 1990).

Be-midbar: **Jewish Unity.** Rabbi Zalman Sorotzkin's comments are from his book, *Insights in the Torah—Oznaim Latorah* (Mesorah Publications, 1994). The quote from Rabbi Abraham Isaac Kook is from his essay, "The Rebirth of Israel," reprinted in *The Zionist Idea*: *A Historical Analysis and Reader*, edited by Arthur Hertzberg (Jewish Publication Society, 1959). The quote from the Sephardic *Birkat Ha-Mazon* (Grace after Meals) is from *A Sephardic Passover Haggadah*, by Marc D. Angel (Ktav Publishing House, 1988).

Be-midbar: **The *Minyan*.** The comments from Rabbi Louis Jacobs and the comments and quotes from Menahem Meiri, Judah Ha-Levi in *The Kuzari*, and the Zohar are adapted from *The Jewish Religion*: *A Companion*, by Louis Jacobs (Oxford University Press, 1995).

Naso: **Lessons from the Priestly Blessings.** For more about Hebrew prayer, see *Emet Ve-Emunah*: *Statement of Principles of Conservative Judaism*, by Robert Gordis and the Commission on the Philosophy of Conservative Judaism (Jewish Theological Seminary of America, 1988).

Be-ha'alotekha: **Roses and Thorns.** Rabbi Samson Raphael Hirsch's commentary is from *The Hirsch Chumash*: *Complete Set*, by Rav Samson Raphael Hirsch

(Feldheim Publishers, 2009). The quote from Joanne Greenberg is from her novel, *I Never Promised You a Rose Garden* (Henry Holt and Company, 2009).

***Be-ha'alotekha*: No Whining.** The quotes from Joseph Telushkin are from his book, *The Ten Commandments of Character: Essential Advice for Living an Honorable, Ethical, Honest Life* (Bell Tower, 2003). The Maya Angelou story is titled "Complaining" and is from her book, *Wouldn't Take Nothing for My Journey Now* (Random House, 1993).

***Shelah-Lekha*: Being Honest to Oneself and Others.** The story about Sam Rayburn can be found in *Memorial Service Held in the House of Representatives and Senate of the United States: Together with Remarks Presented in Eulogy of Sam Rayburn, Late Representative from Texas*, by United States 87th Congress, 2d session, 1962, United States Congress (U.S. Government Printing Office, 1962). Rabbi Louis Jacobs' comments are from his book, *Jewish Values* (Wipf and Stock, 2008).

***Shelah-Lekha*: The Sounds of Silence.** For the full text of Elie Wiesel's remarks on being presented with the Congressional Gold Medal on April 19, 1985, see www.pbs.org/eliewiesel/resources/reagan.html. The quote from Abraham Joshua Heschel and the translation of Psalms 65:2 are from Heschel's book, *Man's Quest for God* (Charles Scribner's Sons, 1954).

***Korah*: The Almond Tree.** The Sherwin B. Nuland quotes are from his book, *How We Die: Reflections on Life's Final Chapter* (Random House Digital, 1994).

***Pinhas*: Teaching by Example.** I. L. Peretz's story, "If Not Higher," is in *The I. L. Peretz Reader*, by Isaac Leib Peretz, edited by Ruth R. Wisse (Yale University Press, 2002).

***Mattot*: Causeless Love.** Rabbi Abraham Isaac Kook's remark about *ahavat hinam* is adapted from *Jewish Wisdom: Ethical, Spiritual, and Historical Lessons,* by Joseph Telushkin (William Morrow, 1994).

***Devarim*: The Meaning of Tisha B'Av.** Rabbi Joseph B. Soloveitchik's teachings about Tisha B'Av can be found in *The Koren Mesorat HaRav Kinot, The Complete Tisha B'Av Service with Commentary by Rabbi Joseph B. Soloveitchik*, edited by Simon Posner (Toby Press, 2010). Isaac Bashevis Singer's comment is from an interview with Sander L. Gilman and appears in *Inscribing the Other,* by Sander L. Gilman (University of Nebraska Press, 1991).

***Devarim*: Constructive Criticism.** The translation of Leviticus 19:18 is based on *The Soncino Chumash* from the Soncino Books of the Bible, edited by Abraham Cohen (Soncino Press, 1947).

***Va-ethannan*: Re-experiencing Jewish History.** Salo Wittmayer Baron first used the phrase "lachrymose theory" in his article, "Ghetto and Emancipation: Shall We Revise the Traditional View?" in *The Menorah Journal*, Vol. 14 (1928). Statistics about how many Jews have visited the State of Israel are from the National Jewish Population Survey (NJPS) 2000–2001.

***Va-ethannan*: Loving Your Fellow, Loving God.** The translation of Leviticus 19:18 is based on *The Soncino Chumash* from the Soncino Books of the Bible, edited by Abraham Cohen (Soncino Press, 1947). The "Field of Brotherly Love" story is found in *Lessons From Our Living Past*, Vol. 2, Part 2, edited by Jules Harlow (Behrman House, 1972).

***Ekev*: Saying Yes.** For more information about Jewish demographics and the number of "Jews by Choice," see the American Jewish Identity Survey, 2001. The Henry Slonimsky quote is from his book, *Essays* (Hebrew Union College Press, 1967). The Dag Hammarskjöld quote is from *Markings*, by Dag Hammarskjöld, translated by W. H. Auden and L. Fitzgerald Sjoberg (Knopf Doubleday Publishing Group, 2006).

***Ekev*: Yirat Shamayim.** Rabbi Harold Kushner's commentary is from *Etz Hayim: Torah and Commentary*, edited by Rabbi David L. Lieber (Rabbinical Assembly, 2001). Rabbi Louis Jacobs' quote is from his book, *A Jewish Theology* (Behrman House, 1973). Rabbi Byron Sherwin's quote is from his essay, "Fear of God" (*Yirat ha-Shem*), in *Contemporary Jewish Religious Thought*, edited by Arthur A. Cohen and Paul Mendes-Flohr (Charles Scribner's Sons, 1987). Rabbi Baruch Ha-Levi Epstein's commentary about *yirat shamayim* is from his book, *Mekor Baruch* (1928).

***Re'eh*: The Prophetic View.** The quote and comments from Norman Podhoretz are from his book, *The Prophets: Who They Were, What They Are* (Simon & Schuster, 2010).

***Shofetim*: The Sin of Indifference.** The full text of Elie Wiesel's speech can be found at www.historyplace.com/speeches/wiesel.htm. Raul Hilberg's comments are from his book, *Perpetrators Victims Bystanders: Jewish Catastrophe 1933–1945* (Aaron Asher Books, 1992).

***Shofetim*: To Be Someone.** Rabbi Haskel Lookstein's story is based on his sermon, "Menschliness Before Godliness II, Rosh Hashanah 2006," which is available at www.ckj.org.

***Ki Tetse*: The Beauty of Small Deeds.** The anecdote about Michelangelo is from *Heart of Wisdom: A Thought for Each Day of the Jewish Year*, by Bernard S. Raskas (Burning Bush Press, 1973).

***Ki Tetse*: Remembering and Forgetting.** The Yosef Hayim Yerushalmi quotes are from his book, *Zakhor: Jewish History and Jewish Memory* (Schocken Books, 1982). The story about Clara Barton is based on *The Life of Clara Barton: Founder of the American Red Cross*, by William Eleazar Barton (Houghton Mifflin Company, 1922). The closing lines of this sermon draw upon the work of Rabbi Sidney Greenberg, *Say Yes to Life: A Book of Thoughts for Better Living* (Jason Aronson, 1999).

***Ki Tavo*: The Blessing of True Happiness.** The Sam Snead anecdote is recounted at pawprints.kashalinka.com/anecdotes/snead.shtml. Rabbi Dr. Jeremy Collick's remarks on happiness are available at opentoepiphanies.blogspot.co.il/p/secrets-to-be-shared.html.

***Ki Tavo*: Tikkun Olam—A True Story.** Rabbi Shlomo Riskin's story appears in his book, *Listening to God: Inspirational Stories* (Toby Press, 2011). The quote from Rabbi Joseph Telushkin is from his book, *Jewish Literacy* (William Morrow and Company, 2001).

***Nitsavim*: Community and Faith.** The story of the mustard seed is based on the Buddhist legend of Kisa Gotami and the mustard seed. The quotes from Rabbi David Wolpe are from his book, *The Healer of Shattered Hearts: A Jewish View of God* (Penguin, 1991). The translation of Psalms 23:4 is from *Likute Tefilah: A Rabbi's Manual*, edited by Jules Harlow (Rabbinical Assembly, 1965).

***Va-yelekh*: No Regrets.** The English translation of Ecclesiastes 1:15 is from the *Tanach ArtScroll Series* (Mesorah Publications, 2011).

***Ha'azinu*: The Singular Soul.** Rabbi Jonathan Sacks' commentary is from "Covenant & Conversation 5769: *Ha'azinu*—Let My Teaching Fall Like Rain," available at www.chiefrabbi.org/2009/09/26/covenant-conversation-5769-haazinu-let-my-teaching-fall-like-rain/#.

***Ha'azinu*: Mitzvot of Heaven and of Earth.** Commentary from Rabbi Baruch Ha-Levi Epstein is from his book, *Torah Temimah* (1902).

About the Author

Rabbi Vernon H. Kurtz is the Rabbi of North Suburban Synagogue Beth El in Highland Park, Illinois. He was born in Toronto, Canada, received his B.A. from York University (1971), his M.A. and Rabbinic Ordination from the Jewish Theological Seminary (1976), and his Doctor of Ministry from Chicago Theological Seminary (1981). He also received a Doctor of Divinity (*Honoris Causa*) from the Jewish Theological Seminary (2003).

Rabbi Kurtz is President of the American Zionist Movement. He is an associate member of the Board of Governors of the Jewish Agency for Israel, has been elected to its Executive, and serves as deputy chairman of its Russian Speaking Jewry Committee. He is past President of the Rabbinical Assembly, the international association of Conservative rabbis, and he was a member for many years of the Rabbinical Assembly Committee on Jewish Law and Standards. He served for ten years as a member of the Leadership Council of Conservative Judaism. Rabbi Kurtz is a member of the Board of Directors of the Jewish United Fund/Jewish Federation of Metropolitan Chicago, and he previously served two terms on the Board, including a term as Vice-Chairman. He is a member of the Board of the Jewish People Policy Institute.

Rabbi Kurtz has held numerous leadership positions in the areas of Jewish communal and interfaith activities and is the recipient of many awards. He has been President of MERCAZ USA; President of MERCAZ Olami, the world-wide Zionist organization of the Conservative movement; President of the Chicago Board of Rabbis; Chairman of the United Jewish Appeal Rabbinic Cabinet; and President of the Council of Religious Leaders of Metropolitan Chicago. Rabbi Kurtz is the recipient of the Rabbinic Award from the Jewish Federation of Metropolitan Chicago, Council of Jewish Federations (1984 and 1985); the Young Leadership Award from the Jewish Federation of Metropolitan Chicago

(1985); the Rabbi Simon Greenberg Rabbinic Achievement Award from The Jewish Theological Seminary (1998); the State of Israel Bonds Jerusalem Covenant Award (1996); the State of Israel Bonds Star of David Award (2008); the Rabbi Mordecai Simon Memorial Award from the Chicago Board of Rabbis (2008); the Julius Rosenwald Memorial Award from the Jewish Federation of Metropolitan Chicago (2010); and the Rabbi Mordecai Waxman Memorial Rabbinic and Community Leadership Award from Masorti Olami (2011). Rabbi Kurtz is Adjunct Professor of Rabbinics at Spertus Institute for Jewish Learning and Leadership. He has authored *teshuvot* for the Committee on Jewish Law and Standards of the Rabbinical Assembly and has published many articles in periodicals and books. Currently, he is a monthly Torah commentator for the *Chicago Jewish News* and a Senior Rabbinic Fellow at the Shalom Hartman Institute in Jerusalem.

Rabbi Kurtz and his wife, Bryna, are the parents of two daughters, Hadassa (Haim) who lives in Israel and Shira who works at the National Rehabilitation Hospital in Washington, D.C. as a neuropsychologist. He is the proud *saba* of Shmuel Binyamin, Meytal Dvora, and Anael Rina.